Roger Manvell, PhD (London) and D Litt (Sussex), specialized in film propaganda at the Ministry of Information during the Second World War, and
subsequently bec [illegible] ilm
historians. He wa [illegible] ish
Film Academy, a [illegible] the
cinema and alliec [illegible] ed
widely in Britain [illegible] da,
Australia, India a [illegible] ow
at Sussex Univers [illegible] at
Boston Universit [illegible] to
nine books on which he has collaborated with Heinrich Fraenkel, Roger Manvell has published novels and biographical studies of the actresses, Sarah Siddons and Ellen Terry, and of Annie Besant, and is a contributor on film, biography, etc. to the Encyclopaedia Britannica. He has received Orders of Merit from both Italy and the Federal Republic of Germany.

Heinrich Fraenkel was born and educated in Germany where he attended a number of universities. He began his career in film trade journalism in Berlin and then worked for two years as a screen-writer in Hollywood where he came into close contact with many of the greatest screen talents of the time. He returned to Germany briefly but became increasingly interested in politics and in 1933 on the night of the Reichstag fire emigrated to avoid arrest by the Nazis. In Paris first, and then London, Fraenkel continued to make a living writing screen-plays but he also wrote political books, lectured on German history and the roots of Nazism. At the end of the war, he went back to Germany as a journalist for the *New Statesman*. In 1949, Fraenkel asked for British nationality and in 1967 was awarded the Order of Merit (First Class) from the Federal Republic of Germany. Apart from his many books, he has also written a chess column for the *New Statesman* for twenty-seven years and is a regular contributor to *New Humanist*.

By the same authors

Dr Goebbels
Goering
The July Plot
Himmler
The Incomparable Crime
The Canaris Conspiracy
History of the German Cinema
Hess
The Hundred Days to Hitler

ROGER MANVELL AND
HEINRICH FRAENKEL

Adolf Hitler

The Man and the Myth

Grafton

This *Grafton* edition published 1996
by Diamond Books
77–85 Fulham Palace Road
Hammersmith, London W6 8JB

First published in Great Britain
by Grafton Books 1978

Originally published under the title *Inside Adolf Hitler* 1973

ISBN 0 261 66907 9

Printed and bound in Great Britain by
Caledonian International Book Manufacturing Ltd, Glasgow

Contents

Introduction

The unique nature of Hitler's character and of his place in the history of our times inspires an endless stream of comment. Our only excuse for adding a book on Hitler to our series of biographical and other studies of the Third Reich and its personalities (writing and research which spreads back over some twenty years) is that we believe we have come gradually to understand something of Hitler's personality and the reasons for his meteoric career by an unusual process, that of studying him as the single, overwhelming influence in the lives of four very divergent men about whom we have written detailed biographical studies – Josef Goebbels, Hermann Goering, Heinrich Himmler and Rudolf Hess. We have seen him, too, from the viewpoint of the men who led the opposition within Nazi Germany, men such as Admiral Canaris, Ludwig Beck, Carl Goerdeler, and Count von Stauffenberg, who all figure in our books, *The Canaris Conspiracy* and *The Men Who Tried to Kill Hitler* (*The July Plot*). Lastly, we have explored the worst aspects of his hideous tyranny in Europe in our book, *The Incomparable Crime*, a study of genocide, how it came to be practised and organized, and who precisely carried it out.

By this prolonged route, with all the ramifications of research inside and outside Germany, we can claim to have acquired a certain perspective about the man himself. Not that this is our first book about him. In *The Hundred Days to Hitler* we studied, on a day by day basis, precisely how he achieved power without ever having actually won a majority vote from the German people, that is, while they remained free to vote as they preferred. Writing this particular book, perhaps more than any other, revealed to us the inner genius of the man – a negative egocentric genius unendowed with any shred of common humanity, but nevertheless one which gave him the strength and pertinacity to seize the rule of Germany from the feeble grasp of men far less competent and dedicated than he.

The vast and ever-growing literature of the Third Reich contains many brilliant studies of Hitler, either biographical or historical, by such historians as Alan Bullock, Hugh Trevor-Roper, A. J. P. Taylor, J. W. Wheeler-Bennett, William L. Shirer, Joachim Fest, Werner Maser and Percy Ernst Schramm. Popular biographies have been written by, among others, Konrad Heiden, Colin Cross and Robert Payne. Personal reminiscences of importance by those who knew him and endured working with him include the recollections of ambassadors, generals, journalists and, perhaps most notably, early adherents, some of whom like Hermann Rauschning, Hjalmar Schacht, Ernst Hanfstaengl, Kurt Lüdecke and finally Albert Speer were to suffer varying degrees of disenchantment in Hitler's lifetime. Most of these volumes are long and detailed both in historical incident and in comment. Our aim here has been to distill in a brief space what we have come to understand about Hitler, the man, the political careerist and the warlord. One of us, Heinrich Fraenkel, a Jew, left Germany in 1933 and later, after the war, finally adopted British citizenship. The other, Roger Manvell, visited Nazi Germany on a number of occasions during the 1930s, and worked in anti-Nazi propaganda in the British Ministry of Information during the war years.

Although Nazi Germany collapsed some thirty years ago in final, ignominious defeat, it took the combined forces of several determined nations (including the massive powers of the USA, the British Commonwealth and the USSR) to overthrow it. The European empire Hitler built during his brief, twelve-year dictatorship is unique in modern times. He invites comparison with Napoleon, who, however, started his career with many more advantages than Hitler ever possessed, or with Stalin, who had the resources of a vast party machine and a fully established socialist state to exploit in the interests of creating personal power and prestige. Hitler derived his power solely from himself. The state was he and he the state; the Party was he, and he the Party.

We begin our book with a chapter that attempts to evaluate the man, and contrast him more especially with Napoleon. Only after this do we trace, as succinctly as we can, the means whereby he rose to be head of state and finally to hold Europe in thrall from the Atlantic coast of France to the northern shores of Norway, from the Baltic to the Ukraine and Stalingrad, from the frozen boundaries of Leningrad to the heat of the north African desert, representing dictatorial rule over countries as widely different as France, Poland, occupied Russia, Yugoslavia, Greece and Italy, an empire won and lost in the short space of five years, 1940 to 1945.

We believe that everyone, whether alive at the time of these momentous events, or born since Europe was re-formed with an uneasy peace, should know something about the man who was the precipitant, if not in every instance the actual cause of it all. Hitler has not been unique in using the challenges of peace to cover the pursuits of war. There is warning to be taken in our own time from the nature of his skilful duplicity, his brilliant deployment to his own advantage of political causes, party factions and the enervating bitterness of men and women ambitious for advantage over each other. The Third Reich offers us a story of this kind, and the violences of our own times are in no small measure the result of his example.

It is wrong, indeed ignorant, to underestimate Hitler because of the exorbitant nature of his crimes against humanity. His lack of human feeling, his wholesale, uncompromising approach to the creation of history at the expense of large numbers of innocent people who lay in his path as he had conceived and determined it, should not blind us to a certain negative greatness in the man, and the significance of the hypnotic power he was capable of exercising over others. Hence, the grave necessity to arrive at some degree of understanding of him, for in him much that is dark, or hidden in human nature surfaced with results that led European civilization to near-destruction, and in its wake, the civilization of the world.

– Roger Manvell. Heinrich Fraenkel.

1

Hitler: The Destructive Genius

It is not difficult to account for the widespread revival of interest in Hitler in the 1970s. He is unique in modern history and likely to remain so. As a man he possessed many characteristics which excite curiosity and rouse varied and fascinating speculations about human nature.

Hitler is the most prominent power figure in world history since Napoleon, and power over peoples and its deployment on a massive scale have become a central preoccupation of the twentieth century. No other great power figure of our time – Lenin, Stalin, Mao – excites the same individual interest as Hitler because all were the product of political bureaucracy, leaders who rose out of an already existing large-scale political movement. Hitler, by a concentrated application of will, created his own movement and his own dictatorship. Like Coriolanus, he could always claim 'Alone, I did it!'

No matter how much we may detest everything for which Hitler and Nazism stood, we must reckon with the incredible fact that in ten years Hitler went from a petty political demagogue, recently emerged from confinement, to absolute master of Germany; ten years later again he would commit suicide after failing to maintain an Empire which had stretched from the Atlantic seaboard to the environs of Moscow and Stalingrad and from the Arctic Circle to the Mediterranean. This imperial *tour de force*, negative and destructive though it was, was solely brought about by his determination, determination which, until his ultimate collapse in war, had overcome every human and national obstacle. It is true, however, that the circumstances of the time were often in his favour and that in the end he was his own greatest destroyer, through 'vaulting ambition which o'erleaps itself'. Like Macbeth, he was indeed the victim of his own delusions.

The essential danger is that the nature of Hitler's character and career possesses all the necessary elements for the creation of legend. Goebbels had little difficulty in making him out to be a mythological figure. He is the lonely, self-absorbed leader and therefore a 'romantic', messianic artist in politics. More than anyone (with the possible exception of Lenin, who died, like Hitler and Napoleon, in his middle fifties) he possessed the mystique of power, the capacity to move great assemblies of people by speech and by his presence at the centre of mass spectacles staged to enhance the legend of his all-pervading will. His is the Cinderella story, the tale of the unlikely boy, born with no social advantages, who rises from orphan poverty, or near poverty, to inhabit great palaces and command great armies. The Cinderella quality is enhanced, rather than diminished, by his nondescript, lower-middle-class appearance; he did not possess Napoleon's aristocratic handsomeness nor Lenin's farouche and bearded face, the very image of the revolutionary leader. Only his eyes and his expressive hands possessed any touch of distinction.

There is, too, the appeal of the monstrous in him. We are still a barbaric species, reaching towards civilization rather than having securely achieved it, and, as our popular newspapers, fiction, drama and films reveal, we are still deeply attracted by the activities of wrongdoers, especially those who operate on the grand scale, the master criminals.

Hitler was, of course, a human being, not a monster, but he caused monstrous things to be done on a scale unparalleled in history. This alone has excited both primitive and sophisticated curiosity and can lead to unhealthy and prurient interest in those Nazis who specialized in acts of torture or who delighted in human degradation. For such people, the appeal of Nazism lies in its evident sadism. Hitler becomes a legendary symbol of evil, much like Macbeth with whom he could have said by 1942:

I am in blood
Stepp'd in so far that, should I wade no more,

Returning were as tedious as go o'er.
Strange things I have in head that will to hand,
Which must be acted ere they may be scann'd.

Hitler's Germany, like Macbeth's Scotland, was indeed 'almost afraid to know itself'.

The comparison with Macbeth is not fortuitous. Macbeth is Shakespeare's most evil dictator-king, keeping himself in power by cumulative acts of murder and ever-increasing repression. Yet it takes the imagination and humanity of Shakespeare to reveal that even Macbeth possesses human qualities, a negative greatness which gives him the stature of a self-destructive, tragic figure. Hitler, like Macbeth, became amoral, inhuman, self-destroying, ultimately bringing down his country along with himself. But had he been, like Napoleon, a man of good-will, his undoubted genius for leadership and intuitive political judgement might have endowed him with an equal greatness, for the genius and the intuition were there. Without something of these supreme qualities, explain them how you will, he would never have been able to take possession of the German people, and, in effect, hypnotize them into supporting, or at least conniving in crimes against humanity which he disguised as the legitimate reassertion of national identity and racial superiority.

In modern history, the only comparable figure is Napoleon, but the points of genuine comparison, though striking enough, are relatively few, while the points of difference are far more instructive. Both were born outside the nations they were destined to rule – Hitler in Austria, Napoleon in Corsica – but whereas Hitler was brought up in a strict and comparatively unhappy home in circumstances which were solidly middle class, Napoleon was raised in a happy household, his father a lawyer and both his parents belonging to the local, if somewhat impoverished, nobility. While Hitler idled away his youth, Napoleon studied at military academies in France and followed a career (made difficult by the successive phases of the French Revolution) which was strictly that of a professional soldier. He was born to Italian-speaking parents, but learned, in childhood, to speak French without an Italian accent. Hitler was born to German speaking parents, and liked to claim he acquired his Bavarian accent (such as it was) in childhood. Whereas at the age of thirty, Napoleon had already reached the height of his professional career, following his stunning successes in the Italian campaign, Hitler, at a comparable age, was still a corporal in the German army, his political ambitions only vaguely sensed.

Both men, however, were instinctive empire builders on the European scene, looking eastward for their major conquests. Napoleon became Emperor in 1804, five years after his initial appointment as First Consul of France. He was thirty-five. Hitler became Führer of Germany in 1934, on the death of Hindenburg. He was forty-five. The period of imperial expansion followed, in Napoleon's case, during the period 1803–14, by the end of which he had reached his mid-forties; in Hitler's case the period of expansion was from 1938–44, by the end of which he had reached his mid-fifties. Napoleon's empire encompassed France, Germany, Austria, Italy, the Netherlands, Poland, Spain, Sweden, Switzerland and (for the brief period of invasion) Russia as far as Moscow. Both Napoleon and Hitler entertained grandiose schemes of extending their arm of conquest into Asia, approached through the vast Russian hinterland, and both overreached themselves despite their brilliant tactical generalship; in Hitler's case with far less natural feeling for his men than Napoleon entertained. Both men, as a result of their campaigns and conquests, changed the map of Europe, with its complex system of states and ethnographical links and divisions, though the aftereffects in Eastern Europe were far greater in Hitler's case than Napoleon's. But in any comparison with Hitler, Napoleon scores by the far keener positive drive of his humanity. Whatever his faults, Napoleon cared deeply about what he was doing, and for the most part tried to use his ascendency in an outgoing, positive way. He was as great a lawgiver as he was a general. He wanted any rule he established to be of benefit to the people as a whole. Hitler, as an empire-builder, was almost entirely negative and inward-looking; as long as his leadership of the German people appeared to benefit him, he did not care about, or remained indifferent to, the sufferings he imposed on the people he conquered. He poisoned the minds of the German people against all races he held to be inferior. If Napoleon's invasion represented a tyranny in the eyes of those he ruled because they did not want French troops on their soil, his intentions in most of the countries he occupied were positive; Hitler's tyranny was utterly negative, oppression without benefit or compensation. Even in the minute island of Elba, Napoleon set about improving the standard of living of the impoverished islanders.

Both Napoleon and Hitler had the 'charisma' of great leaders. Their public appearances always evoked the highest enthusiasm among their supporters, which meant in both cases a great cross section of the people. Napoleon's personal magnetism was specially directed to his soldiers who loved him and would do anything for him. But whereas Hitler in the final years of defeat avoided public appearances and exercised his powers of leadership from remote and heavily guarded points, mostly at some distance from the actual battlefronts, Napoleon, to the last, stood with his men in the field, his visible presence made possible, of course, by the different scale of armament in the wars of the early nineteenth century. But would Hitler have been able, had he been exiled after a decisive defeat such as Napoleon suffered at Leipzig, to land again in Germany in 1945 and command by sheer force of personality the loyalty of his former troops as Napoleon was able to do when he made his dramatic return to France from his exile in Elba? It would be most unlikely.

Napoleon and Hitler had abnormal reserves of energy and could, when needed, work abnormal hours involving great concentration, although Hitler often gave way to prolonged periods of lassitude even when important business had to be considered. Both were quick tempered, but Napoleon took pains to control himself. Both loved music and considered themselves patrons of the arts. Both enjoyed having familiar faces around them, but Napoleon, when he had time, was a far more social man than Hitler, enjoying the position of Emperor. Both, too, talked a great deal and were prone to stride about when excited. Both were abnormally impatient, anxious for immediate fulfilment of their orders, an aspect of their exceptional energy. They knew how important it was to achieve what ordinary men would have held to be impossible, driving their armies to exceptional feats of speed and endurance. Both firmly believed in discipline, and in the absolute unity of command under themselves.

Whereas Napoleon was considered extremely handsome, Hitler, with his small moustache, had to overcome his initial lack of distinction by the use of his eyes, which most people found remarkable for their penetration. Napoleon liked very feminine women and indeed could excite them through the passionate nature of his affection, but like Hitler he held them to be inferior to men and their primary role to be good wives and mothers. Like Hitler, he had little to do with girls before his maturity; he married Josephine for love at the age of twenty-six and, after his divorce from her, married Marie Louise, daughter of the Emperor of Austria, for political reasons. He later came to love her very dearly. Both his wives were unfaithful to him, taking lovers in his stead, while he himself had several mistresses. Hitler, as far as we know, had but one mistress, Eva Braun, and married her formally only before their joint suicide. Napoleon made one serious attempt at suicide after his abdication, but failed.

Napoleon was astonishingly self-effacing in many respects, considerate of other people's opinions and feelings though he could, like most energetic men, be insensitive or lacking in understanding when faced with the unexpected in other people, including women. In religion he was inclined to scepticism, but was essentially tolerant of the beliefs of others. Hitler had little interest in any opinion but his own; in matters of religion he despised the dogma of the church and what he held to be the effeminate quality of Christianity, though he believed in 'Providence', especially when it appeared to favour himself.

Both men died in their middle fifties, their empires lost. Though fundamentally of a healthier constitution than Hitler, Napoleon suffered from recurrent dysuria (a bladder condition making it difficult and painful to pass water), and he died of cancer of the stomach. Hitler's stomach was also his weak point, but his hypochondriac attitude to health made him suffer more than he need have done through the exploitation of his ailments by his private physician, Dr Morell. He suffered grave deterioration of health following the bomb plot of July, 1944, and looked a physical wreck during the last months of his life.

Hitler, therefore, emerges as a negative genius, a great man *manqué* because his fundamental inhumanity denied him the essential virtues of positive genius, the ability to make some lasting contribution to the betterment of the human condition, to human knowledge, to human experience. In the end, Hitler was dedicated, like Mephistopheles, to the destructive element, and his magnitude was expressed only in the widespread confusion and suffering he wrought. He was virtually untouched by love, the greatest of the human virtues. His undoubted devotion to Germany gradually narrowed to a devotion to himself, the Leader appointed by Destiny (as he saw it) to be the greatest power figure the world had ever known. But without humanity, without love of people, such power became destructive, and led him finally to the retributive act of self-annihilation. This is the final significance of the shrunken, angry, deluded figure in the bunker, the ultimate example of *folie de grandeur*.

If He Had Won . . .

If Britain had collapsed during the summer of 1940 under the pressure of blitzkrieg from the air, followed by invasion at key points along the south coast, the probability is that a form of government would have been continued in exile in Canada. A British Commonwealth war effort would have been mobilized from there. But with the British homeland disposed of, Hitler would have turned his attention to the East and, the moment he felt strong enough, he would have invaded Russia.

Everything would have been done to persuade the British people to become the active ally of Germany in the attack on the Soviet Union. Many of those in Britain who, in the circumstances of actual invasion and occupation, had decided to collaborate, would have been put in positions of authority under SS and military control, and some form of British puppet government would have been established. Local SS and secret police forces would have been formed, as in all occupied countries, to assist, in a subsidiary capacity, the German SS overlords. As far as possible, it would have been British representatives who were put in immediate charge of the civilian administration, if only to delude the public into thinking things were, after all, much the same as usual. Naturally the press and all forms of communication would be under a strict censorship. Meanwhile, behind closed doors and in the prisons, people of note known to have opposed Hitler would have been incarcerated and subject to interrogation, torture, prolonged imprisonment or death. Preliminary lists of names had already been drawn up, and have since been published. Hopefully, a strong resistance movement would have developed in Britain, with underground forces working closely with those in France, each encouraging and sustaining the other. But the more active sabotage by the resistance had become, the harder would have been the lot of the population in general. The Nazis made it evident that collaboration paid handsomely, while to remain passively obedient and unresistant might at least ensure a peaceful, if penurious existence.

The next immediate problem would have been the position of the British Commonwealth and Empire. With Canada the centre for the activities of a free British Government, North America would have become the pivot for the continued resistance to Hitler, closely aligned with Australia, New Zealand, South Africa, India, and the great British bases in the Far East. However, there is no doubt Hitler would have deferred direct confrontation with this group of powers for as long as possible. His major interest lay in Eastern Europe.

With the war in Western Europe concluded, Hitler would have assembled his armies for engagement with Russia at the earliest possible date. As we know now, the Soviet Union was ill-prepared to resist wholesale blitzkrieg. Hitler might well have achieved his objectives (the capture of Leningrad, Moscow and the Ukraine) by the end of summer, 1941, launching his campaign as early as possible in the spring. This would have been the plan, indeed was the plan in any case, had not Mussolini intervened with his disastrous attack on Greece, which forced Hitler to divert major forces to occupy Yugoslavia, Greece and Crete, and share with Mussolini what was to prove a wasteful expenditure of valuable men and materials in the long stretches of the North African desert. But, with the British homeland occupied, the war in the African area might well have been won quickly, and Egypt with the Suez fallen into German and Italian hands. Hitler, left to his own devices, would no doubt have done what he wanted to do: taken Gibraltar and closed the Mediterranean to the British, and then roused the Arab peoples to help break the British hold in the Eastern Mediterranean and in Asia Minor. By 1943–44, Hitler's control could have spread far to the East, not only in European Russia but south in the Balkans, the Mediterranean and in Asia Minor. The plan in the North was to release territory for the German people and their chosen racial kin, driving large numbers of unwanted racial groups (Poles, Slavs and others) further east into Siberia; the European Jews would have been totally destroyed by means of the increasingly mechanized death chambers and crematoria due to be set up during 1942–43 in occupied Poland and, no doubt, elsewhere east of the Reich in the mid-1940s. Slave labour and the full exploitation of a 'colonial' system would feed wealth back to the German people from all occupied territories.

Hitler's plans for the United States were more vague and schematic, for this was territory of which he knew little. It was far away, like Japan, which, though cemented into the Axis, was not closely integrated like Germany and Italy. Hitler was satisfied to encourage the Japanese in their desire to become the *herrenvolk* of the Far East, hoping they would attack the Soviet Union to the West, take over Singapore and the British possessions in their area, and threaten the security of Australia and New Zealand, and of the forces of the United States based in the Pacific.

Hitler became convinced that the United States was

bound to enter the war against him at some time in the future. He believed America to be far weaker than Germany was, torn by internal dissension. He held that the large numbers of Americans of German descent would prove to be a strong, if not the strongest element in the population and, therefore, war might be postponed, if not prevented through their influence. Hitler's nebulous schemes for world 'conquest' included bringing every possible pressure to bear on the United States while, in the event of war itself, it would become Japan's responsibility to attack America in the Pacific area. Hitler intended to build up relations with fascist interests in Latin America, and exploit resistance there to North American political and economic infiltration. He was convinced Germany could find a ready response, particularly in Argentina and Brazil. Another highly sensitive area affecting the United States was the Caribbean, with its numerous British and French dependencies. These would be especially vulnerable, following the downfall of Britain in Europe.

Meanwhile, within the United States itself, a substantial pro-German movement was being fostered by the Nazis among Americans of German origin, with ready support from certain right-wing, non-German elements. This widespread movement, the so-called German-American Bund, would, in the event of Hitler's total ascendency in Europe, have become increasingly active, urging American alignment with the great new power in Europe rather than with the British government in exile. This clamour could have delayed American entry into the war, though action by the Japanese like the attack on Pearl Harbor would inevitably bring the United States in against the Axis powers.

But the proliferation of Hitler's world 'conquest' would carry with it the seeds of its own destruction. He himself admitted that National Socialism was not for export; it was essentially an indigenous movement. The more this single European nation widened the scope of its control, the more it would have been forced to rely on kindred political movements in other lands which would, in the end, prefer their own forms of dictatorship to that of Hitler. The German movement was held together by the will of a single personality, that of Hitler himself, and he knew that his time was limited and that his health and strength were insecure. The first and most important phase in his dream of conquest lay in Europe. Only if this succeeded, and succeeded quickly, would Hitler have the personal strength to initiate the succeeding phases, of which the first signs, in the form of fifth column activities in countries far from Germany, were already evident.

But Britain did not fall. Russia, summoning her mighty strength, drove back the invader when he was deep in her territory, while the United States threw off her reluctance to become involved, and added further massive forces to defeat the German millions. Gradually, and at incalculable cost, the power of the Nazis was eroded in a war which became global. So Hitler was finally driven to die by his own hand, his aspirations turned to ashes and his dreams to nightmares.

Few men in human history have exercised such power. Hitler's story is in the end unique, at once primitive and contemporary, barbaric and yet involving twentieth century mechanisms for mass-persuasion and mass-destruction. Though blinding in its melodrama, the significance of Hitler's story must nevertheless be comprehended rationally, for it reveals, more perhaps than any other single episode in history, the impulse for self-destruction which our species carries in its blood.

2

Youth and Young Manhood, 1889–1918

'At the back of his mind he had the idea that his son should become an official of the Government ... He was simply incapable of imagining that I might reject what had meant everything in life to him. My father's decision was simple, definite, clear and, in his eyes, it was something to be taken for granted ... For the first time in my life – I was then eleven years old – I felt myself forced into open opposition ... I could not become a civil servant ... It nauseated me to think that one day I might be fettered to an office stool, that I could not dispose of my own time ...'[1]

It was the turn of the century when Hitler, at the age of eleven, claimed to have confronted his sixty-three-year-old father. Alois Hitler was a formidable authoritarian figure in the small Austrian community at Leonding on the outskirts of Linz. He had taken his family there on his retirement in 1895 after forty years' service as a Customs Officer. When Adolf was born on April 20th, 1889, his father had reached the rank of Senior Assistant Customs Officer at Braunau-on-Inn, though they were soon, in 1892, to move to Passau, on the Bavarian, that is the German side of the frontier, where Alois Hitler reached the highest rank open to a man of elementary education, that of Probationary Higher Collector. Later he was posted to Linz, the first town to impinge on young Adolf's imagination, though the family lived in the countryside nearby.

Alois Hitler ranked as a man of modest substance in Leonding; his pension record shows he was receiving some 2,000 kronen, or approximately £85 a year in the value of the period. After his death in January, 1903, when Adolf was a schoolboy, his widow, Klara, received for herself and her children some 1,700 kronen, or £70 a year, quite adequate for a quiet life in the country. Her step-daughter Angela married (unhappily) a junior Tax Officer named Leo Raubal in the same year, 1903, and Klara was left at the age of forty-three to look after Adolf, at that time a schoolboy of fourteen, attending Realschule (high school) in Linz, and his younger sister, Paula, aged seven. Klara's other son, Edmund, had died in 1900 and two other children had died in infancy. Adolf, therefore, became very much a mother's boy.

Klara was a quiet, homely woman, described by people who knew her as quick in her movements, neat and clean, and dutiful to her husband, whom she had married in January, 1885, when already pregnant. She was also Alois's second cousin and, as Catholics, they had been forced to secure episcopal dispensation to marry at all. She was twenty-three years younger than her husband, who had been married twice before.

In his public life, as distinct from his private life, Alois Hitler was the pillar of small town and rural respectability. He came of peasant stock and was used to the narrow social life of a countryside far removed from fashionable Vienna. He was illegitimate, the son of forty-two-year-old Maria Anna Schicklgruber, a peasant woman, who was later to marry the man who was said to be the father of her child, fifty-year-old Johann Georg Hiedler, another form of the name Hitler, which was probably of Czech origin.[2] Alois, however, kept the surname Schicklgruber until he was forty, when, in 1876, he changed it to Hitler. The local priest had been pressured into eliminating the world 'illegitimate' from the parish register in Dollersheim on the strength of witnesses testifying that Johann Georg (who had died in 1857) had acknowledged paternity, when (as far as we know) he had not. The change of name was officially recognized in 1877. It does not appear that Alois cared one way or other about his illegitimacy; it was a condition of birth common in rural Austria to the extent of some forty per cent. It is more likely he made the change in order to preserve the name of Hiedler/Hitler and inherit money from another member of the family, Johann Nepomuk Hiedler, under whose roof Alois had been raised either after his mother's marriage in 1842, or after her death in 1847.

Whoever his forebears were, the respectable Alois Hitler enjoyed a rousing private life with the girls. Hitler chose to paint a stern and gloomy picture of his father, as he did of all those who opposed his will. The evidence is at least to some extent different. In male company at the tavern where he spent a great deal of his free time, he appears to have been a cheerful man who enjoyed drinking, smoking and even singing. Indeed, he actually died at the local inn. Hitler, who came to dislike smoking and drinking, claimed the latter affected his health, but there is no real evidence that he drank other than moderately. It is unlikely he was ever a drunkard, a reputation he earned solely because a later associate of his, Hans Frank, claimed Hitler told him his father was often drunk. And there are generalized passages in *Mein Kampf* about drunkenness which have an almost autobiographical ring to them. However, Alois Hitler was in fact noted for his frugality, and highly conscious of himself as a self-made man who had started life as a boot-maker's apprentice in Vienna at the age of thirteen. By dint of hard work and self-education he had transferred himself to the Civil Service in which he enjoyed a successful career. At the office he was generally considered a hard man to work with. In private life he handled his money carefully (including the capital acquired through successive dowries), buying and selling a series of modest properties, including a nine-acre small holding. In outlook, he was something of a free-thinker, and his hobby had been bee-keeping. At home, he acted like a typical, lower middle-class authoritarian of the period. He was head of the house, and they all knew it. But he was seldom at home, no doubt to the family's relief. There is no real evidence that he ill-treated either his wife or his children physically. Seeing that he had so capable a wife, he probably left the detailed management of his family entirely in her hands. But he does not seem to have cared overmuch for his children. A friend of the family has said, 'He was strict with his family, no kid gloves as far as they were concerned; his wife had nothing to smile about.' However, he did not beat the children. 'He never touched him,' that is, Adolf, 'but he often scolded and bawled at him.' There can be little doubt, however, that Adolf came to dislike, perhaps even hate his father and identify himself closely with his mother.

With women, Alois Hitler's attitude had shown a peasant-like irresponsibility. When he was about thirty he had an illegitimate daughter by a girl known as Thekla P. Then, in 1873, when he was thirty-six he had married Anna Glassl, a woman of fifty, probably for her money. In 1876, when visiting her foster-father, Johann Nepomuk (probably in connection with his change of name that same year), he had met his second cousin, Klara, then aged sixteen, and soon afterwards introduced her as domestic help into his home at Braunau. Soon she was to become his mistress. His elderly wife was by now a sick woman.

Meanwhile, however, he had fostered another relationship with a young servant-girl at the local inn, Franziska Matzelberger. In this complex situation, Franziska finally prevailed; Anna separated officially from her husband in 1880 and Franziska (aged only nineteen) took up residence with him. Klara was at this stage sent away. In spite of the fact that as Catholics, they could not marry while Anna was still alive, Franziska bore Alois a son in 1882. When, the following year, Anna died of consumption, Alois at the age of forty-six, married his twenty-two-year-old mistress and legitimized his son, whose name was also Alois. In the same year, Franziska had a daughter, Angela. Alois junior was a wastrel, and was to prove a minor thorn in Hitler's flesh when he was Führer of Germany, but Angela was to form, for a while, a closer connection with her half-brother, with dramatic consequences. She was the mother of Geli Raubal, Hitler's niece, with whom he was to fall obsessively in love.

Franziska was no more happy with her middle-aged husband than Anna had been, and like the older woman she died of tuberculosis (a common disease at the time) in 1884, aged only twenty-three. She had left Alois and the children to live in the countryside near Braunau, and was sufficiently indifferent to permit (if she had any option) Klara to return to look after the family. She was known as Alois's 'niece', and was at once mistress, nurse and housekeeper. She was pregnant by the time Franziska died.

So the pattern repeated itself. Securing their dispensation, the cousins (she twenty-five, he forty-eight) were married just in time to legitimize the first child, Edmund, who died in infancy. Whether the marriage could be regarded as adequate or not – it could scarcely have been happy – Klara was to become an exemplary mother. She remained a simple and unpretentious woman. As Hitler put it, 'My mother would have cut a poor figure in the society of our cultivated women. She lived strictly for her husband and children. They were her entire universe.'[3]

Hitler's revenge for his father's opposition to his desire to train as an artist was to do badly at school. He attended the Realschule at Linz from September, 1900, when he was eleven, to 1904, when he was fourteen, and his school record was so poor he was forced to leave. The education given stressed non-classical subjects, educating the pupil for a practical career rather than one requiring academic training. Hitler's own comments on his schooling in the autobiographical section of *Mein Kampf* are almost wholly misleading; he was putting a gloss on his youth for the purpose of building a personal mythology. His one expressed desire was to be a painter, to which his father had replied categorically, 'Not as long as I live, never.' In consequence, Adolf set out to prove he was being given the wrong education:

> I thought that, once it became clear to my father that I was making no progress at the Realschule . . . he would be forced to allow me to follow the happy career I had dreamed of . . . Certainly, my failure to make progress became quite visible in the school. I studied just the subjects which appealed to me . . . What did not otherwise appeal to me favourably, I completely sabotaged . . . By far my best subjects were geography and, even more so, general history. These were my two favourite subjects, and I led the class in them.[4]

He was, he claimed, fortunate in his history teacher, Dr Leopold (actually Ludwig) Poetsch, who turned the subject into a 'living reality'. This was what he wrote in *Mein Kampf* over twenty years later. Much later, in his *Table*

Talk of 1942, he added, 'In Austria, religious instruction was given by priests. I was the eternal asker of questions. Since I was completely master of the material, I was unassailable. I always had the best marks. On the other hand, I was less impeccable under the heading of Behaviour.' And, 'I got bad marks in German! My disgusting teacher . . . asserted that I would never be capable of writing a decent letter! . . . I showed not the slightest aptitude for foreign languages – though I might have done, had not the teacher been a congenital idiot!'[5] The majority of the professors were, he says, 'somewhat mentally deranged', and he boasted of the way such masters were ragged by the boys.

In fact, Hitler's school reports show that whereas he achieved normally a 'very satisfactory' for conduct, in his final year he was given a 'pass' only on condition he left the school. In 1904 (the year he was confirmed a Catholic, at the age of sixteen, in the Cathedral at Linz), he transferred to another school at Steyr, some fifty miles away from Leonding; here his school report (which survives intact) still gives him 'very satisfactory' for moral conduct, and only 'adequate' in Religious Instruction, Geography and History. On the other hand, his only 'excellent' is in gymnastics. His freehand drawing is reported 'good'.

What seems evident is that Hitler was inventing in *Mein Kampf* another, more romantic pupil in place of his true self; the real Hitler was remarkable only for lack of what his teachers called 'diligence'. This was in marked contrast to his success in primary school, where his first teacher, Herr Mittermaier, described him as alert, obedient and lively, or at his second school in the country at Lambach, where his reports were excellent. He learned singing and had a good voice. At his third primary school in the village of Leonding near Linz, he became more addicted to outdoor romps. 'We were always playing at war – war games endlessly,' one of his fellow pupils has recalled. 'I became the leader of a small gang,' is how Hitler put it himself.[6] He was not, however, a fighter. He fought with his tongue. It was at this time, he reports in *Mein Kampf*, that he discovered two illustrated bound volumes on the Franco-Prussian War on his father's bookshelf. Young Adolf's passion for Germany had gone back to his early childhood in Passau, Bavaria, when his father was stationed there in 1895. Although he was only six when he left Passau, he had already begun to assimilate the Bavarian dialect, and felt Bavaria to be, in a sense, 'home'. And he had learned even in play, something of the traditional German (not Austrian) hatred of the French. His favourite boyhood reading, he was later to admit, were the stories of Karl May, the German equivalent of Fennimore Cooper.

With the death of his father and of his younger brother Edmund, Adolf became the only male of the family living at home. Alois, his shiftless half-brother, had left at the age of fourteen after a prolonged and violent quarrel with his father; he was to get work as a waiter and in 1900 received the first of a series of jail sentences for theft. Adolf, on the other hand, became the object of his mother's devotion. In 1905 he fell ill (possibly from a lung infection) and Klara nursed him devotedly now that he was back in her care. It was to be the beginning of a long period of uncertainty and malingering. Meanwhile, she had sold the family property advantageously, and with some capital at her disposal as well as her pension, she set up her household in an apartment at Linz, where Hitler had his own room in which to dream about the future.

Hitler's trouble with authority, both parental and educational, related therefore directly with the period when, as he says in *Mein Kampf*, he had decided that he wanted to be an artist. 'This happened when I was twelve years old,' he wrote. 'How it came about I cannot exactly say now, but one day it became clear to me that I would be a painter – I mean an artist.'[7] This conviction never left him; when he failed as an artist on canvas, he dreamed of becoming an architect, a builder of cities. When this, too, failed, he had passed through the experience of war, he dreamed of becoming an artist in politics. In this he succeeded. But when finally he dreamed of becoming an artist in war, he failed once again. This was to be his final, most extravagant dream, and it cost him his life.

In fact, at the age of sixteen, Hitler was to embark on a prolonged period in which he had no settled occupation. He liked it to be thought of as a period of suffering and gestation, a great man's odyssey through the vale of despair before his ultimate recognition and rise to power as the leader of his country. We have a picture of him sitting at his mother's table in Linz given by a constant visitor to the family between 1905 and 1907:

> Often when we were at table . . . [he] would take a sheet of paper and make a quick sketch of some building, column, archway, window or whatever occurred to him. Often, too, he would draw the heads of people of different races . . . I can recall very clearly an oil painting with a red velvet curtain and a still-life in front of it with which he took special pains, also building plans for the Linz provincial theatre, and some watercolours . . .[8]

The same witness remembered that Klára was in very poor health, whereas 'Adolf was never ill'.

It was at this time that Hitler made a friend. This was August Kubizek, son of an upholsterer in Linz. He was only nine months older than Hitler, and it was their mutual passion for music, especially opera, which brought them together. They were to be virtually inseparable until July 1908, and Kubizek has left a highly idealized picture of Hitler during this period in his book, *Young Hitler*, originally published in German in 1953. Nevertheless, these memoirs with due allowance for the great gap of time, almost half a century between the events and their recollection, are of great importance for understanding Hitler's slow maturation during an extensive period of what was, in effect, prolonged adolescence.

The years 1905 to 1908 were crucial in Hitler's youth. In May, 1906, when he was seventeen, he spent about a month in Vienna, staying possibly with his godparents. He sent four cards to Kubizek, which are preserved, full of comments on architecture and on his visits to the opera. The trip is estimated to have cost his mother some 200 kronen from her savings. Once home, he began to learn to play the piano, and his mother bought him an instrument. He also took endless walks round Linz with Kubizek, replanning the city and drawing innumerable sketches. He wore smart clothes and lived a life of ease and self-indulgence far beyond the meagre allowance of 240 kronen, or £10 a year, which the Authority allowed him as a fatherless child until his twenty-fourth year, or until he became self-supporting.

Pressure was no doubt being put upon him to work. Hitler heartily disliked his half-sister Angela's husband, Leo Raubal, who made no secret of his opinion about Adolf's laziness. So, too, no doubt did his guardian, Josef Mayrhofer, a friend of his father, and at one time Mayor of Leonding. Such pressure had no effect. Hitler was determined to become a perpetual art student.

In this ambition he was, however, unfortunate. In the autumn of 1907, after his mother had had an operation for cancer of the breast early in August, he went to Vienna for a while. In October his application to enter the Vienna Academy of Fine Arts was rejected on the ground that his best work was not good enough. He was eighteen, and he records in *Mein Kampf* the blow this rejection represented: 'I was so concerned of my success that when the news that I had failed to pass was brought to me it struck me like a bolt from the skies.' However, he treated the rejection as a revelation that he was destined for different work: 'Within a few days I ... knew that I ought to become an architect.'[9]

He had drawn his patrimony from his mother before leaving for Vienna – a sum amounting to some £27 – to which his orphan's benefit of just over one pound a month could be added. He could manage to live for a time on this while studying his future. However, a further blow was to follow; in December his mother died. There is some doubt whether he returned to Linz in time to be with her at the end. Kubizek claimed that he did, showing the utmost devotion, but it would seem from the evidence that he was wrong. But his grief was intense. The family doctor, Eduard Bloch has recalled: 'In all my career I have never seen anyone so prostrate with grief.' Dr Bloch was a Jew. After the funeral he stood at her grave long after his sisters had left.

There can be little question that Hitler was devoted to his mother in his own peculiar way. 'I had honoured my father, but my mother I had loved,' he wrote in *Mein Kampf*.[10]

His developing, self-indulgent egocentricity meant that any affection he experienced was coloured by what he instinctively felt to be his own needs; in this sense, he exploited his mother's affection for him in his moody adolescence and felt entitled to draw on her modest resources in order to indulge his genius, as he believed it to be. The importance of the relationship of Hitler to his mother is that it affected his attitude to women of his own generation throughout his life. He venerated them and, when they responded to him, he exploited them. His mother set the example of dutiful affection alike to an unsympathetic husband and to a son who already felt the stirrings of 'genius', stirrings which warned him instinctively against adopting any kind of settled work which must inevitably delimit his freedom and frustrate his vague aspirations.

Psychologists have made their own assumptions concerning Hitler's childhood orientation to his mother. Some see it as Oedipal, with bitter resentment of any physical contact between Klara and her husband. There can be little doubt that Hitler's development was to a considerable degree abnormal. Because of lack of demonstrable evidence, he has been variously accused of being homosexual, a chronic masturbator, impotent, a practitioner of masochistic perversions. Dr Walter Langer, who was responsible during the war for the secret compilation of psychological observations on Hitler for the American Office of Strategic Services, claims there was a strong masochistic streak in Hitler, as well as a powerful feminine element in his psychological make-up, with its pronounced emotional characteristics. Langer asserts that his sexual relations with women were apparently of an unusual nature, and account for the suicide of his niece Geli Raubal and the two successive suicide attempts made by Eva Braun. According to Langer, he was at one stage at least listed by the Vienna police as a sexual pervert, though this could be more by association with perverts than by actual practice. In early middle age during the 1920s, when he was in his thirties, he responded to older women who enjoyed 'mothering' him, such as Frau Carola Hoffman, Frau Helena Bechstein, Frau Victoria von Dirxsen, as well as Frau Winifred Wagner and Frau Goebbels, who were more of Hitler's own age. Finally, there is the evidence published by the Russians that, on the exhumation of Hitler's half-burnt body from its shallow grave in the Chancellery gardens, he was found to have only a single testicle.

Hitler was eighteen when his mother died. His character was already forming in spite of his late maturation. His mother's death threw him virtually on his own resources, and for a brief period he transferred his need for some form of companionship to his friend, Kubizek, whose recollections fill in the gaps left open in Hitler's rationalizations about his youth in *Mein Kampf*. Hitler, it should be said, felt no responsibility to the other members of the family, even his young sister Paula, aged twelve, who went to live with her married half-sister, Angela Raubal. He drew what he could from the slight family patrimony left after his mother's expensive illness. There is no trace of a will, and the money was evidently divided beforehand. Research shows that Hitler's share of his mother's remaining capital could not have been more than 1,000 kronen (£40 50p) to which must be added the orphan's pension (allowable up to the age of twenty-four) of 25 kronen (about one pound) a month; and the records still exist that this pension was applied for in 1908, and paid.[11] In other words, assuming he had already spent the small capital inherited from his father, Hitler possessed the means of existence on the level of a postman (paid then some 60 kronen a month) for well over a year following his departure from Linz for permanent residence in Vienna, posing as a student. There is also evidence he received some further financial help later on from his hunchback aunt, Johanna Pölzl, who was unmarried and died in 1911, the year he voluntarily gave up his pension at the age of twenty-three, following the inheritance of some money from her.

He was to stay in Vienna from 1908 to 1913 without any settled occupation. In *Mein Kampf* he took pleasure in creating an image of himself as a martyr to suffering and neglect, against which he pitted his calm, his resolution, his unconquerable will. His educational qualifications were insufficient for him to be accepted as a student of architecture. He even refers to himself as a 'mother's darling' hurled into a 'world of misery and poverty' and experiencing 'daily hunger'. He claims one pleasure, his books, and one extravagance, 'rare visits to the Opera, paid for in hunger'.[12] He is nearer the truth when he claims that at this time 'there took shape within me a world picture and a world philosophy which became the granite foundation of all my acts.' Since then, he asserts, 'I have had to learn little; and have had to alter nothing.' During the period of his alleged poverty he claims he worked for a brief time on a building site, and describes the hard lot of the labourers, whose trade union he apparently refused to join. His claim to have worked as a labourer is probably apocryphal, he could scarcely have had the stamina. Also he says, 'I painted to make a living and studied for pleasure.'

There remains, however, the picture of him during the first months of 1908 which Kubizek has described so convincingly. He is obviously proud of his early friendship with the future Führer and, like Hitler, sets out to idealize it. Kubizek's father was apparently convinced at a single session with Hitler that he should permit his son to study music in Vienna, which (if true) shows Hitler's strength of character even at this early age. Hitler, in fact, was determined to claim Kubizek for himself. Kubizek joined him in Vienna in February, 1908, and they shared a large damp back room, for which they each paid the landlady 10 crowns a month. It was at No. 29 *Stumpergasse*, near the station.

Hitler's passion was architecture. He studied buildings in Vienna, as he had done in Linz, constantly sketching, planning, discussing, criticizing. It was to become a lifelong interest, revived in his days of power. Kubizek pleased Hitler because he was happy to listen endlessly: 'Because of his overwhelming gift of persuasion, I agreed with him even when in my heart I held a completely different opinion.'[13] Hitler emerges as a young man of deeply serious outlook, enjoying no youthful gaiety, expending his restless energy on walking, reading, drawing. He wrote poetry and plays, although his spelling and grammar were still faulty. He even planned to compose an opera under the influence of Wagner. More important, he was fostering his hatreds to a point when he seemed 'almost sinister'; he hated Viennese society, smoking, drinking, Marxism, the Jews, idling Army officers, the educational bureaucracy which had rejected his work. His humour, such as it was, developed a sardonic, ironic twist. He rejected entirely the idea of military service in the Austro-Hungarian Army. He was a social outsider, obsessed by his own ceaseless, ill-disciplined flow of ideas. According to Kubizek, 'he read prodigiously, and with the help of his extraordinary memory, stored up an amount of knowledge which was far above the normal standard.' He 'absorbed with fervour', but avoided any rational examination of what he took in. He was intolerant, and gave way to rages; 'he would fly into a temper at the slightest thing'. He held forth on every aspect of social injustice, working himself up into paroxysms of anger. Above all, he hated money. 'To hell with it,' he used to say.

In appearance he was still very neat, and his social manners were polite – 'Adolf set great store by good manners and correct behaviour.' But his old-fashioned gentility gave way to an over-bearing manner the moment he was alone with Kubizek and launched himself into an argument. He often went without food rather than miss an opera, and his life became that of an indolent ascetic. He seemed quite uninterested in girls during his period in Vienna. Following a prolonged obsession for a fashionable girl in Linz – which he had entertained only at a distance and fed entirely from his own imagination – he had relapsed into misogyny. This wholly one-sided romance, according to Kubizek, beginning in his sixteenth year when he was still at school, had lasted almost four years. The girl was called Stefanie, she was blonde and slightly older than Hitler; and he had fallen in love with her in the street. She had eventually married an officer in the Austrian Army. Questioned after the war, Stefanie had no recollection of the pale young 'student' with whom Hitler claimed he had exchanged rapturous, secret glances in the street, but whom he had never dared to address openly. Her finally unconscious 'rejection' of her silent lover, who was convinced she was only waiting for the direct declaration of marriage he was not in a position to make, drove him, says Kubizek, seriously to contemplate suicide. It had been a love affair conducted wholly in terms of fantasy.

Kubizek insists that Hitler was sexually quite normal:

> I must categorically assert that Adolf, in physical as well as sexual respects, was absolutely normal ... He had wanted Stefanie for his wife, for him she was the ideal of German womanhood.[14]

He was repelled by homosexuality and refrained from masturbation, and he had insisted Kubizek maintain the same high, ascetic standards as himself. Yet this strange young man always attracted the attention of girls. Kubizek puts it down to his eyes:

> Never in my life have I seen any other person whose appearance – how shall I put it – was so completely dominated by the eyes. They were the light eyes of his mother ... It was uncanny how these eyes would change their expression ... Adolf spoke with his eyes.[15]

'Naturally, I meant far less to Adolf than he did to me,' Kubizek admits. Soon it was July, and, for Kubizek, time to return home after success in his examinations at the Conservatoire. Hitler, who could not bear sentiment, bade him farewell at the station, pressed his hands, and disappeared.

He was not to see him again for thirty years, although he received a few postcards and letters during the summer. Kubizek's mother sent Hitler food parcels, but when her son returned to Vienna after military service in November, 1909, his friend had gone without leaving an address.

Hitler had left, apparently, because he was short of money. He drifted from address to address as winter came on, sometimes disappearing without paying his rent. By December he had joined the large tramp population of Vienna, herding at night into the Meldling shelter with its mass dormitories, its disinfection of vermin-infested clothes, its meals of bread and soup. Hitler's story now falls into the hands of such fellow-tramps and unemployed men as came into contact with him and with the police during this dire period. The first of these was Reinhold Hanisch, who in the 1930s made what capital he could out of this brief association, painting bogus pictures which he claimed were Hitler's and writing accounts of their partnership for the press.

The story is well-known. Hanisch taught Hitler how to look after himself during the severe winter days, doing odd jobs, scrounging food. He roused Hitler from lethargy; with 50 kronen, probably sent following an appeal to his aunt Johanna, Hitler bought a winter overcoat. Hanisch and he set up home in the State Men's Hostel in the industrial suburb of Brittgenau; Hitler painted post-cards of Vienna and other larger pictures which Hanisch sold. The hostel was large and comfortable, and could be used during the day. There was a canteen, and cubicles cost some 3 kronen a week. The working partnership lasted until the summer, when with increasing lapses on Hitler's part and some forgeries by Hanisch, the relationship collapsed.

By this time Hitler had other friends in the hostel, and time was spent in continuous argument on social and political matters. Accounts of indifferent value have come from such witnesses as Josef Greiner, a lamp-lighter, and a broken-down 'intellectual', Karl Honisch, who joined in the recurrent political debates, which, in 1913, interrupted Hitler's painting. He recalls his gesticulations, and his dangling forelock of hair. He produced now a steady stream of paintings which he sold regularly to Jewish dealers. He was shabbily genteel in appearance. His income up to 1913, when he finally left for Munich, has been estimated at 80 to 100 kronen a month. In addition, he retained his orphan's benefit of 25 kronen a month until, on inheriting money from his aunt Johanna, he yielded to legal pressure from Angela (recently widowed) and gave up his orphan's pension in favour of his sister, Paula.

What finally drove Hitler to leave for Munich in May, 1913, at the age of twenty-four, was his conviction that he had been successful in his annual evasion of military service, for which he had been first due to report in 1909. 'Failed to report. Address unknown', is how it had been recorded in Linz. No doubt he considered he could safely leave the country without prosecution as a deserter. In *Mein Kampf* he claims he left because he could no longer stand living in Austria. As a true German, he was 'impatient to know the happiness of living and striving' in the 'common Fatherland, the German Reich'. Once in Germany he registered as stateless. He was, however, finally tracked down with the help of the Munich police; he was summoned to report in Linz in January, 1914, and placed under arrest in Munich. Through the Austrian Consul-General in Munich he sent a long, wordy, slightly illiterate letter claiming, among other things, that he was on the register in Vienna, but never called, offering penury and ill health as an excuse:

> For two years I had no other friend than care and want, no other companion but everlasting, insatiable hunger. I never learned the meaning of that fine word, Youth. Today after five years the tokens are still with me in the form of chilblains in fingers, hands and feet ... Despite the most utter penury, in the midst of often more than dubious surroundings, I have always preserved my good name, am untainted before the law and clean before my own conscience except for that one omission over the military report ... That is the only thing for which I feel responsible. And for that a modest fine should surely offer penance enough and of such I shall not refuse my willing payment.[16]

Through the kindly intervention of the Consul-General, he was spared by the authorities and summoned without further threat of penalty to report to Salzburg for examination the following month. The Commission found that he was 'unfit for combatant and auxiliary duties, too weak. Unable to bear arms.'

Nevertheless, he was soon to volunteer for the German Army. A few months after being declared unfit to serve, he was anxiously seeking permission as an Austrian national to join a Bavarian regiment. This change of front, if not of heart, was caused by the war fever of August, 1914. The celebrated picture of Hitler's upturned face framed in the crowd assembled to hear the proclamation of war shows the ardour of the volunteer, as well as the neat, respectable appearance of a city clerk. After a period of training, he left for the front in October, 1914, serving in the List regiment. His future supporter, Rudolf Hess, was in the same regiment.

The List regiment saw arduous service, at Ypres, at Neuve Chapelle, on the Somme. In December, Hitler wrote a long, vivid letter to his landlord in Munich describing life on the front. By now he was serving as a runner, carrying messages between the regiment and H.Q. He was wounded in the leg in 1916. After further hard frontline service with the rank of Lance-Corporal, he was severely gassed and temporarily blinded in October, 1918. He was still in hospital when the war ended. He was twenty-nine.

His comrades thought him strange; one eyewitness report comments on the way he would sit brooding, silent and unapproachable, while at other times he would rage against the Communists and the Jews. He does not appear to have sought promotion. He received the Iron Cross (second class) as early as December 2nd, 1914, and, after other decorations, the Iron Cross (first class) in 1918, the citation speaking of his 'cold-blooded courage', his 'readiness to sacrifice himself . . . in the greatest peril of his life'. Hitler the dilettante artist and agitator had now become Hitler the militarist. A wholly new dimension had been added to his character.

In Vienna, before the war, he had acquired, as we shall see, his more lasting prejudices: against the Habsburg monarchy and Empire (identified in his mind with his father), against social democracy, against the Marxists, against the Jews and the Eastern Europeans of mixed race who filled Vienna. He hated alike the capitalists and the left-wing trade unionists, both of whom he identified with the Jews. His exclusive German racialism and nationalism were fostered by his dislike of the polyglot humanity which had drifted through the Men's Hostel.

Yet he was by no means ready for a political career. War service was to toughen him and teach him at least to function, if not to sympathize with others, to understand the nature of activity within a disciplined unit. Before this he had been listless and self-indulgent, utterly lacking in discipline and purpose. He emerged from the war ready to adopt a new, far more purposive style of living. He had seen leadership in action.

Kubizek recalls, with how much idealization no one knows, a significant moment in their early days together in Linz. After a performance of Wagner's *Rienzi*, which neither of them had seen before, Hitler was abnormally silent and insisted on walking through the night to the top of the Freinberg. Then he burst out in what Kubizek describes as a state of 'complete ecstasy and rapture'. The influence of the opera, which shows how Rienzi rises to be Tribune of the people, led him to forecast some form of leadership for himself. 'He spoke of a special mission which one day would be entrusted to him.' As they reached Kubizek's house the clock struck three, but Hitler did not walk away in the direction of his home. He turned once again towards the mountain, as if his messianic mood was still upon him.[17] Kubizek was to remind him of this incident when they met again in 1939, shortly before the war which was to be the climax of Hitler's career. The Führer was evidently very pleased, and remembered it all clearly. He was seventeen at the time.

In his biography, The Life and Death of Adolf Hitler, *published in 1973, Robert Payne claims, on the strength of entries in manuscript memoirs written by Bridget Hitler, Hitler's sister-in-law, and preserved by the archive of New York Library, that Hitler visited her and her husband, Hitler's brother Alois, in Liverpool, England, during 1912–13, staying there for five months. If this most unlikely record is correct, the experience was unique in Hitler's life as he was never to live in any foreign country, only Austria and Germany.*

3

Munich, 1919-1923

Bavaria with a population of seven million ranked as the second State in Germany, though it stood far behind Prussia with thirty-eight million. Prussia had its administrative capital in Berlin, the centre also for the federal system of the new German Republic established after the war. Bavaria, with its capital of Munich, was traditionally hostile to Prussia and alien to Berlin, where the Federal seat of government, the Reichstag, met, dominated by the Social Democrats, who were the leading party in Germany. Each of Germany's seventeen states retained its own state government operating regionally and distinct from the Federal governing body.

The capitulation of Germany in November, 1918, came as a traumatic shock to the German people, who had believed they could still win the war. Ludendorff had stood within striking distance of Paris as late as March, 1918. The government was left to deliver what came to be called 'the stab in the back', while the people had turned against the Army they had formerly been led to admire.[1] With the Kaiser in exile, the post-war threat to Germany's trade and bourgeois stability came from the violent clashes between the forces of the extreme left, who wanted Germany to follow Russia into Communism and those of the extreme right, the nationalists who wanted the rule of Germany to be conducted by the so-called elite, the Junkers or landowners, the industrialists and the officer caste.

Revolution was in the air, not least in Bavaria. The King had abdicated. Munich became prey to violence. Social democracy gave way in April, 1919, to an attempted *coup d'état*, which was in turn overset by the right-wing Freikorps movement, manned by ex-servicemen dedicated to the bloody suppression of the left. In March, 1920, another

Social Democratic government fell in favour of an exclusively right-wing administration under Gustav von Kahr, and with the failure of a similar right-wing revolt in Berlin, known as the Kapp Putsch, Munich could be said to have become the principal centre in Germany for right-wing political activity and the Freikorps.

In *Mein Kampf* Hitler was to express his virulent disgust at the state of things in Germany immediately after the war. He was still blinded, and could read no newspapers; he learned by word of mouth that some form of revolution was taking place – led, as he put it, by 'a few Jewish youths' – that the Kaiser had abdicated, that Germany was now a Republic. His reaction, even by his own account, was hysterical:

> Everything went black before my eyes: I tottered and groped my way back to the dormitory, threw myself on my bunk, and lay my burning head on to my blanket and pillow.[2]

He builds the melodrama of the moment to a crescendo, challenging his own despair in the heat of recollection, cursing the 'miserable and desperate criminals who have brought such disgrace on Germany'. What was the future to be? It was then that the moment of decision arrived. 'I, for my part, decided to go into politics,' he writes.

Hitler returned to Munich from the hospital, his sight restored, although it was never to be good. Dr Langer claims that his blindness, and his refusal for a while even to speak, were regarded by his doctor as a 'classic' case of hysteria, and that the gas attack had, in fact, little to do with the symptoms he manifested. However, he was so disgusted with the situation in Munich that he volunteered for duty in a prisoner-of-war camp in Traunstein, and did not return to Munich until early in 1919. He was still in uniform, and he was to remain in the Army (receiving Army pay and rations) until April, 1920. He claims his disaffection with the socialist 'Soldiers' Councils' led to an attempt to arrest him in April, 1919, but that he drove off the three Communists sent to fetch him by levelling his carbine at them. Whatever happened, Hitler allied himself with the forces of the Right, undergoing a training course for agitators privately sponsored at Munich University by Captain Karl Mayr, Army Staff Officer in charge of information and propaganda. They were to be responsible for countering the propaganda of the left, current among men who were in the process of being demobilized. In July he was at work in Lechfeld demobilization centre. He was reported to be a 'born orator, who with his fanaticism and popular manner in a group, compels the listeners to attention and agreement'.[3]

So Hitler, while still a member of the Forces, became a political agent, and as such was sent to investigate an embryonic political group in Munich, the German Workers' Party, led by Anton Drexler, a railway mechanic. Hitler attended a meeting of some twenty-five people belonging to the group in a Munich tavern on September 12th, 1919; he listened to the speeches, and protested with such vehemence to a suggestion that Bavaria should separate from Germany that he was invited to meet the members of the committee of six who ran this small movement. Among them, in addition to Drexler, were Karl Harrer, a journalist, Gottfried Feder, another engineer by trade, with strong views concerning the abolition of high finance, and Dietrich Eckart, journalist and poet, and member of the Thule Society, a seemingly cultural organization which acted as cover for the right-wing political group which had murdered Kurt Eisner, the leader of the Bavarian socialists.

Hitler found the Party most interesting, not least because of its obscurity; its funds stood at only 7·50 marks, and its business seemed to be confined to discussion meetings held in beer-halls. Nevertheless, when they invited him to join the Organizing Committee as its seventh member, he consented:

> This absurd little organization with its few members seemed to me to possess the one advantage that it had not frozen into an 'organization', but left the individual an opportunity for real personal activity . . . The smaller the movement, the more readily it could be put into proper form.[4]

Hitler set about taking possession of this group, largely through his successful apprenticeship as a speaker at public meetings. The gatherings gradually increased in size and soon he was chosen to be head of the Party's propaganda. At a mass rally which attracted some two thousand people on February 24th, 1920, he announced in person a new name for the movement, the National Socialist German Workers' Party (*Nationalsozialistische Deutsche Arbeiterpartei*, NSDAP, or more vulgarly, the Nazi Party). The newly named party had a political platform of twenty-five points drawn up by Hitler, Drexler, Feder and Eckart, involving unification of all racial Germans, the 'right to self-determination' naturally, equal rights for the Germans, the abolition of the Versailles Treaty, the restoration of Germany's confiscated colonies, the suppression of the Jews and confiscation of Jewish-owned capital, the state ownership of trusts and of certain lands, the promotion of small business enterprises at the expense of finance capital (understood to be Jewish), and the establishment of some form of strong central government as yet undefined.

The military putsch which took place in Bavaria the following month seemed to fulfil some part of these hopes, but Hitler decided that his presence in the Army was no longer compatible with his new role as political agitator. He left the Army on April 1st, 1920; henceforward his role was to be entirely that of the politician.

It is at this stage that he began to gather round him as allies and supporters certain of the formidable names which help to spell out the nature of Nazism in the popular memory of the movement: Roehm, Hess and Goering. Their particular roles complement that of Hitler. Captain Ernst Roehm was the professional soldier who believed that the Army should intervene to preserve Germany from the left; he was far more a tough and unscrupulous soldier of fortune than the traditional kind of Prussian officer, and his side activities involved him as much with the *Freikorps* as with the Army (the *Reichswehr*) itself, though he was to remain in the Army until 1923. He was thickset and overbearing, his face fleshy, and he was later to become noted for his homosexual practices. In 1919, at the age of thirty-two, he had become adjutant to General Franz Ritter von Epp, Military Area Commander in Munich, and his interest in the German Workers' Party had led him to join even before Hitler. With the disbandment of the *Freikorps* units by the Allies during 1920–21, the formation of the Party's own squads seemed all the more important to such men as Roehm, and some of the *Freikorps* arms which should have been handed in found their way to Hitler's embryonic SA (*Sturmabteilung*) movement which he established to police his meetings and harass his opponents in the streets. Roehm was one of the original leaders of these squads.

Rudolf Hess, too, had found the Party in April, 1920, when he was twenty-six. Born in Alexandria, of a respectable bourgeois family from Bavaria, he had been educated in Germany, to which his father, a businessman, had returned in 1900. After studying commerce in Switzerland, Hess had served in the First Bavarian Infantry Regiment and (after being wounded in action) in the List Regiment, ending the war in the Imperial Flying Corps as an officer pilot. He shared in the sense of disgrace in Germany's capitulation which obsessed all the officers who retained their traditional, sternly nationalistic outlook. He had taken part in the street fighting which had led to the overthrow of Bavaria's short-lived Communist administration, and was studying history and economics at Munich University under the influence of Professor Karl Haushofer, whose views on what he termed geo-politics (which emphasized the need for Germany to win living-space in the East) Hess was soon to pass on to Hitler.

Hess, like Hitler, was something of an odd-man-out in his youth. He was absorbed by politics, eschewed dancing and social life, did not smoke or drink and was shy and reserved with his girl friend, Ilse Pröhl, a fellow student at the University. His only excitement was Hitler, who served as his model for a prize essay he wrote on the character of a future leader for Germany:

> The deeper the dictator was originally rooted in the broad masses, the better he understands how to treat them psychologically . . . He himself has nothing in common

with the mass; like every great man, he is all personality . . . When necessity commands, he does not shrink before bloodshed. Great questions are always decided by blood and iron.[5]

By 1921 Hitler had adopted this strongly built, well educated and sternly dedicated young man, with his keen eyes staring out from under bushy eyebrows. He became his aide, his confidant, his sounding board. He spoke, in a letter written in May, 1921, to the Bavarian premier, Gustav von Kahr, on Hitler's behalf, of his 'close personal relationship with him' and with Professor Dr Haushofer. He told the Premier, too, of the importance Hitler attached to winning working-class support for German nationalism, and he was prepared to play his part in the street brawls with the Communist faction which had become a feature of Nazi tactics during the troubled days of galloping inflation of the mark. The nation's troubles in 1921–23 were precisely what the Nazis needed to make their first real impact in Germany's political life. The mark was to collapse, finally disintegrating into billions before the currency reform of November, 1923.

By 1921 the Party was wholly in Hitler's hands; he was made the Leader on July 29th, 1921. Attempts to control him by the outgoing forces, such as Harrer and Drexler, led to his overwhelming victory. It was evident that he was the single outstanding personality capable of bringing the Party within sight of some degree of power and influence in Bavaria. Hitler also went to Berlin to make contact with similar groups in the North, where he identified National Socialism with regeneration of the national spirit. The Party's policy, or programme was, in Hitler's private view, solely a matter of opportunism. Whatever was adhered to, from whatever clan, was the policy he advocated in his single-minded pursuit of power for himself, as head of the Party. To the disaffected workers he was anti-industrialist; to the industrialists he was anti-Communist; to all he was pro-German, anti-semitic, and against any action by the Allies which implemented the Versailles Treaty, especially the punitive reparative assessment in April, 1921, of £6,600 million, and the occupation of the Ruhr by the French in January, 1923.

The same policy dictated his choice of new allies and co-workers, such as Roehm and Hess. Through Roehm he managed to acquire the Party's weekly journal, the *Völkischer Beobachter* (literally *Racial-Nationalist Observer*); the money had come partly from Army sources, and partly from Dietrich Eckart. One of the original members of the Party, a poet and writer well-known in Munich, he was also something of a roisterer in the taverns along with his friend Roehm. Hitler accepted him as editor of the *Völkischer Beobachter*; he was replaced in 1923 (when the *Völkischer Beobachter* became a daily) by another member of the Party's 'intellectual' circle, Alfred Rosenberg, who had been born in Latvia, had trained in architecture in Moscow and had fled to Germany to escape the consequences of the 1917 Revolution. Rosenberg appealed to Hitler because he formulated on paper the same prejudices concerning race and culture which had already fomented in Hitler's overheated imagination. Here, it seemed, was intellectual confirmation of the very thoughts upon which his ready intuition had fed.

Hitler did not escape unscathed during this troubled period. A new, more moderate Bavarian government forced him to serve a brief period of imprisonment in the summer of 1922 for violently disrupting a political meeting. The moderates were attempting to keep Bavaria in tune with the Weimar Republic, but the Republic's opponents brought violence and bloodshed into German political life, culminating in the murder of the Jewish Foreign Minister, Walther Rathenau. There were even talks among the extremists on the right that both the Bavarian and Federal Governments should be overthrown by force, using the *coup d'état*, soon to be demonstrated in Italy by Mussolini, whose much publicized 'march on Rome' took place in October, 1922. The Nazi Party, still far too small to act on its own, was in the forefront of demonstrations against the Federal Republic's policy and that of its Bavarian counterpart; the Party's current aim was Bavarian independence and the re-introduction of a right-wing administration. The Bavarian authorities wanted at once to curb Hitler and exploit him, to tone down his more extreme statements while at the same time making use of him and his party. The situation was ripe for exploitation, but the years 1922–23 were to tempt Hitler to overreach himself and misjudge entirely not only the extent of his influence but the right technique for achieving a successful *coup d'état*. Meanwhile, whether he liked it or not, he was forced to ally himself with the various right-wing groups which flourished in Bavaria. At first, their leaders had looked down on this Austrian ex-corporal. But by 1922 they had to recognize his undoubted genius in handling the crowds. He had, according to one prominent observer of the period, Kurt Lüdecke, who joined the Party in 1920, seized the limelight at a mass demonstration of the loose association of right-wing parties held in Munich on August 11th, 1922. 'It needed no clairvoyance to see that here was a man who knew how to seize his opportunity'; wrote Lüdecke later, in the days of his disillusionment with Nazism.[6]

It was at this stage that another ally joined Hitler: Hermann Goering, the most brilliant of Hitler's acquisitions so far. Flying ace and would-be man of the world, Goering had emerged from the war in which he had commanded the celebrated Richthofen Air Squadron, unemployed and angry at the humiliation of Germany. After working as a civil pilot in Sweden and marrying a Swedish countess, he had returned to Germany and settled in Munich, only to be completely won over by Hitler's capacity as a speaker. In Goering's own words, when on trial at Nuremberg in 1946:

> 'He said that . . . a protest is successful only if backed by power to give it weight. As long as Germany had not become strong, this kind of thing was to no purpose. The conviction was spoken word for word as if from my own soul . . . I just wanted to speak to him, at first to see if I could assist him . . . He said that it was an extraordinary turn of fate that we should meet . . . I told him that I myself to the fullest extent, and all I was and possessed, were completely at his disposal.[7]

At the age of twenty-nine, Goering found himself in control of the Party's SA Squadron. As Hitler put it, 'I gave him a dishevelled rabble. In a very short time he had organized a division of 11,000 men.'

Discipline was needed. Only after great difficulty, and Roehm's intervention with the army, was Hitler finally allowed to hold a mass rally of the SA in Munich in January, 1923. The authorities had initially banned it. With his head filled with thoughts of staging some seizure of power, Hitler had inspired 5,000 of his SA supporters with 'the great mission of our movement', to destroy the 'criminal' Republicans in Berlin, 'those betrayers of the people' controlled, as he always alleged, by the Jews.

Hitler's views on the SA were revealed much later in his *Table Talk*: 'I taught them the technique of concentrating their efforts on limited objectives, and at meetings to attack the opponent table by table.' The SA contained, he admitted, 'some extraordinary elements . . . unusable in time of peace, but in turbulent periods . . . quite different. At that stage these jolly rogues were invaluable to me as auxiliaries . . . with what blind confidence they followed me . . . As for their assumed brutality, they were simply somewhat close to nature.'[8] Then he added, 'The bourgeois with whom we flirted at the time of our struggle were simply aesthetes. But what I needed was partisans who give themselves body and soul, men as ready to break up a Communist meeting as to manage a Gau.'

During this period, Hitler's social life had widened considerably. In his field, he had become something of a local 'star' among those members of upper class society who were susceptible to his particular outlook. His effect was much like that of an actor, Lüdecke writes:

> When he stopped speaking, his chest still heaving with emotion, there was a moment of dead silence, then a storm of cheers.[9]

Something of a society man himself, Lüdecke noted Hitler's lack of care about his appearance; he came off the platform in a dirty, dishevelled raincoat, 'his face pale, his nostrils distended ... the whole man was concentrated in his eyes, his clear, straightforward, domineering, bright blue eyes.' So susceptible people, men and women alike, succumbed to him; Friedelind Wagner, the composer's granddaughter, for example, said of him: 'his sharp cheek bones stuck out over hollow, pasty cheeks, and above them a pair of unnaturally bright blue eyes. There was a half-starved look about him ... a sort of fanatical look'. Rich women, such as Frau Gertrud von Seidlitz, and cultured families such as the Bruckmanns, the Hanfstaengls (both publishers) and the Bechsteins gave him friendship, money and hospitality.[10] Both Elsa Bruckmann and Frau Bechstein, of the famous family of piano manufacturers, developed a motherly patronage of this social nondescript, who had to learn how to behave in such elevated society.

Hanfstaengl wrote of him:

> In his early years he had a command of voice, phrase and effect which has never been equalled ... No one who judges his capacity as a speaker from the performances of his later years can have any true insight into his gifts. As time went on he became drunk with his own oratory before vast crowds and his voice lost its former character through the intervention of microphone and loudspeaker.[11]

His effect on women was hypnotic; Hanfstaengl describes a girl listening to him: 'Transfixed as though in some devotional ecstasy, she had ceased to be herself and was completely under the spell of Hitler's despotic faith.'

In upper-class society he was uneasy and exaggeratedly polite until he gradually learned how to mix socially. Ernst 'Putzi' Hanfstaengl was one of his instructors. His manners with society women at that time have been described by another observer. Hitler is attending a reception:

> He came in a very decent blue suit and with an extravagantly large bouquet of roses, which he presented to his hostess as he kissed her hand ... While he was being introduced, he wore the expression of a public prosecutor at

an execution. I remember being struck by his voice when he thanked the lady of the house for tea and cakes, of which, incidentally, he ate an amazing quantity. It was a remarkably emotional voice, and yet it made no impression of conviviality or intimacy but rather of harshness ... Not until the hostess was so incautious as to let fall a remark about the Jews ... did he begin to speak and then he spoke without ceasing. After a while he thrust back his chair and stood up, still speaking, or rather yelling, in such a powerful, penetrating voice as I have never heard from anyone else. After he had for more than half an hour delivered a quite witty but very one-sided oration on the Jews, he suddenly broke off, went up to his hostess, begged to be excused and kissed her hand as he took his leave.[13]

Hanfstaengl claims he tried to civilize Hitler through the influence of music; he played Wagner for him, whole sections of whose works Hitler learned to hum and whistle. He found Hitler's domestic habits completely undisciplined; he devoured unlimited quantities of cakes and cream, and loved sweet things. He was persistently unpunctual, caring as little about time as he did about money. He was hopeless as an administrator, driving his helpers at Party headquarters or at the office of *Völkischer Beobachter* to despair. In private he continued to read voraciously within his limited sphere of interest – history, the life of Frederick the Great, the French Revolution and the works of Clausewitz, the German philosopher of war. According to Hanfstaengl, he had semi-pornographic tastes, at least in art. Also, he was obsessed by powerful cars, studying the second-hand market. With his unsettled habits, he was always on the prowl when not at meetings or appointments, which he invariably kept late. He had an Alsatian dog called Wolf, and he carried a heavy-handled whip. He lived in a small flat at No. 41 *Thierschstrasse*, a small street near the river Isar. His single comfortless room was barely nine feet wide, the floor covered with linoleum and rugs, the furniture a bed, table, chair and bookshelf. He also had the use of an entrance hall, where there was an old piano. When at home he wore carpet slippers, and slouched around in trousers, braces and shirt. This was the period, however, in which Hitler acquired his love for Berchtesgaden. He was introduced to the place which was later to become the site of his luxurious mountain residence, the Berghof, through staying at the Platterholf Inn, to which he was introduced by Eckart and others of the Party circle.

Hitler paid his rent regularly, but otherwise appears to have been careless about money. When he spoke outside the Party, he charged fees. Money came in for the Party from donations from his wealthier adherents, from Party dues, from collections taken at meetings. Men such as Eckart and Hanfstaengl gave money within their means. But Nazi bills were notorious for not being paid, and the Party throughout the decade was always in danger of bankruptcy except, now and then, when more substantial donations were made by such early industrialist supporters as Fritz Thyssen. In any case, money gifts from abroad, especially Hanfstaengl's dollars, became disproportionately substantial in the days of maximum inflation.

Another characteristic was Hitler's appeal to children. He pretended to enter their imaginary world and was an expert and entertaining mimic, his imitations including women and children. In private he also showed a considerable sense of humour. He was not, as might be imagined, a dull companion, though he was a compulsive talker. He loved the society of pretty women, and Hanfstaengl claims Hitler became infatuated with his wife, to whom he constantly sent flowers and adoring looks when kissing her hand. He also had a kind of adolescent 'crush' on his driver's sister, Jenny, and would frequently go off alone with her. Like most women, Frau Hanfstaengl did not find him unattractive. However, she was of the firm opinion that he was sexually impotent. 'I tell you he's a neuter,' she said to her husband.

It was in the year 1923 that Hitler overreached himself. The 1923 putsch in Munich could easily have ended his career. Before this disaster, however, he had an initial warning setback on Labour Day.

There were three elements in the Bavarian community to take into account: the provincial Government, the regional army (under General von Lossow) and the political parties, left, right and moderate. Hitler's ambition was to pressure the Bavarian Government and the regional army into open revolt against the Central Government, and to oppose the left by breaking up their Labour Day rally. Some 20,000 of the SA were assembled on a large parade ground on the outskirts of the city for this purpose, while Roehm had been successful in bluffing a consignment of arms out of the Army barracks to add to the secret store of weapons the Nazis already possessed. Other national groups joined with them. But the Socialist parade passed by unmolested; at the last moment Roehm was detained by General von Lossow, who had already warned Hitler he could act against any party, left or right, who caused violence. Roehm, in fact, was sent with a further stern warning to the parade ground in the hands of a strong Army detachment, which surrounded the SA gathering. After some hesitation, Hitler capitulated and handed back the arms which had been taken from the barracks. It was a grave loss of face in front of the vast body of men standing ready to take part in a decisive putsch. They dispersed, both Hitler and Goering prominent in steel helmets and wearing their decorations.

Hitler disappeared alone to Berchtesgaden to recover his self-confidence and rethink his position in relation to the Bavarian Government and the Army. Roehm also left Munich for the summer. The Bavarian Minister of Justice, Franz Gürtner, who favoured Hitler, saw to it that no action was taken to bring him to justice on this occasion.

When Hitler finally returned to Munich it was to conduct the notorious November Putsch against the Government, a second trial of strength which aimed to succeed by sheer effrontery. Hitler could not afford a second failure. He depended much at this time on Goering's quiet, aristocratic wife, Carin; pale and often sick, she was, nevertheless, kindly disposed to her bombastic husband's chief. He took comfort and refuge very frequently in their comfortable apartment.

With the coming of autumn, martial law was proclaimed in Germany in face of the growing threat of insurrection. The new Chancellor was Gustav Stresemann. Hitler meanwhile had taken part in a great rally of nationalist forces, speaking against the Government at Nuremberg. He had stood beside General Ludendorff, whose name, honoured still in Germany, added a new dimension of respectability and credibility to the movement, and (Hitler hoped) would finally sway the army in favour of the projected putsch. Ludendorff, nevertheless, was something of a liability because of his age and political ineptitude. He was better seen than heard. However, an alliance of the right was formed, with Hitler as one of the signatories. Roehm resigned his commission in the army to be free of all commitments other than that to Hitler.

The political tension in Bavaria was increasing and the Bavarian President proclaimed a state of emergency and appointed Gustav von Kahr as State Commissioner. Kahr was given full executive powers, and he immediately banned the series of meetings Hitler proposed to call in Munich during October. Hitler only swallowed his anger to the extent that he knew he must still attempt to win over Kahr and Lossow, together with Colonel Hans von Seisser, Commander of the State Police, to his idea of a *coup d'état.* He planned to overthrow the hated Stresemann, with his policy of appeasement to Versailles. Kahr, he knew, contemplated separation for Bavaria. But would he go further and join Hitler in a march on Berlin, parallel to Mussolini's march on Rome? With the Army also favouring the right, it was uncertain which element, Hitler or the other leaders, would win the privilege of leading Bavaria. Hans von Seeckt, the army's Commander in Chief, decided, in the long term interests of the state, to support the central Government, and proclaimed this clearly on November 4th, otherwise he said, only civil war could result.

The balance now rested with the Bavarians, and Hitler's position in relation to the disaffected Kahr and Lossow, who refused to have their policies settled for them in Berlin. They openly defied the capital to Hitler's guarded satisfaction. But he was uncertain of these men as allies. They would probably, for all their defiance, restrict their actions to establishing Bavarian separation, and leave the march on Berlin out of account. Communist risings elsewhere were being adequately faced. Timing was important, and Hitler owed it to his supporters to delay as little as possible. The Kahr–Lossow–Seisser combination must be placed in a position where they would be swept into supporting the great Bavarian tide which Hitler planned to lead.

Or so it seemed when Kahr announced that he could speak at a great public meeting in the Bürgerbräukeller on the evening of November 8th. The auditorium there held some 3,000 people. Hitler sensed this chance must be taken or Kahr might steal the initiative. The SA was on the alert and he decided to take over the meeting himself.

On the platform under the Chairmanship of the Bavarian Premier, von Krilling, were Kahr, Lossow, Seisser and other ministers. Hitler let Kahr start to speak, covering familiar ground. He stood by, virtually unseen in the audience, and wearing an ill-fitting morning suit under his trenchcoat. Suddenly, at a chosen moment, there was a pistol shot. Kahr stopped speaking. The audience turned in astonishment and saw Hitler standing on a table, with a pistol pointed at the ceiling. 'No one can leave this hall,' shouted Hitler. 'The National Revolution has begun. The Army is with us.' Simultaneously, some 600 armed SA men led by Goering, secured the building. Accompanied by Goering and Hess, Hitler then mounted the platform. Leaving Goering to calm the audience, Hitler and Hess hustled the platform party into a side room and, with their guns still in their hands, urged them to accept a form of coalition government with Ludendorff at its head. Hitler assured them Ludendorff was at this very moment on his way to the hall. Meanwhile, Goering told the audience to go on drinking their beer (at a billion marks a litre) while matters were being settled.

Receiving no clear answer, since the ministers were in a state of shock, Hitler rushed back on to the platform and shouted that everything was all right. A new government was in process of being formed, and he himself would be in charge. He proclaimed that there was to be a march on Berlin. Ludendorff had by then arrived, grumbling that he had been giving no warning of all this. Hitler obtained what he regarded as a general assent to his proposals from the ministers, given under duress. But he had not thought out any exact procedure; when he was called away to resolve some minor dispute outside, Ludendorff took it upon himself to regard the affair as settled, and released the key ministers on their word of honour to fulfil their undertakings. The audience was in any case breaking up now that the excitement was over. Lossow flatly disregarded his promise to Ludendorff and put the army in a state of readiness to resist the following day when a great march was planned through the city of Munich to take over the government centre. No control whatsoever was exercised on either Kahr's, Lossow's or Seisser's action.

This march of some 3,000 men led by Hitler, Ludendorff and Goering, took place the following day. However, hurriedly printed Government posters appeared all over the centre of the town renouncing the agreement with Hitler. Roehm found himself surrounded by government troops after he had occupied the old War Ministry. The march itself was suddenly halted in a narrow street in the centre of the city by a contingent of armed police, who did not hesitate to open fire. The SA ranks broke up, though Ludendorff, depending on his rank and the respect he commanded, marched on alone, protected, it would seem, by his age and obstinate courage. No one fired at him, but Goering fell, wounded in the groin, while Hitler was dragged to the ground by one of those marching with him, and then in the turmoil was hurried to the rear of the column and spirited away in a car. His shoulder was dislocated in the fall. In the evening he was brought to the sanctuary of Hanfstaengl's house. In the circumstances, Roehm was forced to surrender, and was placed under arrest. Goering was nursed in a nearby house belonging to a Jewish businessman. His injury was serious, and after medical attention during the night, he was driven with his wife over the border to the safety of Austria. Hess, too, fled to Austria, only returning voluntarily the following year to stand trial and share Hitler's confinement in Landsberg Castle.

The putsch had failed miserably, partly because it had been conducted on the spur of the moment by a leader who at this stage in his career was an amateur in revolutionary strategy. According to Hanfstaengl, Hitler was ready to commit suicide when the police came to arrest him. He was only prevented from doing so by the prompt action of Frau Helene Hanfstaengl, who wrenched the pistol from him in time. He was placed under arrest.

Hitler, along with Ludendorff and Roehm, was brought to trial for high treason on February 26th, 1924. The proceedings were kept as veiled as possible in order to shield the behaviour of Kahr and Lossow. Hitler sensed the importance of the occasion, and the possibility of turning the courtroom into a Party platform. Indeed, it could be claimed that he used the trial as an occasion to rehabilitate himself after the failure of the putsch and his apparent desertion. He must, he knew, turn the trial into an act of defiance, and his rout by armed force in the streets into a great moral victory when confronted by the authority of the State and the weakness of his former 'allies', Kahr and Lossow. He fought back where he felt his opponents stood at the greatest disadvantage:

> One thing was certain, however, Lossow, Kahr and Seisser had the same goal as we had – to get rid of the Reich Government ... If our enterprise was actually high treason, then during the whole period, Lossow, Kahr and Seisser must have been committing high treason along with us.[18]

When they accused him of being a mere upstart, an agitator ambitious for power in direct confrontation with the Minister of State and the army, he proclaimed without the least hesitation or loss of self-confidence the light in which he viewed his ambitions:

> My aim from the first was a thousand times higher than becoming a Minister. I wanted to become the destroyer of Marxism. I am going to achieve this task, and if I do, the title of Minister will be an absurdity . . . The man who is born to be a dictator is not compelled. He wills it. He is not driven forward, but drives himself.

He was, he claimed, thankful it was Seisser's police, and not the Army, which had fired upon him in the street. One day, he foretold, the army would stand beside him, his ally in the struggle, never his opponent. Meanwhile his own private army was growing:

> I nourish the proud hope that one day the hour will come when these rough and ready companies will grow to battalions, the battalions to regiments, the regiments into divisions, that the old flag will wave again . . . For it is not you, gentlemen, who pass judgement on us. That judgement is spoken by the eternal court of history . . . You may pronounce us guilty a thousand times over, but the goddess of the eternal court of history will smile and tear to tatters the brief of the State Prosecutor and the sentence of this Court. For she acquits us.

On April 1st, 1924, Hitler received the lenient sentence of five years imprisonment from judges so divided and uncertain of themselves that the proviso was mentioned in court that he could qualify for parole within six months.

4

Landsberg, 1924

At least Hitler had by now achieved notoriety. He was well-known in Bavaria, but less so in the north, where the Party was more closely identified with the Strasser brothers, who were in charge of its development in Berlin, Hamburg and the industrial Ruhr. Hitler at this stage was still strongly identified with the south, and in particular with Bavaria, Germany's second, and highly distinctive state. Bavaria was by tradition alienated from Prussia, with its centre in Berlin, which was both the federal and the state capital.

1924 was to be Hitler's Sabbatical. He was imprisoned in considerable comfort, from November 11th, 1923, to December 20th, 1924, in Landsberg Castle, situated in a pleasant country area west of Munich. The Castle was more like an officers' quarters than a prison, and Hitler, housed on the first floor, was in effect in house-confinement. The trial, which had given him a platform from which to air his views and grievances, was an interlude in a life of some indulgence, since he could receive visitors, and he was showered with presents, largely flowers and food, by his many well-wishers. Emil Maurice acted as his aide and batman, and others of his supporters shared his confinement. The most notable was Hess, who very honourably returned from exile in Austria to face trial in April and join his chief in Landsberg. Goering remained in exile in Austria, recovering from his severely poisoned wound in the groin and acquiring in the process his lifelong addiction to morphine. He ended up finally in a Swedish sanitarium for addicts, and was not to return to Germany, temporarily cured, until 1928. Roehm, though found guilty, had been discharged and released after the trial, and was active outside prison in fomenting disagreements within the various Nationalist splinter groups, disagreements which Hitler chose at this stage to disregard. They awaited his release and resumption of personal leadership; meanwhile, the greater the division the better it suited him. He would reappear, eventually, like a Messiah, to restore unity through his personal magnetism. In July, 1924, he even went so far as to resign the leadership of the Party, but this was a politic gesture to prevent his deportation to Austria, which the Bavarian authorities were threatening. This was a move which Hitler had to frustrate at all costs, and his powerful ally in preventing this action was the Bavarian Minister of Justice, Franz Gürtner, who shared his outlook and was later to become one of Hitler's own ministers when he came to power.

Meanwhile Hitler kept aloof from all party disputes, holding court in his castle residence, where he received his visitors, conducting endless discussions with his friends and fellow prisoners, numbering up to forty from the Nazi putsch. In the summer he walked in the castle gardens, wearing leather shorts. It was, in effect, the best year of his life so far. In April he reached the age of thirty-five. He had also achieved political maturity with the realization that the method of attempting to achieve a *coup d'état* which he had adopted was entirely wrong in a society such as Germany, where the ruling forces were in the end the stable middle and upper classes. With time to think, he adopted an entirely new approach to the problems of seizing power, and he said as much to his supporter, Kurt Lüdecke, who was a frequent visitor to Landsberg, and who recorded Hitler's words during one of his sessions with him:

> When I resume active work, it will be necessary to pursue a new policy. Instead of working to achieve power by an armed coup, we shall have to hold our noses and enter the Reichstag against the Catholic and Marxist deputies. If out-voting them takes longer than out-shooting them, at least the results will be guaranteed by their own Constitution . . . Sooner or later we shall have a majority – and after that, Germany.[1]

Hitler's future insistence on 'legality' must not be mistaken, of course, for a gesture of respect to a Constitution he took every opportunity to revile. It was a new phase of calculation, more realistic than that of the armed coup. The Nazi Party, with deputies in the Reichstag, would become a fifth column dedicated to disrupting the machinery of the new democracy, which had scarcely had an opportunity to take root in post-war Germany in the form of the Weimar Republic.

Hitler in any case was sifting his thoughts. When Max Amann, who was by now the Party's publisher, invited him to write his autobiography, he accepted. The book that he compiled while in Landsberg did not turn out quite as Amann had hoped; he wanted a highly saleable popular account of this sensational young politician's life, with its mysterious background in Austria. *Mein Kampf* (*My Struggle*), which finally appeared in July, 1925, in its initial form, was composed entirely at Landsberg, though Hitler had been planning to write something of this sort since 1922. Although this volume, subtitled *A Reckoning*, contains some pages of autobiographical reminiscence which had been carefully adapted to project Hitler's image of himself, the greater part is a pronouncement of his specific view of recent Austrian and Germany history, together with an emphatic and repetitious assertion of the political and racial prejudices and obsessions. A second part, entitled *The Nazi Movement*, did not appear until December, 1926, and from 1930 these two parts were combined to form the standard edition of *Mein Kampf*. Hitler was to dictate the draft of a third, very similar book to Max Amann during 1928; this, however, was only to be published posthumously, appearing in both German and English in 1961 – *Hitler's Secret Book*.

Hitler loved talking, but disliked writing. He declares in his Preface that 'men are won over less by the written than the spoken word' and that it is orators, not writers, who have headed great movements in the past. However, the record demanded that he commit his principles to paper. It is well-known that *Mein Kampf* is exceptionally badly written in flat and undistinguished prose, sometimes ungrammatical, losing sense in labyrinthine sentences. Hitler mixes his metaphors, and clogs his prose with unnecessary words.

Mein Kampf is therefore the composition of an ill-educated writer, in the sense that Hitler had had little schooling in composing highly literate German prose. On the other hand, he was widely read in the subjects of his intuitive choice, but he drew on his knowledge only insofar as he could use it to support his particular line of argument. His addiction to theatre and opera encouraged sudden dramatic flourishes of style, but his instinct for platform oratory and effect does not suit the printed page. His style is often exaggerated, even sentimental, and coarse in its vituperation. His favourite method of composition was dictation because dictation represents the spoken rather than the written word. This led him to adopt an undisciplined continuity; he goes off on tangents as stock ideas and arguments cue themselves in his obsessive mind. Hess's influence on the first volume of *Mein Kampf* appears to have been limited to constant discussion, which had been the case since he first met Hitler in 1920 and passed on to him Haushofer's views on geo-politics, which were so in tune with his own. Hess's son claims that Hess himself never took dictation from Hitler; in any case, there were plenty of others to do so, and Hitler had a typewriter at Landsberg which a number of people used. Hess also helped in proofing the book before publication. We have the assurance of two of his later secretaries that dictation was Hitler's favourite form of composition, followed by revision of the typescripts.

The first part of *Mein Kampf, A Reckoning,* begins autobiographically. Hitler traces his upbringing in an 'alien' Austria, a 'sham' state in which the German element is mixed with other 'inferior' racial groups. Only when he was alone in Vienna were his eyes opened, he says, to the poison represented by the combined threat of Marxism and Judaism; he underwent a 'hardening process' under the influence of the 'goddess of suffering'. He claims the 'granite foundation' of his viewpoint was established through his contact (as a 'petit bourgeois') with the workers in Vienna, whose lives he portrays with violent emphasis on their drunkenness, brutality and the degradation of their family life. They were betrayed by trade unionism and the flaccid weakness of Social Democracy, the political tools alike of Marxism and Judaism. Similarly, the Viennese press is subject to the Jews, who have corrupted the arts, journalism and social life, through the exploitation, for example, of the white slave traffic. The Jews, in fact, represented to him a racial conspiracy to dominate the earth.[2]

Meanwhile, Hitler says he had begun his long course of study. The art of reading as he sees it is 'to retain the essential, to forget the non-essential', that is, he drew on books to support his gathering obsessions. 'I had ceased,' he writes, 'to be a weak-kneed cosmopolitan and became an anti-Semite.' He learned much from the anti-Semite mayor of Vienna, Karl Lueger. In spite of his general admiration for imperialist Britain, he claims that the British example of parliamentary democracy was a bad one, betraying the idea of true leadership by submitting decisions to the will of a majority. 'Must not our principle of parliamentary majorities lead to the demolition of any idea of leadership?' Meanwhile, he was training himself, or so he claims, in the art of persuasion and debate. 'I had carefully avoided any public appearance . . . Only in the smallest groups did I speak of things which inwardly moved or attracted me . . . I learned to orate less, but to know people with their opinions and objections that were often so boundlessly primitive.'[3]

His concept of Germanic democracy lay in leadership, not parliamentary debate; he speaks of 'the truly Germanic democracy characterized by the free election of a leader and his obligation fully to assume all responsibility for his actions and omissions'. Parliamentary debate, he argues, only erodes leadership, and so plays into the hands of the Marxist conspiracy for power. It is, he believes, the prelude to full-scale Marxism. As against this, Hitler looks forward to the redevelopment of the pan-German spirit, the integration of all racial Germans as the superior people of Europe. This ideal, identified historically with Frederick the Great and Bismarck, but betrayed by the polyglot Austro-Hungarian Empire into which he himself was born, must be pursued with 'cold ruthlessness'; even Lueger had not been strong enough to achieve this. But Hitler knew when writing

Mein Kampf that he was this god-given leader, and he claims that he even sensed this during those difficult days in Vienna: 'Vienna was and remained for me the hardest, though most thorough, school of my life. I had set foot in this town while still half a boy and left it a man, grown quiet and grave.'

His aspirations led him to Munich, the centre for him, at the time, of true Germanism. But Germany was faced with dire problems which he analyses in his own fashion. Its lack of space to expand should not, he claims, be met by population control, or by living artificially on industrial exports, or by pressurizing the home production of food to an unnatural extent. The answer (learned through Haushofer) was to win *lebensraum* (living space) by occupation of lands to the East – a 'geo-political' solution. 'For Germany . . . the only possibility for carrying out a healthy territorial policy lay in the acquisition of new land in Europe itself.'

Hitler's concept of a state is ethnic, not economic: 'the urge to preserve the species is the first cause for the formation of human communities . . . Thus, the most sensible prerequisite for the formation and preservation of a state is the presence of a certain feeling of cohesion based on similarity of nature and species.' The heroic virtues (which he believed the English, for example, possessed) develop from the promotion of racial, not economic persuasion. Here lay, for him, the fallacy of Marxism, which emphasizes the economic struggle in society, and the fault with the Jews, whose cohesion is both economic and religious. The outcome of the First World War as the betrayal of Germany by Marxism and Judaism was a cornerstone in his propaganda.

Hitler then examines the nature of propaganda, a new factor (he claims) in politics. He learned a great deal from the effectiveness of British propaganda during the war. Propaganda is a means to an end; it is emotional, not rational; it is aimed exclusively at the unthinking, basically stupid mass of people, who he terms 'feminine by nature and attitude'. This chapter on propaganda is perhaps the most celebrated in the book for its frank exposition of mass-persuasion techniques.

> The function of propaganda is . . . not to weigh and ponder the rights of different people, but exclusively to emphasize the one right which it has set out to argue for . . . Its task is to serve our own rights, always and unflinchingly . . . It must confine itself to a few points and repeat them over and over . . . (Its) purpose is . . . to convince the masses.[4]

Hitler then reverts to autobiography: his period of blindness, his post-war army service, his introduction to the German Workers' Party, and his final determination to take it over for himself. He reveals touches of an inferiority complex in his constant attacks on the 'so-called intelligentsia' who look down on those who lack conventional, academic education, a 'costly envelope' for the 'biggest empty-head', as he puts it. His work for the Party, and his determination to devote himself entirely to politics, led him to analyse the weaknesses of post-war Germany. Germany deserved her defeat, he declares, because of the poor quality of her working-class, the lack of moral fibre in the monarchy, the nation's subjection to a Jewish-dominated press, and the corruption of youth not only by the mentally diseased intelligentsia but by the physical corruption of widespread prostitution. Art became degenerate; as far as he is concerned 'the Bolshevistic present is embodied in a cubist monstrosity'. All this culminates in the final betrayal of the German Army by the Austrian authorities through the infiltration of cowardly, second-class soldiers into its ranks. Germany failed to recognize the menace her racial problem represented, and almost succumbed after the Armistice to a Marxist-Jewish *coup d'état*: 'the deepest and ultimate reason for the decline of the old Reich lay in its failure to recognize the racial problem and its importance for the historical development of peoples'.

The climax of the first part of *Mein Kampf*, therefore, lies in its final chapters, with the special attack on Jewish influence in German life. He accepts the argument of natural selection, and the survival of the fittest; racial crossbreeding, in his view, lowers the value of the stock and leads to its evolutionary decline, reflecting at the same time the decline of culture. The so-called 'Aryans' (a word borrowed incorrectly from linguistics, in which it has no racial significance) are for Hitler 'the founders of culture', the originators of standards, the inventors. On the other hand, he regards the Jews as destructive parasites, mere middlemen and profiteers in business, the seducers of the workers. He accepted *The Protocols of Zion* (the notorious, fake documents produced by the Russian police in 1902, and published in German) as genuine, with their implication that the Jews were plotting to dominate the world.

It was to fight the battle for German nationalism and racial purity that Hitler took over the Party. He organized the first mass rally in 1920, where he presented his twenty-five points amid tumult – 'one after another was accepted with steadily mounting joy . . . There stood before me a hall full of people united by a new conviction, a new faith, a new will.'

So ends the first volume. The second has virtually no narrative and consists almost entirely of exposition. It opens with one of Hitler's sardonic passages mocking the democratic system and its procedure. He insists on the importance of the Nazi Party as a fighting movement, opposing Marxism and its aim 'to hand the world over to the Jews'. Once again, Hitler insists on racial purity as the basis for a state organism, preserving intact what is best and noblest in mankind. 'The German Reich as a state embraces all Germans and has the task, not only of assembling and preserving the most valuable stocks of basic racial elements in this people, but slowly and surely of raising them to a dominant position . . . It must set race in the centre of all life. It must take care to keep it pure.' He holds up the Catholic Church as a model, with its priesthood drawn continually from the people instead of being self-perpetuating, and its 'iron will-power' and discipline.

Nevertheless, Hitler looks to the individual to provide invention and leadership: 'all inventions are the result of an individualist's work'; 'an organization can only exist if a broad mass, with a more emotional attitude, serves a high intellectual leadership'. Again he returns to the importance of the spoken word in the hands of a master of propaganda:

> I gradually transformed myself into a speaker for mass meetings ... I became practised in the pathos and the gestures which a great hall, with its thousands of people, demands.[5]

In his opinion, 'a brilliant speaker will be able to write better than a brilliant writer can speak'. He goes out of his way to praise Lloyd George as a mass orator: 'the great English demagogue had set out solely to exert the greatest possible effect on the mass of his listeners.' He speaks of 'plastic headlines', and the importance of the mass meeting 'for the reason that in it the individual who at first ... feels lonely ... for the first time gets the picture of a larger community, which in most people has a strengthening, encouraging effect.'

His party, he claims, boldly set out to challenge the Communist Front, meeting violence with violence, unlike the timid bourgeoisie, who were terrified by the outward strength of the Communists on the streets. The SA, with its special technique of handling opponents, was essential to the Nazi movement. He describes some of the early rallies and the dangerous confrontations he encouraged with the enemy, the Marxists. As a symbol of party unity he describes his careful choice of flag and insignia: like a 'poster', a 'symbol of our struggle', using the swastika because of its supposed link with 'Aryan' origins in the East, and its association with German extremists going back to the previous century.

Hitler argues at length about the SA, seeing it in part as the inheritor of the wartime 'volunteers' who later joined the nationalist Free Corps. All revolutions, he says, depend not only on 'a great, creative, renewing idea', but must be backed by strong-arm forces. The bourgeois parties were too cowardly to oppose Marxism with any show of force. The problem lay in disciplining the younger members of the SA when universal military training was abolished after the war. The SA, which was formed solely to protect the movement, gradually had to assume paramilitary discipline following the French occupation of the Ruhr, which, according to Hitler's belief, the German government accepted supinely.

As for the Weimar republic and its federal government, he calls these an 'intermezzo', a sham phase through which Germany is passing before the establishment of the fully centralized, pan-Germanic state envisaged by the Nazi movement. For this, he emphasizes yet again the importance of leadership: 'Leading means being able to move masses.' He distinguishes, too, between supporters of the movement, and actual members: 'a supporter ... is one who declares himself to be in agreement with its aims, a member is one who fights for them.' The leader, in absolute control, sets the pace for all.

Hitler concludes the second part of *Mein Kampf* by repeating other basic points in his programme: the abolition of the trade unions, with their false emphasis on a class struggle, and their replacement by a Nazi labour organization, the re-uniting of all German 'National' territories in Europe, the expansion east to win proper living-space for the growing German peoples. In all this he sees Britain as a potential ally, not as an opponent. 'In the predictable future there can be only two allies for Germany in Europe – England and Italy.' But Germany's true opponents remain the Jews, originators of Marxism and the devisers of the iniquitous Versailles Treaty. Their influence must be utterly purged, and their presence in Europe removed.

5

Reconstruction of the Party, 1925-1930

Hitler's assessment of the bourgeois parties and their bureaucracy as spineless is ironic in the light of his release from confinement on December 20th, 1924. He was freed on parole. The State Police had wanted to deport him, sending him back to Austria. Gürtner, Bavarian Minister of Justice, had resisted this. The Nazi-Völkisch Coalition did so badly in the December Reichstag elections, polling under a million votes, that it was felt Hitler's political influence had disintegrated. In any case, he had made a temporizing gesture of resigning the leadership of a party which appeared to have lost its momentum through fragmentation. The coalition leadership, which in the absence of Hitler included Ludendorff, Strasser, Roehm and Rosenberg, was at loggerheads.

Meanwhile, the moderate party, the Social Democrats, had increased its vote by thirty per cent, and was to hold the lead in the Reichstag until 1932. Indeed, during the period Hitler was in prison, Germany had achieved a new phase of social stability, owing to Schacht's control of inflation and the re-establishment of the currency, and Stresemann's negotiation of the Dawes Plan for German reparations. The Ruhr was evacuated, and Allied troops left the demilitarized Rhineland. When the aged conservative, Field Marshal von Hindenburg, was elected President in 1925, Germany gained a monolithic figure as head of state, a dedicated monarchist and a nationalist of a kind utterly without sympathy for Hitler's racial concepts of nationalism.

Hitler secretly welcomed the dissension which thrived among his followers and his nominal allies. It showed clearly enough what could happen without him. His policy in any case in dealing with his immediate sub-leaders was already a policy of 'divide and rule'. His power became absolute when his potential rivals expanded their energies among themselves in rivalry for his favour. Now a fresh start had to be made by the one man who knew what leadership meant. Hitler said to Hess, in a remark which became celebrated: 'I shall need five years before the movement is on top again.' His forecast was accurate; the Party was to revive minimally at the close of the 1920s which brought the decline of the German economy.[1]

His most severe loss was Roehm, whose friendship he ruthlessly sacrificed because of disagreement over the paramilitary formation known as the Frontbann, which Roehm took over after the SA had been prohibited. Hitler wanted to reconstruct the SA as a strictly political force. He turned his back on Roehm, who resigned in disgust in April, 1925, and later left Germany to act as a military adviser in Bolivia, only rejoining Hitler in 1931. Hitler sacrificed the 'Völkisch' support, which he did not want largely because of its (to him) wasteful anti-clericalism, losing its alliance with the aged Ludendorff in the process. In any case, Hitler did not like old men. The Nazis were to be essentially a youth movement in politics.

With the decks cleared for action, Hitler re-launched the *Völkischer Beobachter* on February 26th (with banner headlines – 'A New Beginning'), and the day after held a mass rally which Gregor Strasser, Alfred Rosenberg and Roehm pointedly omitted to attend. Hitler spoke out, reestablishing in a single two hour speech his former authority over an audience of thousands.

> If anyone comes and wants to impose conditions on me, I shall say to him – 'Just wait, my young friend, and see what conditions I impose on you ... I alone lead the movement, and no one can impose conditions on me so long as I personally bear the responsibility ... If in the struggle I should fall, the Swastika banner shall be my winding sheet.[2]

But Hitler's brilliance on the platform had the effect of a boomerang; he was forthwith forbidden by the various state authorities to speak again, not only in Bavaria (where the ban lasted until May, 1927) but elsewhere in Germany, notably Prussia (the ban lasting there until September, 1928). This was most serious, it meant that the man who relied almost entirely on oratory for the maintenance of his leadership had to remain silent on the platform for up to three years, and rely on others to speak for him. Hitler had to be circumspect; he was on parole; he could be deported. So his leadership was for a while confined to organization and the imposition of his viewpoint and personality on those whom he chose to speak for him.

With Roehm gone, Goering in exile combating drug addiction, and Goebbels still serving his apprenticeship as a Party agitator in the north-west, Gregor Strasser was undoubtedly the strongest figure left among the Party hierarchy after Hitler. He was a Bavarian who had served as a lieutenant in the war and now owned a pharmacy in Landshut in Bavaria. His influence ranged from Berlin to the Rhineland and in the mid-twenties his viewpoint was more immediately effective in the north than Hitler's. With the help of his brother, Otto Strasser, he controlled this area for the Party, and his success both as speaker, party administrator and publisher of the *Berliner Arbeiterzeitung* was considerable. He crossed swords with Hitler over policy and he appeared to be genuine in his radical outlook. While Hitler's aim was solely to pioneer his way to power using any nationalist platform which was expedient, either radical-sounding or right-wing, Strasser was more the traditional politician with a left-of-centre bias in his interpretation of Nazi policy. He appeared, in other words, a much safer man than Hitler from the standpoint of other politicians.

It was the Strassers who had appointed Paul Josef Goebbels in 1924 to be an assistant in their office in Elberfeld in the Rhineland. His salary was 200 marks a month. This brilliant, volatile, waspish and over-emotional young man, was, at twenty-seven, bitterly resentful because he had failed to make any mark as a writer and dramatist. Politics was a last resort, a final outlet for his wounded vanity and still adolescent exuberance. He had a fine voice, and he was out to impress, and he soon discovered he could be very effective as a political orator. But he was a born intriguer, and his self-interest was always paramount. He was by nature a radical, and as a speaker he had a special appeal for working-class audiences. Of working-class origin himself, he had obtained his university education with the aid of charitable grants, and his search for palatable employment had come at the time of the collapse of the mark during 1923. Like Hitler, he wanted to be successful in the arts.

It did not take long for Hitler to discover this young man, or for Goebbels to discover on which side his bread was buttered. Although strictly identified with the opposition, he was able to figure the relative strength of the Strassers and Hitler at two conferences for Party officials which were to become celebrated in Nazi history, the first convened by the Strassers in Hanover in January, 1926, and the second by Hitler in the southern town of Bamberg the following month. Hitler was not present at the first of these confrontations, at which Goebbels, though still in a very junior position represented himself (in his private diary for the period, which survives) as an equal of the Strassers. One question at issue (indeed, the subject of a national referendum) was Party policy over the expropriation of the property of the former German royal houses. Strasser and his followers, including Goebbels, naturally were for this, just as they were also for nationalization of heavy industry and of the properties of the big landowners, but Hitler strongly opposed this policy because at this point he was seeking the moral and financial support of both the Hohenzollerns and certain industrialists. Goebbels, however, never uttered the remark so frequently attributed to him, 'I demand that the petty bourgeois Adolf Hitler be expelled from the National Socialist Party.' Even so, the Hanover Conference represented an open revolt against Hitler's policy and leadership.

Goebbels always refers in his private diary to the 'breathless tension' he inspires when he speaks at such conferences, or on the public platform. At Bamberg, however, Hitler's own territory, he was circumspect. His temperament was in the end far more responsive to Hitler's emotive appeal than to Strasser's semi-respectable logic. 'I would love to have Hitler for my friend,' he records, and he speaks of Hitler's 'big blue eyes, like stars!' Yet he still found Hitler's views reactionary. However, he listened rather than spoke at Bamberg, and found himself inspired by Hitler's personality. Hitler had seen to it that his supporters out-numbered Strasser's, and in any event Strasser was never able to match Hitler in any face-to-face confrontation. Partly by pressure and partly by blandishment, Hitler persuaded Strasser to play it his way.

Hitler, still forbidden to speak except at these private conferences, saw in Goebbels the very orator and firebrand he needed to win over the working-class from Marxism. He invited him south to speak on a number of occasions ('I told them of my growing fame,' says Goebbels, 'they received me with considerable acclaim.') Then, during the summer, Hitler invited Goebbels to come to the mountains as his guest. It was almost like a love affair. Goebbels, weary of the industrial north, was transfigured. He felt Hitler to be a genius.

> He is a creative instrument of Fate and Deity . . . Good and kind, but also clever and shrewd . . . What a man. He speaks about the State and how to win it and he speaks about the meaning of political revolution. He seems like a prophet of old . . . He is an artist in statesmanship . . . To him I feel deeply linked. Now the very last of my doubts have vanished. Hitler gives me a bunch of flowers – red, red roses.[3]

The seduction was complete. Hitler appointed Goebbels *gauleiter*, or district Party leader, in Berlin. It was a position of considerable trust, since the capital was a recognized centre for Communist and other anti-Nazi activity. So the young man with the fervent, acid tongue and the radical appeal was instructed to go and fight it out on the streets and on the platforms of Berlin and earn a place for himself in the Nazi hierarchy. He proved an outstanding success. He made himself a master of rhetoric, and a brilliant campaign manager and organizer. His success was aided by the growing threat to German economic stability. Apart from Hitler himself, he became the most professional propagandist in the movement, understanding how to co-ordinate the spoken and the written word, and words with actions on the streets in the form of rallies, demonstrations and confrontations with the Left which led to bloodshed and bans from public speaking. But in 1928, when Goebbels was thirty, Hitler made him head of Party Propaganda, and gave him one of the Party's twelve seats in the Reichstag. This rendered him immune from police interference, and removed any ban on his speaking in public.

This was the Party's most difficult period for reformation and recruitment. During the period 1924–29 the Weimar Government achieved its best record, and Germany enjoyed some years of prosperity after the currency reform. Germany entered the League of Nations, and signed as an equal partner the Kellogg–Briand pact outlawing war. The Allied Military Control Commission withdrew in January, 1927. Above all, economic recovery was very rapid; the United States poured money into the country in the form of investment following the Dawes Plan (1924). There was a marked temporary rise in wages and in the standard of living. Reparations, however, still hung like a millstone round the nation's neck (2,500 millions marks a year by the Dawes Plan), but Stresemann even managed to get this reduced somewhat through the Young Plan before his death in 1929.

Hitler spent the years up to and immediately after the 1928 Reichstag elections gradually re-shaping the Party and its organization. In 1926, having dealt with Strasser, he held a Party rally in Thuringia, where he was still allowed to speak. It was a small-scale rehearsal for the later annual rallies at Nuremberg. Nevertheless, some 5,000 attended. The SA was reestablished under new leadership, but there was still the tendency among the men who joined to prefer drinking beer and brawling to politics. Eventually Hitler found it necessary to establish a small 'elite' corps, manned by people of more dedicated political outlook: the SS (*Schutzstaffel*). He was to lean increasingly on this group, especially after its ranks of some 200 men were taken over in

1929 by a quiet, self-effacing young fanatic, Heinrich Himmler. Himmler, at one time a devoted follower of Roehm, had stood at the barricades during the Munich putsch of 1923. Strasser was put in charge of Party organization, and the country divided into regions (*gaue*) under Party *gauleiters.* Germany had thirty-four *gaue,* which corresponded to the electoral regions for the Reichstag. The organization, too, began to cater to youth, including schoolchildren and students, women and certain influential professions, such as law and teaching.

With firm leadership and better organization, Party membership rose gradually – 1925, 27,000; 1926, 49,000; 1927, 72,000; 1928, 108,000; 1929, 178,000. In the 1928 election for the Reichstag, the Nazi vote was only 810,000, which entitled the Party to twelve seats in a House of some 500 deputies. In contrast, the ruling party, the Social Democrats, polled 9·15 million, and the Communists 3·26 million. Goebbels, as we have seen, became a deputy. So did Hermann Goering.

Goering had recently returned after long years of exile (1923–27). Rather nervous of his reception, he had sought out Hitler and offered his services. Without showing immediate enthusiasm, Hitler had been prepared to let him work his passage with the Party, and this he had done so successfully that Hitler permitted him to return to the Party hierarchy. Goering, with his social background and breezy way with men, was an asset in just those spheres where Hitler, at this stage in his career, tended to be weak. He was not yet at ease with the top echelon of society: diplomats, industrialists, generals, senior civil servants, the landowning class. Goering was a good shot, a good talker, and a club man. He took over this side of the Party's work, contacting German society at the opposite pole from Goebbels.

For Hitler needed money, and plenty of it. His personal resources and those of the Party became inextricably mixed. Income came from a number of sources: dues from Party members (one mark a month), entry tolls and collections at meetings and rallies, sale of newspapers and other literature, gifts and grants from supporters. The initial sales of *Mein Kampf* scarcely helped. However, as Hitler became better known and his party came to represent a real challenge in German politics, he was able to sell exclusive interviews for considerable sums, especially to the American press. Similarly, he charged high fees for interviews or articles in the German press. In his tax returns for 1925–29 he described himself as a writer with an annual income varying between some 11,000 and 20,000 marks.

Hitler undoubtedly lived well because he drew liberally on such Party funds as there were, and virtually lived on expenses. Nevertheless, he was often in debt (as indeed was the Party organization). In 1926 he acquired a powerful Mercedes, which cost more than 20,000 marks. In addition to living in Munich, he stayed for considerable periods in *pensions* at Berchtesgaden, where he wrote the second volume of *Mein Kampf*. By 1928, he was able to rent a property, the *Haus Wachenfeld*, which he later bought; this was the house which he eventually developed into the *Berghof*. Angela Raubal came from Vienna to look after the property for him. She brought her two daughters with her; the elder, Geli, was twenty. She was a provocative blonde, and Hitler was to fall disastrously in love with her. In the following year, 1929, he was well enough placed (if not actually endowed) to rent a fine apartment in one of the best areas of Munich, the *Prinzregentenplatz*, where he had a paid housekeeper to look after him, and where he installed Geli.

Hitler was therefore no longer living the life of a deprived person, and was taking his full place in society. He continued to count on his wealthy friends for help and hospitality. For example, in 1926 the Duchess of Sachsen-Anhalt was giving him some 1,500 marks a month. He could also rely for financial support on the Hanfstaengls, the Bechsteins and others of his society friends. The first industrialists to give him and the Party money were Emil Kirdorf and Fritz Thyssen, more particularly around 1930, when Hitler pleased them because of his violent opposition to the Young Plan. It was with this money that he was able to acquire the mansion on Munich's *Briennerstrasse* which was to become the luxurious Nazi headquarters, the Brown House, formally opened early in 1931.

However, from 1925–29, the Nazi Party remained a comparatively small force in German politics, vocal, potentially rather than actually powerful, increasingly well organized and experienced in political manoeuvre, and capable of assembling large and impressive annual rallies in Nuremberg. Hitler joined forces with the rich and influential figure of the right-wing nationalists, Alfred Hugenberg, forming an uneasy relationship which was to last on and off until Hitler came to power. The association brought him some peripheral prestige, and eased his position when it came to tapping industrialists for funds, notably Emil Kirdorf and Fritz Thyssen. It helped him, too, to achieve what might appear to be a fantastic success for the Party in the 1930 election.

This success was to a considerable extent due to the negative shift in the German economy both before and after the crash late in 1929. This led to the substantial withdrawal of American investment in Germany, which shared to a spectacular extent the trade recession and consequent unemployment which hit both the United States and the industrialized nations in Europe. The Weimar Republic appeared powerless to check the rise in unemployment – 1,320,000 in September, 1929, 3,000,000 in September, 1930, rising eventually to over six million by the time Hitler became Chancellor in January, 1933. Many of those registered as employed were on short time. Hitler was able to show that his prophecies of disaster had come true, and the Nazi Party with its firm, aggressive policy was able to drive a massive wedge into the comparatively weak and divided party system which made up the Reichstag, with its fragmentation into over ten diverse parties. Whenever the government in power failed to win a majority the President was empowered under Article 48 of the Weimar Constitution to step in and govern temporarily by decree, while the Republic was weakened by having to face fresh elections at increasingly short intervals. It was this instability which gave Hitler his real opportunity to take over power.

Meanwhile, Hitler had to deal with dissension in his ranks. In the north, the identification of the radical wing with the Strasser brothers brought about another crisis, and split the two brothers apart. After prolonged argument with

Hitler, Otto decided to break away and found his own movement emphasizing the socialist slant which Hitler now chose to repudiate, criticizing it as a soft, liberal version of Marxism, with its demand for the nationalization of industry. Gregor, however, stayed with Hitler. On the eve of the election, Otto created his own so-called Black Front movement, which was to achieve nothing in the face of Hitler's landslide victory in September, 1930.

In the new poll, victory went to the two hard-line parties: the Nazi vote rose from 810,000 (1928) to 6,409,600 with 107 seats in the Reichstag as against 12, making them the second party in the State. The Communist vote rose from 3,265,000 (1928) to 4,592,000 with 77 seats as against 54. Together this represented support from one third of the nation, while the previous ruling party, the Social Democrats, lost half a million votes, and the right-wing Nationalists some two million. The coalition Government was led by Dr Heinrich Brüning of the Catholic Centre Party: the Social Democrats were still the first Party, with 8·5 million electors, but their power to carry the house was now greatly diminished. Four million more voters had gone to the polls than in 1928, and this too had counted in Hitler's favour.

It should be stressed that Hitler's sole interest in achieving power for his party in the Reichstag was to frustrate the machinery of parliamentary government. He had said as much in *Mein Kampf*. He repeated his views unequivocally in a speech made in Munich shortly after his great electoral victory:

> For us Parliament is not an end in itself, but merely a means to an end ... We are not on principle a parliamentary Party – that would be a contradiction of our whole outlook – we are a parliamentary Party by compulsion, under constraint, and that compulsion is the Constitution. The Constitution compels us to use this means ... and so this victory that we have just won is nothing else than the winning of a new weapon for our fight ... We win seats in Parliament in order that one day we may be able to liberate the German people.[4]

Hitler had other problems to face: convincing the roughnecks of the SA that the 'legal' way to power was the right way, not bloody revolution, and achieving some kind of rapport with the standing army, the *Reichswehr*, which was hostile to the Nazis. The old problem was to what extent the army might itself engage in politics, a matter which came to a head in late September, 1930, when three young officers with strong Nazi sympathies were brought to trial in Leipzig for spreading propaganda in the army. Hitler himself was introduced as a witness for the defence by the defence counsel, Hans Frank. Hitler went out of his way to claim that the SA was a purely defensive force to protect the Party from assault, and not, as was often assumed, a force intended to confront the army. He claimed that 'we will see to it when we have come to power, out of the present *Reichswehr* a great German People's Army shall arise'. He protested under examination that he was seeking only a legal way to power, a legal way towards achieving the German National Revolution:

> For the Nazis it means simply an uprising of the oppressed German people ... Our movement represents such an uprising, but it does not need to prepare it by illegal means ... Our propaganda is the spiritual revolutionizing of the German people. Our movement has no need of force ... We will enter the legal organizations and will make our Party a decisive factor in this way. But when we do possess constitutional rights, then we will form the State in the manner which we consider to be the right one. (The President: This, too, by constitutional means?) Yes.[6]

Hitler's statement in court did much to alleviate the graver suspicions of the Army High Command, but little to mollify the street gangs of the SA who expected a take-over of government by force now that the Party had won a major triumph. Hitler needed a strong man to control the SA which had actually mutinied in Berlin shortly before the election, a dangerous situation which Goebbels preferred not to handle. Hitler had been forced to come to Berlin in person to restore order. He assumed a temporary personal command of the SA and induced his former strong man and confidant, Ernst Roehm, to return from Bolivia and take over once again as Chief of Staff of the SA now that prospects for victory in the State were so much brighter. In January, 1931, Roehm arrived, and at once put the SA under a stricter discipline, and firmer organizational control. During 1931 he was to increase the force from 100,000 to 300,000 men.

The next two years, 1931 and 1932, were to be crucial in Hitler's campaign for power. He had cast his principal lieutenants carefully: Ernst Roehm in charge of the SA and keeping good relations with the army, Goering developing relations with the industrialists and acting as roving ambassador with the upper class inside and outside the Reichstag, Frick heading Party organization in the Reichstag, Gregor Strasser controlling and tightening Party organization throughout the country, and Goebbels developing Party propaganda and organizing the many electoral campaigns, both national and provincial, to come. Hess remained Hitler's constant companion and personal aide in the drafting of documents, letters and memoranda.

Hitler's base remained in Munich, with the Brown House as his headquarters from early 1931. In Berlin, when he chose to visit the capital, he took a suite of rooms at the Kaiserhof Hotel for himself and his staff at a cost of some 10,000 marks a week. The Party was frequently in debt, although its income from rallies, party dues, subscriptions and donations, and the sale of publications was considerable. Hitler was now a world celebrity, and he could charge increasingly high fees for exclusive interviews. This, he was to claim, paid the hotel bills at the Kaiserhof, where he held court on a scale suitable to a great leader in German political life. He was poised and ready for the struggle to come.

6

Seizure of Power, 1931-1933

Hitler was now a leading actor in the German political scene. His successful deployment of this new eminence was to be the real test of his skill and judgement. It would have been only too easy to throw away the sudden advantage his success had brought him by compromising with other parties of the right and assuming some ministerial office of secondary importance, such as the Vice-Chancellorship. His unthinking, unruly followers wanted quick results, and had constantly to be reminded that the Führer's decisions were absolute, and that he was biding his time. Only the Chancellorship itself was good enough for him. His more immediate supporters understood the importance of holding out; some, however, especially Strasser, were to urge compromise. Hitler's mystical belief in his own power and destiny restrained him from taking any false step, though he was sometimes slow in reaching decisions. Often he would retire behind a wall of silence, ruminating among the mountains of Berchtesgaden, searching for the right decision, for example, whether or not to stand for President in opposition to Hindenburg, a contest in which he was almost certain to lose, but in which a substantial vote in his favour would be of great importance in developing the Party's position in the Reichstag. During the greater part of the period the Party was virtually bankrupt, yet by combining bluff, and even charm with intimidation, Hitler managed to maintain an expensive front office both in Munich and Berlin, where he stayed always at the Kaiserhof Hotel. At the same time he lived well domestically whether at Munich or Berchtesgaden.

Behind the stern front of the Leader, however, there was still a certain vulnerability. He was not yet entirely certain of himself in the society of the 'elite'; although he knew now how to behave and possessed the appropriate clothes, his inhibitions led him to exaggerate the courtesies, over-playing the part of the gentleman, especially in the company of women. He posed as the gallant, forever kissing hands and presenting flowers. He preferred to be accompanied by Goering or Roehm on formal occasions, such as meeting the President, the aged and formidable Hindenburg. He knew Hindenburg despised him, and he was formally presented to the President for the first time only on October 10th, 1931, over a year after his great electoral success. He appeared nervous and uneasy in his formal clothes, and apparently talked too much. Hindenburg, aged eighty-four, was unimpressed. Such a man was only fit to become, at best, Minister of Posts, was the President's comment to his aides.

Both Hitler and Goering, who had attended the President with him, were under great emotional strain. Goering's Swedish wife was dying, and he had been forced to leave her in order to support Hitler at what they had believed to be this crucial interview, during which Hitler had hoped, in vain, to make some impression on the monolithic Field Marshal. Carin Goering died in her husband's absence. Three weeks before, on September 17th, 1931, Geli Raubal, Hitler's deeply-loved niece, had been found dead in Hitler's apartment in Munich.

Before entering the relatively undocumented area of Hitler's sex life, it is necessary to understand that everything in Hitler's image of himself, his 'persona', had in the end to conform to his concept of his ultimate destiny: his leadership of the German people. Nothing could be allowed to stand in the way of this great objective, including any thought of marriage. Hitler realized that his hold on the German people (whom he had already characterized as 'feminine' and 'emotional') depended on his remaining single, the unattached object of every German woman's dream. Speer has reported him as saying, 'Lots of women are attracted to me because I am unmarried. This was especially useful during our days of struggle.' Speer also adds that 'Hitler believed that he had a powerful sexual appeal to women. But he was also extremely wary about this.'[1]

Hitler's name was therefore constantly linked with individual women, older women who fulfilled the role of foster-mother and younger women who appeared in the guise of potential sexual partners. Among the latter was one woman of some social position, Winifred Wagner, the English-born daughter-in-law of Richard Wagner, whose husband, Siegfried Wagner, died in 1930. Winifred Wagner was about Hitler's age, and she built a house for him on the Wagner estate after he had become Chancellor. He was always to be on terms of close friendship with her. She called him 'Wolf', and the intimate 'Du' was used by the whole Wagner family in addressing him. This relationship, however, did not lead to marriage.

But Hitler's pleasure lay far more in impressing women with his genius through talk and winning a warm, admiring response from them than in actually inducing them to become sexual partners. This is in line with Kubizek's extraordinary account of his adolescent relationship with Stephanie, when Hitler had been convinced the girl was mesmerized by the sight of him and had fallen deeply in love without any direct contact. Rauschning claims that 'women's gushing adulation, carried to the pitch of pseudo-religious ecstasy, provided the indispensable stimulus that could rouse him from his lethargy'.[2] On the whole, Hitler was resistant to intimacy with really intelligent women, preferring to relax with pretty and undemanding ones. 'A highly intelligent man should take a primitive and stupid woman,' he would say later, even in the presence of Eva Braun, whom he came to know well around 1932. He liked actresses, not only for their beauty and free manners, but because they were often lively without being too serious. It is notable that he chose Leni Riefenstahl, whom he admired as a dancer, actress and film director, to make the film designed to project his personality, *Triumph of the Will*, in 1934. However, her powerful self-assurance, according to Speer, was resented in Nazi circles. There was gossip that she was Hitler's mistress. She stoutly denies this, and, indeed, doubts that Hitler's sexual needs were ever very strong. Magda Goebbels, who was a profound admirer of Hitler, wanted him at this period to associate with some sympathetic woman of her choice. It was useless.

On the other hand, Rauschning, Otto Strasser and 'Putzi' Hanfstaengl have given a more sinister slant to what they claim to have been Hitler's sexual interests. Hanfstaengl accepted his wife's intuitive judgement that Hitler was impotent though he nevertheless appeared to adore women. He had, says Hanfstaengl, a fixation for Frau Hanfstaengl herself. Hanfstaengl has stressed Hitler's liking for pornography (including, of course, Streicher's anti-Jewish publication, *Der Stürmer*); Rauschning claims that Hitler spoke of the *Stürmer* as 'the form of pornography permitted in the Third Reich', and that he had a room 'with obscene nudes on the wall, concealing nothing'. Rauschning went on to accuse him of maintaining a social milieu of sexual perversion. 'Most loathsome of all is the reeking miasma of furtive, unnatural sexuality that fills and fouls the whole atmosphere around him, like an evil emanation.' This was no doubt partly inspired by his association with Roehm, and tolerance (until 1934) of his notorious homosexuality. Otto Strasser told the American psychologist, Walter Langer, that Hitler preferred his bodyguards to be homosexuals. On the other hand, there is no evidence whatsoever that Hitler was homosexual. Rather, he remained adolescent in his relations with women. He liked performances of musical comedies (such as *The Merry Widow*, featuring an American strip-tease performer), cabaret and other shows featuring semi-nude girls. Otto Strasser, questioned by Langer, offered it as his opinion that Hitler was a masochist, deriving satisfaction from 'having a woman urinate or defecate upon him'.[8]

However this may be, Hanfstaengl claims he has seen what he terms 'pornographic' studies of Geli drawn by Hitler, drawings which were later alleged to be destroyed after her suicide. She was a lively, sexually active girl, who studied music, and it appears that she was hedged in by her uncle's jealousy. Her death may have been caused by a frustrated desire for other men, notably Hitler's chauffeur, Emil Maurice, with whom Hitler discovered she was having an affair. Also, she was said to be deeply in love with a student in Vienna. The extent of her relationship with Hitler will most likely never be known, though he appears, according to Heiden, his early biographer, to have declared his passion for her as early as 1929; Frau Winter, Hitler's housekeeper, considered she took her life because of her love for Hitler. Whatever the truth of the matter, her death at the age of twenty-three (after a violent quarrel with her uncle, according to Heiden) was the single tragedy in Hitler's private life. His emotional nature was such that he never recalled her memory without tears. Her room remained untouched in the form of a shrine. Her photograph always hung in his private room, wherever he might be, Berlin, Munich, Berchtesgaden. He claimed many times to friends that she was the only woman he had ever deeply loved. The State Attorney declared her a suicide, but she was nevertheless buried with Catholic rites in Vienna. Hitler was so distraught that Gregor Strasser stayed close to him for two days, fearing he, too, might commit suicide.

As if to compensate for his private loss, Hitler concentrated on public gain. The odds were formidable. The economic recession was his opportunity to consolidate the victory he had won, since he wore the mantle of a prophet of doom so long as Brüning and the Social Democrats headed the government. The divided Reichstag could only continue by means of uneasy coalitions which concealed the personal rivalries of the various party leaders contending for power. Over all stood the autocratic, senile Hindenburg, a monarchist at heart and subject to the influence of the men of the right, such as the aristocratic Franz von Papen, of the Catholic Centre Party, and the *eminence grise* at the Ministry of Defence, General Kurt von Schleicher. He was watched over by his son, Oskar von Hindenburg, and his Secretary of State, Otto Meissner, a career civil servant. Von Papen was elegant, charming, the essence of the landed gentry, with a somewhat shady, if thoroughly gentlemanly, diplomatic past. He was an experienced horseman, and still handsome in his fifties. Schleicher, who was also something of a socialite and in his fifties, enjoyed wielding power in the background. He sheltered in the Defence Ministry, and spent his time in intrigue, making and unmaking ministers. In an atmosphere of growing hostility, Brüning (who managed to remain Chancellor, or Prime Minister, from 1930 until May, 1932) was the only honest politician in the high place.

In these circles, few bothered themselves about Hitler, whose party, though powerful in the House, could do little but make Brüning's conduct of affairs as difficult as possible. Hitler continued his uneasy alignment with Hugenberg, whose Nationalist Party held forty-one seats, but the association with this wealthy autocrat was difficult for anyone of Hitler's intransigent nature.

1932 was the year which finally saw the democratic system crumble, largely under pressure from the Nazis. Brüning feared there would be further disintegration when Hindenburg's term of office as President expired, and he had already approached both Hitler and Hugenberg to try to persuade them to agree to Hindenburg being re-elected, even at the age of eighty-five, unopposed. Hindenburg, as a figurehead, represented stability. Neither agreed, so an election had to be held. Hindenburg agreed to stand in open election, but Hitler, to the consternation of Goebbels (who had to promote the campaign) remained in a state of silent uncertainty as to whether or not it would be wise for him to offer himself in direct confrontation with Hindenburg.

It was not until February 22nd that he announced his decision to stand, less than three weeks before the poll on March 13th. He was formally made a German citizen on February 25th (a necessary preliminary) and the ceaseless round of speechmaking began in Berlin and the provincial centres. Goebbels made twenty-eight major speeches. In the first election Hindenburg only failed by 100,000 votes to win his absolute majority. Hitler, however, with 11,339,285 votes, polled over twice as much as Thaelmann, the Communist contender, who gained just below five million. In the second ballot, on April 10th, Thaelmann fell below four million, while Hitler rose to 13,418,051 votes (36·8 per cent of the poll). Hindenburg strode home with over 19 million, or fifty-three per cent. There was some evidence that, had Hitler won, the SA would have staged a *coup d'état* in defiance of their leader's policy of 'legality'.

The Party, desperately short of money, had to conduct a long series of national elections (two of them for the Presidency), as well as provincial, State ballots of no little importance, all during 1932. In Prussia, the Nazis became first Party in the Diet in April; this was an influential election, since Prussia was by far the largest and most central of the German States, containing two-thirds of the population of Germany. Hitler conducted his campaigns by air; he spoke twenty-six times in the nine days prior to this election. The Party did well also in Bavaria (the second State in importance). Hitler was becoming more and more a figurc who had to be reckoned with, and Schleicher began initial discussions with him to explore how he might be brought into some kind of coalition government. Gentlemen such as Schleicher and Papen thought that Hitler would be comparatively easy to manage once he was involved in government, and ceased to operate solely in opposition. Hitler, however, kept aloof, biding his time, watching the shifts of power. What concerned him was that the economic misfortunes of 1930–31 which had done much to win him mass votes were, if anything, beginning to recede, and the tide could therefore turn against him. Time was of the essence in this prolonged manoeuvre for power.

On April 14th, the SA and SS were banned, and tension ran high yet again. Hitler's judgement was once more put to the test in his determination to keep to the 'legal' path. He could see the power of Brüning waning; the Chancellor was unpopular with landowners (including Hindenburg) because of certain projected land-reforms, and he was unable to secure agreement from France for alleviation of reparation payments or for parity in German arms. Hitler knew the Chancellor must fall, and that further elections should play into his hands.

Schleicher, too, was preparing for Brüning's collapse; his aim was to put Papen, whom he regarded as his puppet, in his place as Chancellor. Brüning's government finally resigned in May. Again, Hitler and Goering went to see Hindenburg, but they were received with the utmost coldness. Papen, they were told, was to be the new Chancellor. As far as Hitler was concerned, this at least meant the ban on the

SA would be lifted. Schleicher was to be Minister of Defence, and he was determined to keep in with Hitler. These corruptible people would be easier to exploit than the incorruptible Brüning.

Papen was to be Chancellor for just over six months, but by a curious turn of events he was never to address the Reichstag. He raised the ban on the SA, and he ordered new elections in July. Papen has recorded his first impression on meeting Hitler at this time: 'I could detect no inner quality which might explain his hold on the masses. He was wearing a dark blue suit and seemed the complete petit bourgeois. He had an unhealthy complexion, and with his little moustache and curious hair style had an indefinable bohemian quality. His demeanour was modest and polite, and although I had heard much about the magnetic quality of his eyes, I do not remember being impressed by them.'[4] Nevertheless, Hitler did not fail to tell him he was determined to win the Chancellorship for himself. The projected idea of buying Hitler off with the Vice-Chancellorship, which both Papen and Schleicher felt he should accept with gratitude, tempted him not at all. Goering told Papen, 'Hitler could become any number of things, but never a Vice.'

In the streets there was rising disorder between the left and the right, and Papen himself took over the government of Prussia as Reich Commissioner. There was fear of civil war. Again, the campaign aircraft flew Hitler to rally after rally, and speech-making was conducted alongside riots. The Altona riots in Hamburg, with 13 killed and 300 injured, were among the worst.

In this July election Hitler achieved the highest vote he was ever to be given by the German people in a freely conducted democratic election. The Party received, in fact, virtually the same poll as Hitler had received in the second ballot for the Presidency – some 13·7 million votes (37·33 per cent), approaching twice the vote of the Social Democrats. The Communists achieved only 5·27 million votes. It was plain that Hitler had won substantial support not so much from the working-class as from the bourgeois ranks of the centre and right-wing classes. Nevertheless even with 230 seats in the Reichstag, the Nazis were far short of commanding a majority vote. But his position was very strong as head of the leading party in the house.

Hitler waited for the President's summons, with an offer of the Chancellorship. It did not come. Papen remained Chancellor. So the bargaining grew harder. Papen describes meeting a new Hitler: 'the modest air of deference had gone, and I was faced by a demanding politician.' These demands Hitler was now prepared to make directly to the President himself, and he did so at a meeting on August 13th, 1932. No longer would he seek to form a coalition government; in Meissner's words, 'he was adamant in refusing to put himself in the position of bargaining with the leaders of other parties and in such a manner to form a coalition government'. Hindenburg and Hitler failed to reach any agreement concerning participation in the government by the Nazis. Hitler insisted that only a strong government led by the Nazis could abolish the threat of civil war which he alleged was coming from the left. Papen, who was also present, says the atmosphere was 'icy'. Hitler, angry and despondent, retired to Berchtesgaden.

The Party organized its revenge. In September, Goering, who had been elected President of the Reichstag, which involved him in controlling the conduct of business in the House, tried by a trick to subject Papen to a vote of 'no confidence' and dismissal from office before he, as Chancellor, could use Hindenburg's authority to dissolve the Reichstag, and continue his rule by decree. Goering failed, but nevertheless fresh elections had to be held in November. In these, the Nazis lost two million votes; although remaining the leading party in the House with 196 seats, they were in a less commanding position than before. The tide appeared to be turning strongly against them. The middle-class Nationalists who had deserted their parties and responded to Hitler in the July election left him, while the poll itself was substantially lower than in July. It is symptomatic that the economic depression, Hitler's principal ally, was beginning to recede, and this undoubtedly affected the size of the poll. The Communists increased their deputies from 89 to 101. Papen was still Chancellor, but his position remained ineffective, and this was Hitler's principal strength. Papen felt increasingly that Hitler must somehow or other be brought into a coalition government, if only to ensure that his elders and betters secured a proper hold over him. This was to be Papen's greatest error of judgement. Hitler refused to compromise, in spite of the dangers of the time. He wrote to Papen on November 16th: 'Your endeavours, Mr Reich Chancellor, appear to me vague and thereby as much a waste of time as they are useless ... This wastage of the hope, faith and trust of the nation in a German future is what fills me with sorrow and pain, but at the same time confirms me in my unswerving resolution to insist on my demands.' On November 17th, Papen resigned.[5]

Hitler was again summoned to discuss the situation with Hindenburg. The tension was so great he had to calm himself by listening to music beforehand with Goebbels. Hindenburg wanted Hitler to serve in a supra-Party government, Hitler replied he could only lead. However, if he were made Chancellor, he would be content to select the majority of his Cabinet from the other parties. Once again the meeting was abortive. The celebrated correspondence between Hitler and Meissner (writing on behalf of the Reich President) followed, lasting from November 21st to 30th. Meanwhile, Hindenburg was under pressure behind the scenes from certain prominent industrialists to offer Hitler the Chancellorship on the grounds that he commanded the following of a great national movement which threatened national and economic stability if not given its due recognition. They felt, as did many others, that civil war was not impossible, with the growing menace (as they supposed) from the Communist millions. Among the signatories were Schacht (a staunch supporter at this period), Thyssen, Krupp, Siemens, and the banker Baron Kurt von Schroeder, who was to figure in the notorious meeting between Hitler and Papen the following January.

Another action was also being planned behind the scenes: to split the Nazi movement by inviting the Nazi 'moderate', Gregor Strasser, to become Vice-Chancellor in Hitler's place, and carry with him a substantial number of fellow-moderates among the 196 Nazi deputies in the Reichstag, perhaps amounting (in Papen's estimate) to as many as 80. The protagonist in this plot was Schleicher, who, somewhat unwillingly, left his back-room shelter to accept the Chancellorship on December 2nd, 1932.

Hitler was not slow to scotch this threat of recession within his own movement, nor was he ever to forgive it. Strasser's long record of dissent had strained relations between himself and Hitler. Nevertheless, it was a fundamental part of Hitler's nature that he hated to sever relations with old comrades, perhaps also a dislike of admitting his failure to dominate every wing of the Party, or of acknowledging that there could be some other, active point of view than his own. Everyone, even the difficult, must be retained in orbit. This probably accounts for the tolerance he extended to his principal Party administrator when Strasser made speeches during 1932 in favour of compromise with the other parties, criticizing Hitler's 'all or nothing' policy. It also accounts for the emotional confrontation between Hitler and Strasser on December 5th during which Hitler let himself go at a meeting of all the 196 Nazi Reichstag deputies and annihilated his opponent. Strasser simply did not possess the strength of personality, rather than the courage, to beat Hitler at this game of public recrimination. He left the assembly, sent in his resignation from the Party, and (after an emotional meeting with his closer supporters) left the capital. Hitler, his emotionalism deeply stirred, summoned his Party leaders and the regional gauleiters to Berlin and treated them to a charismatic lecture on the 'legal' way to power, combined with a fervent appeal for their absolute loyalty, which they swore in his presence.

Goering, re-elected President of the new Reichstag, though with a reduced vote, used his authority to put the House into an early recess for Christmas. This left Schleicher isolated, as unpopular and ill-fated a Chancellor as Papen had been. After a comfortless Christmas – Magda was seriously ill – Goebbels staged a remarkable election campaign in Germany's smallest state, Lippe-Detmold, which had an electorate of a mere 100,000. Nevertheless, Hitler himself and the Party's top speakers concentrated on winning a 'spectacular' victory, symbol of a Nazi comeback which might be blazoned nationwide.

On January 4th, Hitler had a 'secret' meeting with Papen in Cologne at the house of the banker, von Schroeder. It would appear that Papen arranged this behind the Chancellor's back, since he had said nothing of it to Schleicher, to whom he no longer felt any loyalty. Nevertheless, Schleicher knew of it and saw that it was prominently publicized in the press. Papen acted from now on as Hitler's 'broker' with Hindenburg, seeing himself as the future paternalistic partner of this bright, untamed young demagogue who would come to heel as soon as he gained the coveted office of Chancellor. The celebrated meeting on January 4th, was only exploratory, but Hitler saw in it a glittering chance. Papen was as near a trusted figure in the President's frigid circle as there was; news of the meeting was not slow to take effect among those industrialists who were anxious to see Hitler in government. It must always be remembered that, until he came to office, Hitler and the Movement were chronically short of money; even after the Schroeder–Papen meeting, it would seem unlikely they received any substantial sums from industrialists. However, as Rauschning puts it, 'The question of finance has never troubled Hitler much.' Money had to be borrowed to conduct even the diminutive Lippe–Detmold election, in which they won 33,000 votes, beating the Social Democrats. The Nazi press proclaimed the victory, and on January 20th, Hitler staged a mass parade outside Communist headquarters. Demonstrations in the streets followed. But still Hindenburg and Schleicher remained inactive, while the Reichstag remained in recess. On January 22nd, Papen met Hitler again informally, this time at the house of Joachim von Ribbentrop; Meissner and Oskar von Hindenburg were also present, representing the President. Again, Hitler refused anything less than the Chancellorship.

Schleicher, unpopular with Hindenburg and, as a last resort, planning to establish a military dictatorship, was at last forced to resign on January 28th. The Nationalists, led by Hugenberg, wavered, always uneasy about coming to terms with Hitler. Finally, Papen managed to persuade the President to appoint Hitler Chancellor, with himself, Papen, as Vice-Chancellor, and Goering and Frick the only Nazis in the Cabinet. The rest of the Ministers would come from the old, right-wing menage – including Franz Guertner (Justice). Count Schwerin-Krosigk (Finance), Baron von Neurath (Foreign Affairs) and General von Blomberg (Defence). Hindenburg, old and exhausted, gave way. Hitler became Chancellor on January 30th, making as part of his hard-won bargain, that his colleagues consent to the immediate dissolution of the Reichstag and new elections. Alarmed at Hitler's recalcitrance, the new Cabinet, arriving late at the President's office, was sworn in.

Goebbels recalls the emotion of this great moment in Hitler's career, coming a bare eight years after his release from Landsberg and reformation of the Nazi Party, which had only managed to achieve twelve members in the 1928 Reichstag, five years earlier. Hitler emerged from the President's office after his appointment and hurried to the Kaiserhof. 'He says nothing, and we all remain silent also,' wrote Goebbels. 'His eyes are full of tears. It has come. The leader is appointed Chancellor . . . Germany is at a turning point in her history . . . Everyone clasps the leader's hand; it could seem as if our old pact of loyalty were renewed at this moment.'[6] As the winter darkness fell, crowds of Nazi celebrators, carrying lit torches, processed in the clear, starlit night in front of the Chancellery, where Hitler, Goering and Papen stood on a balcony. Hindenburg, half hidden behind a closed window, stared down also at the mass of Storm Troopers, Hitler youth and Nazi women supporters, excited and triumphant, whom his grudging decision to grant Hitler his dearest wish had brought out on the street: 'hundreds of thousands of delirious people from every level of society,' according to Papen. '*Heil, Heil, Sieg Heil* rang in my ears like a tocsin. When Hitler turned round to speak to me, the sound of the new Nazi anthem, the *Horst Wessel Lied*, died away.' 'We close the windows and are surrounded by absolute silence,' writes Goebbels. 'The leader lays his hands on my shoulders.'

But Hitler was by no means supreme. His hold on the

Reichstag, even after freak elections, could be as unstable as that of previous Chancellors. The intervening weeks before the election of March 5th, must be used to the fullest advantage. Goebbels flew into action, 'Radio and press are at our disposal. We shall achieve a masterpiece of propaganda. Even money is not lacking this time.' Behind the scenes, Goering began a rapid cleaning-up operation among the Prussian police and civil service; Prussia, its Diet dismissed from office, was at the mercy of Papen and Goering, now appointed his Deputy Commissioner for Prussia. Everything possible was being done to forestall retaliation by the Communists (or, for that matter, by the left-wing Social Democrats), which might prevent the elections from becoming a landslide for the Nazis. Hitler broadcast that 'fourteen years of Marxism has ruined Germany', and promised that a new 'Third Reich' would be born. The 'Reichs' of Charlemagne and Bismarck were recognized as the previous ones.

Hitler was astute enough to play the part of Prime Minister very quietly and co-operatively with his Cabinet colleagues. But behind his soothing phrases Goering's threats in Prussia sounded formidable; in Goering's words, 'Out of thirty-two police chiefs I removed twenty-two. Hundreds of inspectors and thousands of police sergeants followed in the course of the next month. New men were brought in, and in every case these men came from the great reservoir of the Storm Troopers and Guards.' Papen and his colleagues in the Cabinet found themselves swept aside.

Papen himself admitted later, 'In practical terms, the mistake was to consider the apparatus of the State sufficiently intact and independent to assert itself, under Conservative leadership, against the propaganda methods and machinery of the Nazi movement.' He was gravely in error about Hitler. 'My own fundamental error was to underrate the dynamic power which had awakened the National and social instincts of the masses ... With me (Hitler) was invariably polite, even modest ... It took me a long time to see through him.'[7] But he should surely have seen through Goering, Hitler's principal strong-arm man at this time, who on February 17th proclaimed, 'Police officers who fire their revolvers in the execution of their duty will be protected by me without regard to the consequences of using their weapons.' And later, 'I know two sorts of law because I know two sorts of men; those who are with us and those who are against us.' On February 22nd, Goering made the boldest of his moves, he recruited a force of 50,000 from the SA and SS, and their allies, the Nationalist Stahlhelm (the Steelhelmets) to be auxiliaries to the Prussian police. The streets were filled with Nazis during the election campaign, and fifty-one people were officially listed as killed in the clashes with the left.

What Goering wanted most to prove was that the Communists were planning a *coup d'état*; with this in mind he raided their headquarters in Berlin, the Karl Liebknecht House, claiming (though he never produced the evidence) that he found plans for the intended coup. Then, on February 27th, came the firing of the Reichstag building, which Hitler and Goering immediately claimed to be a Communist act, their tool being a half-demented young Dutchman, Marinus van der Lubbe, found in the building. It would seem now that it was indeed the Nazis themselves who fired the Reichstag as an excuse to take action against the Communists before the election, and swing the voters still further to the right. The fire played into their hands, and many prominent Communist candidates were arrested.[8] A decree of February 28th gave Hitler and Goering sweeping powers over the liberties of citizens, though the Communist Party itself was not officially outlawed until after the election. It was, however, persecuted.

On March 5th, 17,269,623 votes were cast for Hitler, representing 288 seats and forty-three per cent of the electorate. Hitler still lacked his absolute majority, but both the Social Democrats (with 120 seats) and the Communists (with 81) suffered heavily in the poll. This was the last, relatively free election in which the voters were still able, if courageous enough, to resist. Coercion was represented by the constant presence of Storm Troopers in the streets. Protests came from sections in the Churches, and in the Trade Union movement, but by now they were powerless to oppose the Nazi avalanche. Hitler proclaimed in Munich on March 12th, 'Years ago I took up the struggle here, the first phase of which may be considered now as ended. A co-ordination (*Gleichschaltung*) of political life, such as we have never before experienced, has been completed.' Two days later, Goebbels took up his new appointment as Minister for Propaganda and Public Enlightenment. The forces of the press, film, radio and theatre were soon to be brought to heel, and the expulsion of Jews from the media effected.

Meanwhile a great, traditional ceremonial act was being planned to accompany the opening of the new, Nazi-dominated Reichstag. The Weimar years were to be forgotten; Hitler's regime was to be seen as restoring a direct link with the pre-war past, with Hindenburg in the role of antediluvian monarchical representative. The inaugural ceremony took place at the Garrison Chapel in Potsdam on March 21st, with all the glitter of Prussian military pageantry. Hitler was careful, however, not to compromise himself by attending either the Protestant or the Catholic services which preceded the ceremony.

Behind the scenes, Hitler was preparing the so-called Enabling Act which was to be pressured through the new Reichstag assembly, due to meet in the Kroll Opera House. Records of Cabinet Meetings survive to reveal in formal terms how easily Hitler overrode his non-Party colleagues when preparing them to accept this act which was to give him dictatorial powers, a 'legal' permit to rule thereafter by decree. For this he needed a two-thirds majority in a House which had 647 deputies. The arrest, or forcible exclusion, of deputies who would vote against Hitler was discussed. All Communists and Social Democrats were in any case excluded from the ceremony at the Garrison Chapel, at which both Hitler and Hindenburg made formal speeches, and exchanged a handclasp for the photographers.

The Enabling Bill was presented to the Reichstag on March 23rd, 1933. The Social Democrat leader, Otto Wels, was courageous enough to oppose it in open debate. When the bill was finally put to the vote it was passed by 441 votes; there were 94 Socialist opponents. Many deputies were absent either voluntarily or by force.

It is of the greatest significance that in spite of the excessive pressure exerted by the Nazis, Hitler never secured more than a forty-four per cent vote of confidence from the German people before becoming Dictator. Opposing parties had their publicity suppressed, and many of their prominent members put in prison. But Hitler never achieved a majority vote in any free election in Germany.

Nevertheless Hitler's twelve years rule of Germany had begun.

7

Retribution, 1933-1934

Simultaneously with the passing of the Enabling Bill, Hitler passed a second law imposing Reich Commissioners (*Statthalter*) on the various States, with power, under his supreme authority, to dissolve the State Diets (for which Hitler had no more future use than for the Reichstag itself), and the power to appoint officials, judges and others. The states, at a single stroke, lost their autonomy, and Hitler began the great task of bringing the whole of Germany under a single, centralized form of government. The Diets themselves were, in fact, to be abolished in January, 1934, and the States were formally merged into the single unified German Reich. Treating Bavaria as a special case, on March 9th, 1933, Hitler instigated a *coup d'état*, replacing the elected government with Nazi deputies. The local Army Commander was ordered from the Defence Ministry in Berlin not to intervene in this 'purely political' matter, the political-administrative aspect of national co-ordination (*Gleichschaltung*). But there were other aspects, as the German people were soon to learn.

Decree followed decree with the inevitability of retribution on the German people who had allowed Hitler to seize power. In April, 1933, came the first major act against the Jews: a general prohibition from any further employment by the State or in the professions, together with a national boycott of Jewish shops. The same month came a ban on all newspapers out of sympathy with Hitler. The following month 'May Day', the Trade Unions were abolished; a Nazi Labour Front was established under Robert Ley to look after workers' rights. In June, the Social Democratic and Communist parties were disbanded, and their properties confiscated. On July 14th, a further decree proclaimed: 'The National Socialist German Workers' Party constitutes the only political party in Germany.'

Hitler then began the prolonged process of coming to terms with the churches. In this his attitude was complex, for he was as calculating in the way he made use of religion for political ends as he was determined, at this early stage, not to tamper with a hornet's nest by issuing any open challenge to the Churches, either Protestant or Catholic. He had already written in *Mein Kampf*: 'For the political leader the religious doctrines and institutions of his people must always remain invisible . . . especially in Germany any other attitude would lead to a catastrophe.'[1] In the rare references to religion in that book, he accepts its importance for the 'unthinking' masses, because it provides the basis of their morality; without it they would drift into moral nihilism. At the same time, he would not brook the 'misuse of religious convictions for political ends'. However, he sees religion, properly used, as an ally of the leader and the 'folkish-minded man', interpreting the will of God as the maintenance of racial purity. 'Anyone who destroys His work is declaring war on the Lord's creation, the divine will.' He was against strife between the denominations, Protestant and Catholic.

In private, however, he was to become increasingly outspoken about his attitude towards religion. Although *Table Talk* was not recorded until seven to eight years later, there is little reason to believe Hitler greatly changed his fundamental views about religion in later life. Rauschning's *Hitler Speaks* recording his views on the subject in 1933 proves this. 'One is either a German or a Christian. You cannot be both,' he said in Rauschning's presence in 1933.[2] Christianity stood for 'pity-ethics', the German god must be strong and heroic: 'God in Nature, God in our own people, in our destiny, in our blood.' He was merely not prepared to publish what might appear cynical in the eyes of his people. 'The heaviest blow that ever struck humanity was the coming of Christianity,' he said then. 'Bolshevism is Christianity's illegitimate child. Both are inventions of the Jew . . . Christianity is a rebellion against natural law, a protest against nature . . . the systematic cultivation of the human failure.' Hitler's faith, if he could be said to have had one, was in the survival of the fittest, of the racially pure and strong. He believed the doctrines of the Christian Churches had 'reached the peak of absurdity' in the face of modern scientific discovery; 'consequently the more Christianity clings to its dogmas, the quicker it will decline.' 'I shall never believe that what is founded on lies can endure forever. I believe in truth. I'm sure that, in the long run, truth must be victorious . . . I shall never come to terms with the Christian lie . . . I rebel when I see the very idea of Providence flouted in this fashion.' The Bible is regarded as 'Jewish mumbo-jumbo'. However, Hitler supported the idea of belief in God, especially for the unintelligent or uneducated. 'The notion of divinity gives most men the opportunity to encompass the feeling they have of supernatural realities.' In a typical piece of mental effrontery, he claimed Christ could never have been a Jew. 'He must be regarded as a popular leader who took up his position against Jewry . . . The Galilean's object was to liberate his country from Jewish oppression. He set himself against Jewish capitalism, and that is why the Jews liquidated him.'

Hitler was quite definite about what lay ahead:

> I envisage the future, therefore, as follows: first of all, to each man his private creed. Superstition shall not lose its rights. The Party is sheltered from the danger of competing with the religions. The latter must simply be forbidden from interfering in future with temporal matters.[3]

Faced by Hitler, the churches in Germany were divided. Among the Protestants there were the supporters of Hitler, led by Reich-Bishop Müller, and that section which refused to support him, led by Pastor Niemöller. Supporters of Hitler, such as Pastor Joachim Hossenfelder, could assert: 'God speaks in a more powerful language through blood and talk than he does through the idea of humanity . . . Bismarck had forged the Reich on the anvil of war . . . God had again chosen his man . . . a man compact of purity, piety, energy and strength of character, our Adolf Hitler.'

Substantial sections among the German Catholics followed suit; one Catholic newspaper, for example, went so far as to claim: 'The best minds of Catholicism, particularly among the youth, must not be content with a simple and inadequate adaptation, but must devote themselves with passion to the historic task of National Socialism.' On the political front, the Catholic Centre Party dissolved itself in July. The culmination of the rapprochement between Hitler and the Catholic Church on a diplomatic level was the signing in the same month, July, 1933, of the Concordat with the Papal See, the signatories being Papen and Monsignor Eugenio Pacelli, the Germanophile Papal Secretary of State who later, in 1939, was to become Pope Pius XII. Pacelli had for eleven years been Papal Nuncio in Germany, and spoke German fluently. The Concordat was the first agreement to give Hitler international recognition. It was a specious gesture by Hitler guaranteeing the freedom of the Church and its right 'to regulate its own affairs', in return for an undertaking that the Church would not interfere with Germany's political life. New Bishops, too, had to be approved, and to swear loyalty to the German Reich. The Catholic Church in Germany was almost immediately affronted by Hitler's enactment of a sterilization law. So Hitler dealt, in a matter of four months following the Enabling Act, with political and administrative matters. But there was much else to be done. In the Cabinet, Papen had become a lay-figure; the right-wing ministers whom Hitler retained as nominal advisers were only those prepared to support him without further question, such as Schwerin-Krosigk (Finance) and Guertner (Justice). To them he added Goebbels and, in December, Hess and Roehm. Goebbels' special concern with the cultural life of Germany extended to everything but the theatre and opera, which Goering liked to keep under his special jurisdiction. Goebbels controlled the press, radio and cinema. To co-ordinate the whole cultural life of Germany, a Reich Chamber of Culture was established, with separate sections for each form of art and communication – broadcasting, journalism, literature, fine arts, theatre, music and films. Every worker in each field had to belong to his appropriate section. Jews naturally were barred and all elements antipathetic to Nazism purged from participation in any form of communication.

The Jews, as was Hitler's intention, began to leave Germany – some 50,000 by the end of 1933, paying expropriation taxes during the years 1933–34 of some 50 million marks. During the five year span, 1933–38, 235,000 Jews were to leave Germany to take refuge primarily in Britain, the United States, Austria and Czechoslovakia – the latter two, unfortunate choices. Some also managed to reach Palestine. Hitler was fully prepared to sustain the severe loss of genius, talent and skill involved. For him such loss was gain.

In Hitler's view the German revolution had to be phased. In this he showed his wisdom, and the superiority of his judgement over that of many of his colleagues, who believed the Nazi take-over bid meant the total squeezing of Germany in favour of Party followers, the 'respectable' and the hoodlum alike. It is true that by February, 1934, when Hitler exacted his first oath of personal allegiance – from Nazi officials – the total number of these officials was claimed by Rauschning to have reached as many as one million men. This only followed the official proclamation of Germany as a Nazi State the previous December, and the remodelling of the Constitution to conform to this. But Hitler thought that the second phase of the revolution should be more carefully and subtly won, and had said as much at successive sessions of his *Reichstatthalters* and *Gauleiters* in July, 1933.

> The stream of revolution released must be guided into the safe channel of evolution ... We must not dismiss a business man if he is a good business man, even if he is not yet a National Socialist, and especially if the National Socialist who is to take his place knows nothing about business ... History will not judge us according to whether we have removed and imprisoned the largest number of economists, but according to whether we have succeeded in providing work ... The ideas of the programme do not oblige us to act like fools and upset everything, but to realize our trains of thought wisely and

carefully ... Political power we had to conquer rapidly and with one blow; in the economic sphere other principles of development must determine our action. Here progress, must be made step by step without any radical breaking up of existing conditions which would endanger the foundations of our own life.[4]

Hitler had never held the radical views of many of his followers and he was determined to consolidate his power in the second phase of his revolution by broadly maintaining the *status quo*, and by encouraging the industrialists to encourage him. It was not easy, however, to cope with the unruly mob of SA men (numbering between two and three million) or, for that matter, with Roehm, whose aggressive ambition was to merge the SA with the official army under his head. Hitler, on the other hand, realized the importance of keeping the army chiefs like the industrialists, at least neutral during this period of national adjustment.

In his dealings with the Army he was especially discreet. The army, after all, owed its allegiance to the President, Hindenburg, as head of state, and not to the Chancellor. Hitler spoke to a private assembly of the leading generals and admirals on February 2nd, 1933, almost immediately after he had become Chancellor. He assured them of his support over the question of re-armament, and promised to keep them out of any internal political strife. In July he made a public declaration before the SA leaders that they 'as political soldiers' had 'no wish to take the place of our Army', or compete with it. In July he ended the jurisdiction of the civil courts over the military, which the army had greatly resented. In October, he withdrew Germany from the League of Nations and from the Disarmament Conference.

Neither Roehm nor the SA were so easy to deal with. Neutrality was not their style. *They* had put Hitler in power. Now that he was there, it was his turn to put them in a similar favourable position. But the truth was, Hitler no longer wanted them. They had performed their function, and ideally speaking, should now be disbanded and returned to the civilian life from which they had come in such extensive numbers on the wings of unemployment, the figures for which were now rapidly receding. Their radical indiscipline was spoiling the new all-dignified image which Hitler, as Chancellor-Dictator of the Third Reich, was determined to create.

Divide and rule. The 'sanctions' Hitler had been establishing to exercise against inveterate opponents lay in the new political police, originated by Goering as the Gestapo (*Geheime Staatspolizei*) in Prussia immediately after coming to power. Hitler had already given command of his 'elite' political soldiery, the SA, to young Heinrich Himmler, who had been rewarded after the seizure of power with the seemingly small appointment of Acting Police President of the City of Munich. Himmler, however, was the precise opposite of Goering in character; he was quiet, unpretentious and unaggressive in his nonetheless determined pursuit of power. His ambition lay entirely in dedicated service to the movement and to Hitler himself; he was fanatical to a fault. Whereas Goering had no permanent desire to hold down the unpopular job of political 'policeman', Himmler, a born desk man, was ideal for the important task of co-ordinating political police activities in the name of security. Hitler allowed him, as part of the policy of *Gleichschaltung*, to become head of political police in a number of states. At the same time, camps for correction and political indoctrination (largely under maltreatment) were set up, notably by Goering at Oranienburg (later Sachsenhausen) near Berlin, and by Himmler at Dachau in Bavaria. Other concentration camps, authorized and unauthorized, were established throughout Germany, and the cruelties associated with Nazi imprisonment began to establish a reign of terror in Germany. When the unofficial camps were closed, the official ones (often initially quite small) amounted, by the end of 1933, to around fifty, with some 27,000 internees. At Christmas an amnesty was declared, but few were released. Nazi promises were for publication, not fulfilment.

At this stage, Himmler's SS in their black uniform with its silver braid, were technically under the overall command of Roehm, while the political police, the Gestapo (in April, 1934, transferred entirely to Himmler's command) remained separate. The SS during 1933–34 expanded rapidly, reaching some 300,000, not all the recruits conforming to Himmler's absolute standards of racial purity, athletic skill and dedication to and understanding of Nazism. But there were special reasons for this expansion, since, although both formally under Roehm's control, the SS and the SA were increasingly to become rivals. Hitler's policy of 'divide and rule' was being extended from individuals to armed forces. The matter was complicated by the need to absorb into the SA (and therefore yet again increase its numbers) of such allied para-military formations as the Stahlhelm, which took place at the end of 1933; Stahlhelm officers who objected had suffered rough treatment, while some had even been arrested.

It is one of Hitler's strongest character traits, that he could not easily bear profound disagreement with men whom he regarded as old and trusted colleagues. He had had a major disagreement once before with Roehm, but nevertheless had enticed him back into his service, while his qualms about taking Goering back in 1927 had been quite soon overcome. He liked the familiar faces around him, and there can be little doubt that if Gregor Strasser had come to heel he, too, would have been welcome. There was a strong paternalistic streak in Hitler's nature, though of the somewhat negative kind which demands that his close associates accept wholeheartedly the general tenor of his policy and follow implicitly his intuitive judgement. In the next few months, the first half of 1934, Hitler had to force himself to do one of the most unpalatable acts of his career: eliminating Roehm, who was potentially, at this stage, by far the most dangerous man in his hierarchy. It is nevertheless very characteristic that Hitler sent him a most complimentary letter at the New Year, expressing gratitude for all he had done for himself and the Nazi movement. He undoubtedly meant this.

Roehm made no secret of his unwelcome ambitions, even in Hitler's Cabinet to which he had recently been appointed – another gesture Hitler hoped would go some way to mollify, or at least flatter him. He was there, sitting alongside General von Blomberg, the Minister of Defence, whose office he coveted. Blomberg, however, was Hitler's man, fulfilling whatever Hitler said he wanted. Roehm, who considered himself, and indeed was, a career soldier, felt he was the ideal man to place in the charge of the enlarged army which he knew Hitler intended to create. Roehm's own SA Commanders were mostly ex-Army, ex-Freikorps men, and they felt the same as he did, that the SA should, in effect, take over the standing Army. Roehm grumbled in private to Rauschning:

> Adolf's a swine . . . He only associates with reactionaries now. His old friends aren't good enough for him. Adolf is turning into a gentleman. He's got himself a tail-coat! Adolf knows exactly what I want . . . Not a second edition of the old imperial army. Are we revolutionaries or aren't we? . . . The generals are a lot of old fogeys . . . You won't make a revolutionary army out of the old Prussian NCOs. But Adolf is and remains a civilian, an 'artist', an idler . . . What he wants is to sit on the hilltop and pretend he is God . . . I'm the nucleus of the new Army, don't you see that.[5]

Roehm, Rauschning admits, was a little drunk at the time, but the truth came out. Roehm was no appreciator of Hitler's second phase of revolution. What Hitler had in mind was to take Hindenburg's place as absolute head of state when the President died, inheriting with this position the army's allegiance. Since Hindenburg's death was, in the early months of 1934, expected at almost any time, Hitler had to prepare the army for so substantial a change as delicately as he might, and part of this indirect form of negotiation was, in effect, to assure the army that Roehm's ambitions were void.

In Hitler's calculations, therefore, the SA was increasingly discounted, while the 'elite' corps of the SS, commanded by that devoted loyalist Himmler, came correspondingly to the fore. During 1934 Himmler and his second-in-command, young Reinhard Heydrich (as blond and cold-blooded an 'Aryan' as even Himmler could wish) were drawn nearer to Hitler, and indeed required to construct a dossier on Roehm and his associates which, at least in terms of their private behaviour, was not difficult to do. From Himmler's point of view, release of the SS from its nominal command by Roehm was long overdue; he regarded the SA as an ill-bred, ill-disciplined rabble with whom the SS should never be remotely associated. Himmler, however, knew how to keep his own counsel, and there was no open breach between him and the man who was technically still his Commander-in-Chief.

But there were constant 'incidents' between the various rival factions, and it was plain that at some time a classification of the position would have to be made. And the only man who could do this was Hitler. But Hitler played for time, his eye on the President's waning life. In April he steeled himself actually to go to sea (an element for which he had a peculiar dread, as he never had for the air) on the cruiser Deutschland during naval manoeuvres; he did this solely to cement his good relations with the Generals and Admirals, and he may even on this occasion have put out feelers, quite informally, to discover their reaction to his assuming the presidency after Hindenburg's death, probably at the same time promising to curb Roehm's ambitions, of which they were so suspicious. Hitler was also on his best behaviour when Anthony Eden (Britain's youthful Lord Privy Seal) visited Germany in February, 1934 on behalf of the British and French Governments. Eden was most surprised to discover how ready Hitler was to agree to delimiting the SA – Eden's visit, in fact, was very timely for Hitler, adding sound international to sound internal reasons for suppressing the SA. Eden found Hitler 'restrained and friendly . . . As I spoke he fixed me quietly with his pale, glaucous eyes, which protruded slightly, a feature often associated with an over-active thyroid.' Eden considered him 'much more than a demagogue . . . as the long interviews proceeded, (he) showed himself completely master of his subject'. Roehm, whom he also met, he found, 'a flamboyant figure, scarred and scented', but with an 'intelligence of a kind'. He thought him like 'a condottiere of the Middle Ages'. Hitler agreed privately to a reduction of the SA by two-thirds, and that they should receive no instruction in the use of arms or military training.

The campaign against Roehm intensified after April, when Hitler felt secure with the army. Goering, Goebbels (a potential sympathizer with Roehm's impatience for revolutionary deeds, since he had been impatient himself), and Himmler, were all party to these growing tensions. Goering and Himmler, in particular, were anxious, for their own prestige, to see Roehm pushed aside. Once they had assimilated Hitler's own doubts, they brought increasing pressure on him during May and June to take some drastic action. For Goering it was the same sort of situation which had surrounded the Reichstag fire – cry out that a *coup d'état* was afoot, and at the same time make a surprise move to stop it. So Hitler allowed himself to be persuaded that Roehm and his immediate associates in the SA were plotting to take control of the State.

For Hitler these difficult months were evidently agonizing. He liked Roehm personally; along with Hess, he was the oldest of his Nazi friends and colleagues. Without Roehm, his 'old comrade', he could never have reached his present eminence. He realized by now that he would have to purge him, but he could not easily bring himself to do it. The Himmler dossiers grew, involving once again Schleicher and Strasser (neither of whom Hitler could now tolerate) as taking part in the planning of the alleged *coup*. When he was unhappy and uncertain, Hitler became restless, constantly on the move, or, if he were free to do so, he would retire to the restful isolation of Berchtesgaden. At the beginning of June he actually met Roehm himself and (by his own account as given to the Reichstag after the purge was over) warned him against becoming involved in any disruption of the State that might be in the minds of disaffected people. He had, he said, received Roehm's assurance of collaboration. Nevertheless, on June 7th the SA was ordered to go on leave the whole month of July, and at the same time Roehm announced that he was going away immediately on 'sick leave', though at the same time issuing what sounded very much like a threat: 'If the enemies of the SA are nursing the hope that the SA will not return from its leave, or that a part only will return, we are ready to let them enjoy this hope for a short time. At the hour and in the form which appears to be necessary they shall receive the fitting answer.' Hitler, however, had agreed to meet the SA leadership at Bad Wiessee on June 30th.

Hitler's own engagements were rapid and varied. On June 14th, he was in Venice at Mussolini's invitation, meeting the Duce for the first time. Since Mussolini tried to maintain an ascendency, the meeting did not go particularly well. On June 17th, Hitler met his Party leaders in Gera, Thuringia, and was in a sour mood, which was not at all alleviated when he heard about a speech Papen had read the same day at the University of Marburg in which he had voiced the unease many German conservatives were experiencing at the nature of some of the changes taking place in Germany, and in particular the absence of freedom of speech. Goebbels pounced on this and forebade its publication, but not before some account of it had become generally known. Papen, for once, had acted with courage. Hitler was summoned to visit the President on June 21st, and told he must calm the nation or face the consequences of the army taking control. Meanwhile Himmler and Goering pressed him to take action against Roehm; they never ceased to urge that the evidence for the *coup d'état* was mounting. On June 24th Himmler held a briefing conference of the SS High Command in Berlin. On June 25th the army was placed on the alert; all leave was cancelled, and the men were confined to barracks.

Hitler retired briefly to Bavaria, then went with Goering to Essen on June 28th, visiting the Krupp plant and attending the wedding of a local *gauleiter*. Through Himmler he was in constant touch with the capital. On June 29th he visited labour camps, but that night after travelling to Godesberg he came to a final decision to act. He telephoned Roehm at Bad Wiessee to confirm he would speak to his senior officers at ten o'clock the following morning, June 30th. At the same time he summoned Sepp Dietrich, one of his most trusted SS officers, to join him at Godesberg. Dietrich found both Goering and Goebbels there, together with his namesake, the press officer, Otto Dietrich, when he arrived by air early in the evening. Sepp Dietrich was then ordered to fly immediately to Munich and await orders. Goering returned to Berlin, where he was to take charge of the purge which was to follow Roehm's arrest the next day.

Hitler finally left Godesberg by air for Munich at 2.00 a.m., accompanied principally by Goebbels, Otto Dietrich, and Viktor Lutze, a loyalist SA officer who was later to be given command of what was left of the SA after Roehm had gone. According to Otto Dietrich, 'The monstrous side of Hitler's nature for the first time broke loose and showed itself for what it was'. In fact, he was in a state of high nervous tension, having passed the night entirely without sleep. At the airport he tore the insignia off the uniform of Roehm's Chief SA Officer in Bavaria, who had been specially taken by the local SS to the airport for this ceremony of degradation. Then Hitler, in a motorcade, set off in the dawn light along the empty, tree-lined road leading to the quiet Tegernsee where Roehm lay sleeping in the sanitarium at Wiessee.

They arrived unannounced, taking Roehm and his companions entirely by surprise. Heines, his favourite, was caught in bed with a youth; both were led out and shot, the execution undertaken by Emil Maurice, Hitler's driver. There is no certain account of what actually took place between Roehm and Hitler; Roehm was alone, and under sedation. Otto Dietrich has recorded that Hitler 'paced up and down . . . with huge strides, fiery as some higher being'. Eventually it would seem he decided to take Roehm and those with him at Wiessee back to Munich under arrest. They were taken to the Stadelheim prison. All those SA officers due for the ten o'clock conference were told to report instead to the Brown House in Munich.

It would then appear that a mood of indecision seized Hitler. He returned to the Brown House, suffering from nervous exhaustion. At noon he made a speech saying all those involved in the alleged *coup* against himself and the army would be shot. But Sepp Dietrich, who had found himself in charge of a large contingent of SS men sent specially from Berlin, was left virtually without orders until late in the day, when he was suddenly instructed by Hitler to form shooting squads to execute some 110 men 'guilty of high treason'. He found himself opposed on formal grounds by the prison governor and Hans Frank, the Bavarian Minister of Justice, because he had been given no legal warrant. In the end only nineteen men are said to have been actually shot that evening. Roehm, strangely, was not among them. By order of the Führer, he was given an opportunity to shoot himself in his cell on Sunday July 1st by the SS Commandant of Dachau concentration camp, Theodor Eike, and his deputy. When he refused to do so, they shot him down themselves.

Hitler, meanwhile, had flown back to Berlin with Goebbels and Otto Dietrich on the evening of June 30th. He had not slept for forty hours. He was met at the airport by Goering, Himmler, Frick and others. There was quite an assembly to receive him, mainly police officers and officials. His appearance, according to one witness, was pale, gaunt and pallid, and he was unshaven. He held a hasty conference on the tarmac with Goering and Himmler, who had been conducting executions of SA and others since dawn that day with the greatest efficiency. They were showing him lists of names of the dead and those still due to be shot. With a violent toss of his head, Hitler appeared to leave it all to them. As the sun set with a blood-red light, he sped away with his fleet of cars to the Chancellery. For him, the purge was over. In fact, he was giving a garden party the following day, and thought it expedient not to cancel it.

According to Rauschning, Hitler had lost his nerve during the action against Roehm. 'His nerve had,' it was alleged, 'completely deserted him at the crucial moment, and everything had been done without his knowledge, though in his name.' The full extent of what had happened had been withheld from him; following the event, he suffered from night fears, afflicted with bouts of weeping and convulsions like ague. His sleeplessness was indeed chronic, but it would seem unlikely that Hitler suffered such dire effects. It is true that, after the initial confrontation with Roehm, he had withdrawn entirely from the action, staying in the Brown House until his flight back to the security of the Chancellery. On the occasions when he was to be seen – facing Roehm at Wiessee, holding a conference at the Brown House, on the tarmac in Berlin – he had appeared worn out by sleeplessness rather than distraught by conscience.

No one knew how many died on June 30th and July 1st. The purge extended throughout Germany. Hitler, in the carefully edited account he gave the Reichstag, assessed the dead at seventy-seven. Other estimates reached two hundred. Accounts were being settled on a wide basis. Schleicher and his wife were shot down in their home. Gregor Strasser was arrested and shot in prison. Only Papen, through the intervention of Goering, was spared. It would not be right to shoot the Vice-Chancellor on the grounds of an incautious speech. But all those who were known to have written the speech for him were shot. The killings only stopped, by the order of Goering, on that Sunday evening. Pressures were brought to bear to ensure that public congratulations for Hitler appeared from Blomberg on behalf of the army and from the President, who sent him 'profound thanks and my sincere recognition'. Sepp Dietrich was promoted to SS General. The shine of 'Legality' was still bright.

A month later, on August 2nd, Hindenburg was dead. Hitler immediately announced that the office of President and Chancellor would be merged, and that he would become supreme Head of State. He ordered all units in the Army to parade and take collectively the new oath: 'I swear by God this holy oath: I will render unconditional obedience to the Führer of the German Reich and People, Adolf Hitler, the Supreme Commander of the Armed Forces, and will be ready, as a brave soldier, to stake my life at any time for this oath.' Hitler was careful to endorse this further seizure of power with a published testament by the late President, in effect 'bequesting' the nation to him. Oskar von Hindenburg proved willing to broadcast to that effect. But Hitler wanted to secure himself at every point. He announced a plebiscite would be held on August 19th to give the German people an opportunity to confirm him as their national leader. Some 43 million went to the polls, and over 38 million voted in his favour. Let Germany and the world take note. Nothing could be more 'legal' than that.

8

Dictator, 1934-1939

What mattered most in the consolidation of Hitler's power during the six years of peace preceding the war in September 1939 was success. It was easier to drain opposition at home and centres abroad by representing that Germany had recorded an almighty voice in his favour, the voice of a nation rescued from decline. One of the most obvious signs he had to offer was the receding unemployment, which had in fact begun before he came to power but which had fallen dramatically from six million to two and one-half million by December, 1934. Labour was to be absorbed in extensive public works and new industrial developments identified with Germany's 'recovery' largely in the form of armaments manufacture and innovations designed to make Germany more nearly self-supporting.

Hitler was in his early forties when he came to power. He was already set in his private habits, and did not change them substantially now that his days had to be planned to take account of the demands of State business. The expenses of his official residences were now being met by the nation. In Berlin he lived in the Chancellery, a building he disliked and planned to exchange for a massive modern block more in keeping with his grandiose architectural concepts. This was built for him in a single year, 1938–39, by the young architect, Albert Speer, who, at the age of only twenty-eight, was promoted to Reich architect. Speer, by using 4,500 workers in two shifts, finished this vast building two days ahead of time, in January, 1939. Hitler's sole criticism was that the final reception hall, reached only after walking 480 feet down a large, marble-floored gallery, was too small. The Chancellery was, in Hitler's own words, 'the first architectural creation of the new great German Reich.' He wanted, he said, to awe visiting dignitaries and diplomats who had to pass through gates into what Speer called a 'court of honour', then ascend an exterior staircase, enter the first reception room from which double doors seventeen feet high led into a large hall. After ascending more stairs, the visitor passed through a domed room to face the long gallery with its slippery marble floor. Hitler said to Speer, 'on the long walk from the entrance to the reception hall they'll get a taste of the power and grandeur of the German Reich.' He did not care about the slipperiness of the marble floor in the gallery, 'that's exactly right; diplomats should have practice in moving on a slippery surface.' Hitler's own study (over 1,500 square feet in dimension) had four doors with gilded panels above in which the four virtues were depicted – Wisdom, Prudence, Fortitude and Justice – extending their benign influence to the occupant of the great desk below, inlaid with the symbolic design of a sword half drawn from its sheath. 'When diplomats sitting in front of me at this desk see that, they'll learn to shiver and shake,' said Hitler, when he first saw the desk. A large marble-topped table stood by the window, to be used in the later, wartime years for spreading maps needed during military conferences.[1]

The Chancellery was the only great structure Hitler achieved in Berlin. He and Speer had plans for a grandiose boulevard, flanked by trees and public buildings, transecting central Berlin; it was to have a massive Arch of Triumph in the middle, and a huge domed hall at the farthest end. Photographs of the models for this boulevard with its public buildings appear in Speer's book, *Inside the Third Reich*. Speer managed with great skill to enshrine Hitler's love for 'inflated baroque'. This was a symbolic Empire building looking to the past rather than to the future. According to Speer, Hitler's 'sense of political mission and his passion for architecture were always inseparable'.

So much for Hitler's more grandiose dreams. He still retained his modest apartment at Munich, but in 1936 his other small residence, the Villa Wachenfeld in the

Obersalzberg above Berchtesgaden, was totally converted into the celebrated Berghof; this involved acquiring the whole surrounding territory, expropriating many other properties in order to give Hitler a carefully guarded mountain estate of some 27 square miles: the outer fence was some 9 miles in circumference and the inner some 2 miles. The man responsible for this enterprise was Martin Bormann, Hess's principal aide at Party Headquarters in Munich. To create the Berghof estate Hitler let Bormann tear down old farms and wayside shrines and ruin parts of the afforestation with paved walks, which in fact Hitler disliked and seldom used. Bormann's only virtue was that he could be trusted with money; he administered an 'extraordinary' fund maintained for Hitler's private spending by grateful industrialists. Bormann used this large fund for the conversion and expansion of the Berghof which continued to be Hitler's retreat for relaxation as well as business, with its round Tea House situated at a place commanding a fine view of the Berchtesgaden valley. The estate included the mountain top 6,400 feet high, which could be reached by an elevator shaft excavated in the mountain itself and reached by means of a steep road blasted out of the solid rock. It was a waste, since Hitler seldom used it. But the main house, the Berghof itself, was entirely Hitler's personal design, incorporating the original wooden house which was very small, with a dining-room, long room and three bedrooms, furnished (according to Speer) in a bogus old-fashioned German peasant style, with cacti and rubber plants, and swastikas embroidered by devoted women on the cushions. To this Hitler added a luxurious centre with a great picture window in the living-room capable of being raised and lowered, but with a penetrating smell of oil coming from the cars housed in a garage beneath. It had the appearance of a weekend cottage blown up to suit the tastes of some *nouveau riche* occupant. Hitler at least pretended to be using his private income (the greatly expanded royalties from *Mein Kampf*), but Bormann had to draw on other funds to pay the inflated costs of the Berghof, with its many attendant outbuildings needed to house guests, SS guards, staff and the like. It was through his work at the Berghof that Bormann first ingratiated himself with

Hitler; by making himself appear indispensable, he quietly attached himself to Hitler's private entourage, finally replacing Hess himself after the latter's ill-advised flight to Scotland in 1941.

In one respect Hitler made a substantial change in his private life. He took a mistress. This was Eva Braun, a blonde, athletic, good-looking woman who devised such a sex life as Hitler was able to enjoy. Hitler had met her when she was working in Hoffmann's showrooms and had taken to her, paying her compliments which she received very seriously, and inviting her to occasional parties. She fell deeply in love with him at some period just before or just after Geli Raubal's suicide in 1931, when Eva was nineteen.

Her father was a senior employee at Oetker's, a firm specializing in baby foods, in Simbach, a town near Munich. She had two sisters, an elder, Ilse, and a younger, Gretel. A fellow pupil at the school she had attended during 1928–30 has described her as 'stunningly beautiful ... always very elegant ... with lovely, fair straight hair parted on one side and falling down the side of her face on the other side ... a happy girl who smiled a lot.'[2] Nevertheless, a few months after Geli's suicide, in the summer of 1932, Eva herself attempted suicide out of love for Hitler, or perhaps because of jealousy over his feeling for Geli. The attempt was covered up as far as her family was concerned, since her father disapproved of her attempted relations with Hitler. According to Hoffmann, this demonstration of love was successful, and Hitler decided it would be best to take her into his care. Hoffmann professes complete ignorance of when she actually ceased to be his companion and became his mistress. Speer, however, holds her to have been his mistress from the beginning of his acquaintance with her, which was to ripen into friendship in later years. Speer joined Hitler's more intimate circle in the winter of 1933, and found Eva to be part of the permanent household, though her position was accepted entirely without comment and carefully concealed from any outside gaze. She travelled to Berchtesgaden separately, along with Hitler's secretaries, and kept herself aloof. The only sign of intimacy between them was when Hitler would from time to time sit relaxed, holding her hand, and when, late at night, the prolonged period of talking over, they would retire to their adjoining bedrooms together. She was never permitted to appear at lunch or evening meals if ministers, senior officials, or other outside visitors, such as diplomats, were being entertained. She was, for a considerable period, nervous of her position, even intimidated, and unhappy when Hitler absented himself from her. In her uncertain state, she easily grew jealous and in 1935 she made a second suicide attempt by taking an overdose of barbiturates. Eva destroyed a letter sent to the Führer by her father complaining of his treatment of her before it came into his hands. Hitler bought her a villa in Bogenhausen, a fashionable suburb in Munich, by way of an attempt at compensation.

She was plagued by insecurity and loneliness. Hitler often neglected her for weeks on end. It would appear that his affection for her, though genuine enough, lacked any profound feeling. He gave her many presents, largely inexpensive jewellery, and made her an allowance which was paid through Hoffmann's establishment as if to some male employee. There are touches of pathos in the diary she began to keep around 1935, when she was twenty-three – she wishes she had a little dog 'so as not to be alone all the time'. (Later she was to be allowed to keep two Scotch terriers. Hitler had his own Alsatian, called Blondi. 'Leaders should be seen with big dogs,' he said.) She writes how delighted she is to receive flowers from Hitler. However, 'he didn't even ask me what I'd like for my birthday.' 'It looks as if he *will* take me to Berlin. But I shan't believe it till I'm actually in the Chancellery.' These entries were all written about three months before her second suicide attempt. During the rebuilding of the Chancellery, she stayed at the Adlon Hotel when Hitler permitted her to come to see him in Berlin. In his will of 1938 he left all his property to the Party, but stipulated, among other bequests, that Eva Braun, his sister, Paula Hitler, and his half-sister, Angela Raubal, should each receive a thousand marks a month for life.

Later, in somewhat happier times, Eva Braun became relatively proficient at making 'home movies', and considerable captured footage survives in American archives recording her domestic life with Hitler at Berchtesgaden. Also she grew a little bolder in asserting her position. When Goebbels made his celebrated remark in 1939 about the Führer being much too busy to have a private life, Eva said, 'I am his private life.' She would go shopping in Berlin (unrecognized, of course), charging her purchases to the Führer's secretariat. She spent a great deal on clothes.

It would appear that Hitler had, at least for a while, normal sex relations with Eva Braun. She admitted as much to Speer, implying once, in the middle 1930s, that Hitler was less potent than she liked. Then, when Hitler's concern over his health was paramount, he said to her, 'I'll soon have to give you your freedom. Why should you be tied to an old man.' Eva repeated the words to Speer, sobbing. Hitler was still under fifty at the time.

In his purely private, domestic life, Hitler remained remarkably *petit bourgeois*. Speer, one of the most candid and accurate observers, found him, like others, completely undisciplined as a worker, a 'bohemian' who had to be put under some form of pressure in order to summon the energy and concentration to work. He would relax into time-wasting lassitude at Berchtesgaden, putting off until tomorrow anything which need not absolutely be done today, such as speech preparation. The lassitude, however, was not total, since the steam of his ideas built up a full head during the days or weeks of apparent idleness. He did not like beginning work before mid-day or even later; he caught up a little with immediate business before taking a prolonged lunch with those guests who happened to be present. In the dining room (with walls and ceilings panelled in larchwood, the chairs covered in red moroccan leather) a long table seated up to twenty people; the waiters, in close-fitting white jackets and black trousers, were in fact drawn from the SS Guards. Eva Braun sat on his left, while Hitler usually chose some other lady to sit on his right. The circle included wives of officials and female secretaries, while the men who were constantly present included the photographer, Hoffmann, and Bormann. Such 'minister-friends' as Hess, Goering and Goebbels appeared less and less often in Berchtesgaden as their responsibilities in Berlin increased. Speer found

Berchtesgaden very enervating and boring, and professionally time-consuming. So he, too, absented himself, his position in Hitler's favour now assured. Like the others, he hated Bormann.

The conversation in the circle round table was dominated by the expression of his views and reminiscences, those constantly present became a perpetual sounding board for twelve years of incessant, repetitive monologue. The food served was simple but plentiful, and Hitler did not impose his vegetarian and teetotal tastes on his guests. Meat and wine were served. After lunch Hitler might take his guests to the Tea House, walking in pairs, preceded and tailed by SS Guards. At the Tea House, coffee, tea, chocolate and cakes were served, followed by liqueurs. This lasted until about six o'clock. Then, after a rest period at the Berghof, the evening meal was served at eight and the company returned afterwards to the lounge with the long picture window and red-upholstered easy chairs. Here records would be played, or films shown, the screen concealed behind a moving tapestry. Hitler liked simple, banal films, both German and foreign, which were also shown at the Chancellery in Berlin. Tragic films were avoided, or the kind of critical comedy represented by Buster Keaton or Chaplin. Hitler favoured romantic films, historicals, epics, musicals, operettas and revues. His demand for new films (including those from abroad which had been banned) was so great that many had to be shown twice. He liked, for example, *Lives of A Bengal Lancer*, and said so to Anthony Eden when the latter paid a second visit to Berlin.

Hitler's behaviour in public and private differed. With Speer, for example, he was pleasant and informal; one evening he invited him suddenly to dinner at the Chancellery, and loaned him one of his own coats because Speer's had become accidentally soiled on the building site. But if anything went wrong (such as a car not arriving when it should) he could be merciless to a nervous subordinate. Rauschning bears this out: 'He would throw his entourage into confusion by well-timed fits of rage, and thus make them more submissive. People began to be afraid of his incalculable temper.'[3] According to Speer, 'with enormous histrionic intuition he could shape his behaviour to changing situations in public while letting himself go with his intimates, servants or adjutants.' He was always ungracious when crossed.

Another observer, the right-wing British Ambassador in Berlin from 1937 to 1939, Sir Nevile Henderson, was told by those in close touch that Hitler's chief quality was his *Fingerspitzengefühl* (finger-tip feeling), 'his sense of opportunity, allied with clearness of mind and decision of purpose'. He could give exactly the right answer to silly questions such as that Henderson put to him after a four-hour march past in which he had had to stand with arm outstretched in the Nazi salute: 'I asked him afterwards how he managed to do it. His reply was "Will-power." ' He had in fact once asked an actress of our acquaintance whether she could advise him on any technical trick of the theatre to assist him to do just this. Henderson, who was unfortunate in that he always had to meet Hitler when the Leader was in a bad mood, felt that 'his continual outbursts were not spontaneous, but that he deliberately worked himself up into a state of excitement . . . He may have thought that, since demagogical eloquence swayed the masses, it must have a similar effect on the individual.'[4] Ambassador William Dodd of the United States, first meeting Hitler as early as October, 1933, wrote in his diary, 'My final impression was of his belligerence and self-confidence. If Hitler ever paused to listen to a diplomat after the mid-1930s it was largely to prepare his riposte, rather than to consider the arguments being put to him.'

Eden, meeting him again in 1935, found him 'definitely more authoritative and less anxious to please than a year before'. Henderson also noticed that 'contradiction was insufferable to him', and that therefore 'his entourage steadily and inexorably deteriorates into mere "yes-men".' As a diplomat, Henderson compared him to a chess-player waiting for his opponent to make a false move from which he could score some immediate advantage, his movements the result of 'long-headed calculation and violent and arrogant impulse'. Worse still, he had, according to Henderson, a capacity for self-delusion, which enabled him to work himself up into believing anything he chose to believe, and impress this on others. As his prestige grew in the later 1930s, he took even less notice of the advice of others. Goering once said to Henderson (who was friendly with him, since they went shooting together), 'When a decision has to be taken, none of us counts more than the stones on which we are standing. It is the Führer who decides.'[5] This was to become the standard excuse for all Nazis once the enormities of the regime became known.

Hitler, however, learned the technique of being the cordial host at the big diplomatic receptions he had to hold as head of State. He knew how to make guests feel welcome. Eden, for example, writes of a dinner party at the Reich President's house in 1935: 'The occasion was informal and much pleasanter, the decoration and lighting restrained ... Hitler was an easy host, moving about among his guests and making sure that all wants were satisfied.'[6] At a diplomatic reception in September, 1934, shortly after Hitler's assumption of the Presidency, Dodd writes, 'When the corps, some fifty in all, were properly arranged around the reception salon, Hitler, von Neurath ... came into the room in full dress, and the Nuncio (as senior member of the diplomatic corps) read his conventional document congratulating (him) ... Hitler replied in German avowing his good-will to all the outside world and his one objective: peace. When he finished, he advanced in perfect form, bowed and shook hands with the Papal representative ... As the happy Führer extended his hand to me, I reminded him of the peace note in his speech ... Hitler bowed pointedly and talked for a moment as though he were a pacifist, a type he always damns in his public statements ... He assumed that I actually believed what he had said! I have never seen Hitler quite so happy-looking ...'[7] At a dinner-party given in 1937 to the diplomatic corps, Dodd speaks of 'close to seventy-five servants marching in and halting in military fashion before the tables,' but comments on the fact that, 'there were no champagne toasts, the rule here at big dinners.'

Speer is perhaps the soundest guide to the problem of Hitler's health. Hitler shrank from any revelation about his physical disabilities, he felt any sign of sickness would be fatal to the image of strength he and his propaganda had built up. According to Speer, from 1935 on (when he was only forty-six) he became obsessed by the idea that he was going to die. He was experiencing spasms of acute gastric pain and treated himself by reducing his diet to a minimum: soup, salads, the lightest foods. He complained in private of cardiac pains, insomnia and excessive wind. Yet he refused every pressure put upon him by his entourage to submit to a proper medical examination. The news, he felt, would be bound to leak out. He prepared to treat himself at this stage. However, he was examined by a recognized specialist for a throat infection, and a harmless node was removed. Hitler, who had feared cancer of the throat (of which Frederick II, father of the last Kaiser, had died), was greatly relieved.

But this was the limit of Hitler's orthodox treatment. In 1935 his photographer, Heinrich Hoffmann, was cured of a serious illness by the fashionable Dr Theodor Morell, a ship's doctor who claimed to have studied under the Nobel prizewinner Ilya Mechnikov, a bacteriologist who had been a professor at the Pasteur Institute, and had died in 1916. Hoffmann urged Hitler to consult Morell, an ambitious and money-loving man who sprang at this opportunity to make the Führer his permanent patient. He injected Hitler with intestinal bacteria and other drugs which he kept secret. Hitler was fascinated by this unorthodox specialist, and when he began to experience alleviation from his pains he made Morell his private physician. For the rest of his life, the full ten years, Hitler's body became the chemical testing laboratory for an increasing quantity of drugs originating from sources as varied as the testicles of bulls, or extracts from plants. Morell was to take every advantage of his position, making Hitler an addict to his drugs and patenting the many medicines he devised for the Führer. Morell had smart consulting rooms on the Kurfürstendamm, and a country house on Schwanenwerder Island near Berlin, where Hitler became a frequent tea-time visitor. Morell was noted for treating film stars, and advertised himself as a specialist in venereal diseases; however, there is no hard evidence, only rumour, that Hitler was suffering from the long-term effects of syphilis contracted in his youth. The Crown Prince was another of Morell's patients. So, also, through heavy-handed pressure from Hitler, were most of the entourage. However, after 1937, the temporary improvement in Hitler's health began to lapse, and the refrain was constantly repeated in his private conversation, 'I shall not live much longer . . . my health is growing worse all the time.' A copy of his will, made in May, 1938, survives, with bequests to his friends and members of his domestic entourage. As his health appeared to deteriorate, Hitler accelerated his plans of the future. From 1938 he was ever more impatient to realize his more grandiose schemes before an anticipated, premature death. This probably explains his increased peremptoriness after 1938, and the precipitate way he entered on the war campaign of 1939–41. The wars on which the imperial expansion of the greater German Reich depended had to be engaged upon while Hitler felt he still had the strength to direct them.

It was Rauschning, a frequent visitor from Danzig to both Berlin and Berchtesgaden between 1932 and 1934, who recorded Hitler's 'table talk' of this earlier period. After this he 'defected'. Rauschning describes Hitler's monologues as a 'passionate self-interpretation', revealing not only the character of the man in his maturity, but the less inhibited expression of his instinctual desire to shape Germany, Europe, and even the world according to his will. He regarded Germany as synonymous with Europe, its heartland: 'It will be Germany, only when it is Europe as well. Without power over Europe we must perish. Germany is Europe.' To achieve this, the Germans must be hardened, rescued from the degeneracy which has afflicted them and the rest of Europe. 'I must be a harsh master,' he said, 'we must be ruthless'. He wanted to shock. 'We are barbarians!' he shouted. 'We want to be barbarians! It is an honourable title. *We* shall rejuvenate the world . . . It is our mission to cause unrest.' On another occasion he said, 'Brutality is respected . . . The people need wholesome fear. They *want* to fear something. They want someone to frighten them and make them shudderingly submissive.' And again, 'Unless you are prepared to be pitiless, you will get nowhere . . . Terrorism is absolutely indispensable in every case of the founding of a new power.'[8]

There are a number of passages in which Rauschning tries to penetrate Hitler's weaknesses as a human being. He found him always 'filled with an immeasurable hatred ... He seemed always to feel the need of something to hate. But equally, the transition from anger to sentimentality or enthusiasm might be quite sudden.' In certain respects Hitler possessed the very opposite character to that he professed to admire: By nature he was impressionable, romantic, easily moved to tears and to nervous storms. His ruthless pose, says Rauschning, was 'the desolation of a forced and artificial inhumanity', his cynicism and vulgar abuse to some extent the product of a hypersensitiveness which he was anxious to cover up. Rauschning found it significant that he had to bolster his confidence by surrounding himself with somewhat 'overblown' young women and the admiring wives of his aides. Yet he was fundamentally an unattractive man. His very appearance was dead. His famous eyes were 'neither deep nor blue' and his look was 'staring or dead', without 'the brilliance of a sparkle of genuine animation'. His voice was 'harsh' and 'repellent', his tone 'guttural and threatening'. He was charmless except for his hands, 'which are strikingly well shaped and expressive'.

Hitler's insomnia was especially acute in Berlin, as were his nervous derangements, especially following the horrors of the Roehm purge. It was said, reports Rauschning, quoting a man he holds to be a reliable source, that he would wake from fitful sleep weeping, shaking as in an ague, calling for lights and the presence of someone he could trust, such as Hess or his SA guards. It appeared that he constantly feared he was being poisoned, and would wake sweating profusely and calling for help, crying out some unnamed man had been in the room. He would mutter unintelligible phrases, or figures, or unknown German word-formations.

Not all Hitler's rages must be thought to be assumed. Rauschning describes one which appeared real enough. 'He behaved like a combination of a spoilt child and an hysterical woman. He scolded in high, shrill tones, stamped his feet, and banged his fist on tables and walls. He foamed at the mouth, panting and stammering in uncontrolled fury ... He was an alarming sight, his hair dishevelled, his eyes fixed, and his face distorted and purple ... Suddenly it was all over. He walked up and down the room, clearing his throat, and brushing his hair back. He looked round apprehensively and suspiciously, with searching glances at us.' He then proceeded to talk quite rationally.

Hitler claimed to Rauschning he was not a dictator. He was, rather, a leader. A dictator he held to be a fool, imposing arbitrary decisions on his people. He claimed that, as a leader, he was merely fulfilling the will of the Party. 'There is no such thing as dictatorship in the accepted sense,' he said. 'Even the most extreme autocrat is compelled to correct his absolute will by existing conditions. Considered soberly, there are only various means of giving shape to the public will ... It is my foremost problem – never to find myself in opposition to my party. If I am of a different opinion, then it is my duty to change either my own, or the Party's view.' In any case, he disliked the term Party for his movement. 'I should prefer "order" myself. But perhaps this is romantic.' He saw the Party as 'taking over the function of what has been society', as 'representative of the general good'. National Socialism was 'more even than a religion; it is the will to create mankind anew'. In this, elite man (*Herrenmensch*), the man of the future, rules the earth in the place of, and at the expense of the man of the herd, past man (*Herdenmensch*). 'Politics,' said Hitler, 'is completely blind without a biological foundation and biological objectives.'

To hasten the fulfilment of this objective, Hitler was prepared to abandon all the rules of conventional social dealing. 'Where should we be if we had formal scruples?' he demanded. 'I am prepared to commit perjury half-a-dozen times a day.' He could take everything on his conscience. His romantic cynicism became a form of moral nihilism which permitted him to overlook the crimes against humanity committed by the SA and SS, by the Gestapo, by the Guards of the concentration camps. He permitted, or turned aside from, the speculations, large or small, of Party members, from ministers down to local officials. His concern was solely with his own purpose. His aim was to make, within his lifetime if possible, the German revolution a

European one and, after that, a world revolution. He intended, he said, to undermine the morale of the weaker nations – 'how to achieve the moral breakdown of the enemy before the war has started – that is the problem that interests me . . . We shall not shrink from the plotting of revolutions . . . I shall never start a war without the certainty that a demoralized enemy will succumb to the first stroke of a single gigantic attack.' This was the blitzkrieg. He saw the future of warfare in a combination of air and land forces; he always tended to discount navies, probably because of the vulnerability of shipping to the submarine, and partly because of his irrational dislike of the sea.

Meanwhile, no international agreements would stand in his way. 'I shall shrink from nothing,' he said to Rauschning. 'No so-called international law, no arguments will prevent me from making use of any advantage that offers. The next war will be unbelievably bloody and grim. But the most inhuman war, one which makes no distinction between military and civilian combatants, will at the same time be the kindest, because it will be the shortest.' In the pursuit of this aim, Hitler said, he would use temporary treaties of friendship, non-aggression pacts: 'I am willing to sign anything . . . There has never been a sworn treaty which has not sooner or later been broken or become untenable . . . Anyone whose conscience is so tender that he will not sign a treaty unless he can feel sure he can keep it in all and any circumstances is a fool . . . I shall make any treaty I require.'

Of his generals he spoke disparagingly in private only at this stage. 'They are blind to the new surprising things . . . The creative genius stands always outside the circle of the experts,' he said. In the end, it was he who would command, in war as in diplomacy. As he looked west, he saw only the weak and divided democracies, riddled with pacificism. To the East he still saw the main area for German expansion beginning with Austria, Bohemia and Moravia (with alien races removed), the Baltic countries (where 'we shall easily Germanize the population'). In 1934, the latest period of the conversations at which Rauschning was present, he was wary about Russia: 'perhaps I shall not be able to avoid an alliance with Russia,' but nothing must stand in the way of the ultimate confrontation between a greater Germany and 'the greatest continental empire in the world'. As for the United States, this was permanently on the brink of revolution, with its millions of unemployed. It was in the 'mire' of progressive self-destruction. It was a fictional democracy, and could be overcome initially through agents, perhaps spreading destructive bacteria. Or it could be taken over by the powerful German minority in the population acting as a fifth column. As for Latin America, Brazil appeared to him the most suitable starting point for a National Socialist revolution. 'We shall create a new Germany there,' he declared. North American and Hispano-Portuguese influence would be squeezed out. The further Hitler was removed from Germany itself the more fanciful his schemes became. He saw every German outside Germany as a secret agent for National Socialism. Opposition would crumble until the world itself, no less, in one way or another would fall within Germany's sphere of influence.

Returning to the world of practical affairs, Hitler's arbitrary control extended to his non-Party ministers. Papen, out of favour but at least preserved from Schleicher's fate by Goering, lost his Vice-Chancellorship. He capitulated, along with Neurath and Schwerin-Krosigk, and signed the law making Hitler supreme head of State after the death of Hindenburg. Papen was then dispatched to become Minister Extraordinary in Vienna, a position he lost after the Anschluss in 1938. He subsequently became German Ambassador in Turkey. Hugenberg had been dropped as Minister of Economy as early as June, 1933. Neurath was summarily removed as Minister of Foreign Affairs in 1938 in favour of Ribbentrop; Neurath, in due time, was sent away to become Reich Protector of Bohemia and Moravia, following the occupation of Czechoslovakia, a position he held from 1939 to 1943. Of the original right-wing ministers, Franz Guertner, Minister of Justice, and Count Schwerin-Krosigk, Minister of Finance, retained their posts throughout the regime until 1945; they were both compliant men and subservient to Hitler's will.

One of the worst cases of the bare-faced removal from

office of a man Hitler no longer wanted was that of Field Marshal von Blomberg, Minister of War, known as 'Rubber-Lion' (*Gummi-Löwe*) on account of his original subservience to the Führer following his original appointment in 1933. The method adopted for his removal in 1938 became a scandal and strained relations with the army. Hitler took a grave risk in consenting to the treatment of so senior an officer in this way, and his action can only be attributed to his acerbity. Blomberg was inadequate to supervise Hitler's daring plans for the war to come. Both he as Minister and the Army's Commander-in-Chief, General von Fritsch, insisted the Army was wholly unprepared for war. The Army had been increased from eight divisions (1933) to thirty-six, which was far too many in peacetime. Blomberg's protests only led to his downfall. The Nazi leaders looked for his Achilles heel, and found it in an infatuation Blomberg, aged sixty, entertained for a young woman, Erna Grühn, who was scarcely of a class or character suitable for a Field Marshal. Nevertheless, after taking private advice from Goering, he married her, with both Goering and Hitler acting as witnesses. While Blomberg was on his honeymoon, files were placed on Goering's desk showing the girl had a police record as a prostitute. Hitler consented immediately to Blomberg's dismissal and disgrace. Thereafter, he lived in retirement. Fritsch, his natural successor, was framed by the Gestapo as a homosexual, although the evidence produced was faked and turned on mistaken identity. Although finally proven innocent after an inquiry upon which the army chiefs insisted, Fritsch was so broken by the case that, at the beginning of the war, he returned to active service and committed virtual suicide during the Polish campaign. Whether or not Hitler and Goering knew in advance of the trap which Blomberg was entering can only remain an open question; the Fritsch case is less doubtful, and Goering's behaviour as President of the Court of Honour concerned to clear Fritsch's name was, to say the least, specious, permitting Fritsch to be exonerated while at the same time protecting the Gestapo from the exposure the army had planned to stage.

Only one of Hitler's ministers proved recalcitrant – at

least by his own account of what happened. This was Hjalmar Schacht, former President of the Reichsbank, and one of Hitler's supporters among the financiers immediately prior to the seizure of power. Schacht accepted Hitler's invitation to become Minister for Economic Affairs in August, 1934, and remained in office until November, 1937. He then resigned because of what he regarded as Goering's intolerable interference in his sphere of work, which was to turn Germany rapidly from a peacetime to a critical wartime economy. Goering, a many-headed monster in the Nazi hierarchy because of his greed for offices of state, was appointed in effect Controller of the German war economy as plenipotentiary for Hitler's Four Year Plan, an appointment announced by Hitler at the annual Party Rally in Nuremberg in 1936.

Hitler did not consult Schacht in this matter; it was a flagrant case of 'divide and rule'. Schacht, authoritarian in his own right who knew he had done much since 1934 to achieve Hitler's wishes, was entirely unwilling to run in double harness with Goering, whom he held to be an overbearing amateur. Differences soon arose between them; Goering, without consultation, ruthlessly decreed whatever he wanted, commandeering in July, 1937, for example, the iron and steel industry. The whole economy, management and labour force, was by now hemmed in by law. Hitler wanted to retain Schacht's skill, but refused to intervene with Goering, urging always that it was for Schacht to come to terms with him; Hitler's personal interest never lay in economic affairs. Schacht forced his resignation on Hitler, but remained a nominal minister without portfolio and President of the Reichsbank to conceal from the public his quarrel with Goering. Hitler finally dismissed Schacht in January, 1939, with the words, 'You don't fit in to the general National Socialist scheme of things.' 'I entirely agreed with his remark,' is Schacht's only comment.

Thereafter, Schacht, according to his own account, became involved in the German resistance to Hitler, of which there were to be growing signs from 1938.

Above Hitler's obsessive interest in fast cars was indulged to the full once he was in power. The compressor-Mercedes was the most expensive and powerful of Germany's cars of the period.

Below Hitler constantly retired to the Berghof, his mountain retreat in the south, to replenish his energies. The Berghof developed with the years from a mere chalet to a palatial establishment.

Although Hitler increasingly left routine desk-work to his ministers and aides, he insisted on being presented to the world as a hard-working and punctilious administrator.

Hitler concealed in public his innate aversion to the Christian religion and the established Churches, whom he could not afford to antagonise. His diplomatic relations with the Vatican were facilitated by the German sympathies of Cardinal Pacelli, the Papal Nuncio in Berlin, seen here with Hitler, Pacelli was later to become Pope.

Above Hitler used his minister Goering in the multiple capacity of controller of war economy, leader of the newly-established Luftwaffe, and his diplomatic aide in his relationship with the upper class and rich industrialists. Goering, seen here on Hitler's right, was also Master of the Hunt.

Below Hitler's Minister of Propaganda and Public Enlightenment was Joseph Goebbels, controller of all Hitler's initial election campaigns and, during the war, increasingly in charge of German civilian life and morale. Goebbels always boasted that it was he who created the 'myth' of the Führer; he is seen here on Hitler's right.

Hitler and Child. Hitler and Goebbels were always careful to emphasize in their propaganda, Hitler's devotion to children of blonde, Nordic descent.

In his public relations with women, he wishes to be considered as 'married' to the nation's entire womanhood, sacrificing, as it seemed, all private happiness.

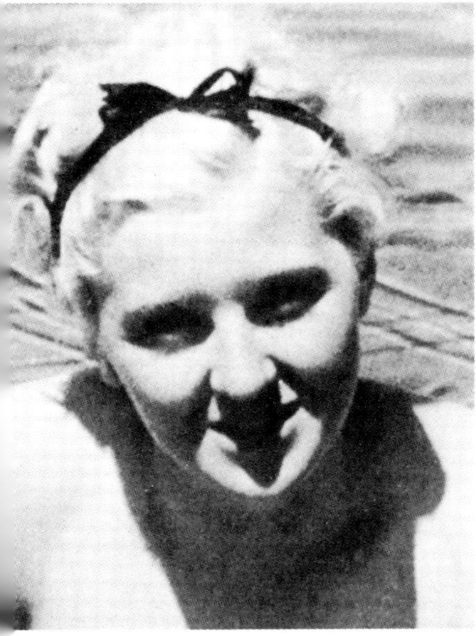

Left Eva Braun was Hitler's secret mistress for more than a decade only becoming his wife a few hours before their great suicide. Only their intimate circle of friends knew of their actual relationship. (*Keystone Press*)

Below Hitler was photographed by official press photographer Gerhard Baatz immediately after the attempt on his life on 20 July 1944. Caught off-guard, Hitler's nervous movement of the hands reveals his condition. (*Photograph by Gerhard Baatz, archive Helmut Laux*)

Little over two hours after the assassination attempt, Hitler stands in pouring rain ready to welcome Mussolini. Note the defensive 'flak' wagon. Baatz was ordered by Hitler personally to photograph him copiously to demonstrate his survival. (*Photograph by Gerhard Baatz, archive Helmut Laux*)

Spectacular Party rallies formed an essential part of the Nazi public image, emphasizing the Führer's leadership, and displaying the rigid disciplines of military power under the swastika insignia.

Hitler's initial relationship with the Duce Mussolini revealed a certain nervous admiration for the man who had set the pattern for dictatorship. Their relationship was eventually to reverse, with Hitler as by far the dominant partner in the Rome-Berlin Axis, established in 1938.

After the Night of the Long Knives purge of the SA and the assassination of Roehm, Hitler placed national security in the hands of the black-uniformed SS under Himmler, seen here on Hitler's right.

9

The Violent Peace, 1936-1939

Hitler's unscrupulous brilliance as international diplomatic gambler reached its peak during the years between 1936 and 1939. From the beginning he determined to outwit the professionals in the interest of German advancement. Increasingly he delegated to his ministers the issue of decrees and legislation concerning the home front, in particular to Hess, who (on the principle of divide and rule) had responsibility to supervise decrees issued by the civil ministries. Hitler hated such routine. He was never to be an administrator, though his phenomenal memory meant that those responsible to him had to face the onslaught of his unexpected knowledge of what was going on in their departments.

What appealed now to his burgeoning imagination was the deployment of a new Europe, with Germany at its heart and head. As Goering said during the Nuremberg Trial after the war, 'Foreign policy above all was the Führer's very own realm.' The chains of Versailles must be cast off, and Germany (impregnated by the will of the Führer) would rearm in preparation for re-alignment with her more immediate neighbours. This included, as a first priority, the expansion of the frontiers of the Third Reich to encompass those areas where Hitler claimed there was a predominantly German population. Hitler felt himself to be surrounded by States old and new, anxious to hem him in and pin him down. Germany had to rearm, while at the same time her Leader preached peace with all the fervour of the true propagandist. Schacht, who was made responsible by Hitler for the economy governing rearmament, said in 1935, 'The accomplishment of the armament programme with speed and in quantity is *the* problem of German politics.' Schacht's adroit and brilliant mind worked on this problem until he was eventually displaced by Goering in 1937. Secretly at first, Schacht began to absorb Germany's unemployed as armaments workers. But as early as May, 1933, Hitler was proclaiming his desire for peace, in direct response to Roosevelt's plea for disarmament:

> Germany is entirely ready to renounce all offensive weapons if the armed nations, on their side, will destroy their offensive weapons . . . Germany is prepared to agree to any solemn pact of non-aggression, because she does not think of attacking but only of acquiring security . . . On the other hand, the disqualification of a great people cannot be permanently maintained, but must at some time be brought to an end. How long is it thought that such an injustice can be imposed on a great nation?[1]

The Disarmament Conference was in session at Geneva, and Hitler was well aware that if he talked peace, it would come as a surprise and relief to the divided democracies. But when by October, 1934, it was clear that the Allies would only grant parity by the end of the decade, Hitler took his first great gamble outside Germany; he abruptly withdrew his representation from the Disarmament Conference and the League of Nations. At the same time he issued a challenge, rather than a plea, to the nations declaring that force solved nothing, and that he would give them another chance. 'We will put up with no more of this persistent discrimination,' he said to Ward Price, correspondent of the London *Daily Mail*. To add strength to his position, he declared a plebiscite in order to invite the German people to confirm his withdrawal from the League. He challenged the democracies to bring sanctions to bear on him for the rearmament which had already begun, and the German people supported him with a ninety-five per cent vote of confidence.

Next in this two-faced diplomatic contest, Hitler did the second unexpected thing. In January, 1934, he concluded a non-aggression pact with Poland. Since it was realized that Germany bitterly resented what it saw as an artificial state incorporating territory which had formerly been German, the pact was utterly unexpected. In spite of Hitler's affirmation to Ward Price in the interview – 'I will sign no document with a mental reservation not to fulfil it. What I sign, I will stand by. What I cannot stand by, I will not sign' — he only made the pact as a blind, since any attack on Poland by Germany was at this stage well beyond his capacity. The pact was also a gesture against France, which was supposed to be the ally of Poland in the European balance of power. German relations with Poland were to be persistently pursued until 1939. Goering was given the task of keeping the Polish diplomats and politicians in line, which meant that negotiations were conducted during boar-hunts in Poland or shoots at Goering's huge estate north of Berlin.

Meanwhile Hitler secretly fostered the growth of the Nazi movement in Austria, with some 40,000 supporters in Vienna alone. Chancellor Dollfuss was assassinated by members of the Austrian SS on July 25th, 1934. Hitler was attending the opera at Bayreuth when this happened, and the news at first delighted him. According to Friedelind Wagner, 'the Führer was most excited – this excitement mounted as he told us the horrible news ... he could scarcely wipe the delight from his face.' Nevertheless, his first act was to free himself from any involvement in the assassination. 'I must go across for an hour and show myself,' he said to Wagner's granddaughter, 'or people will think I had something to do with this.'

The Austrian putsch was as ill-timed as that in Munich eleven years previously, and Hitler was anxious no one should think he was to blame. Many Austrian Nazis had to take refuge in Germany, and Papen was sent to represent Hitler in Vienna and placate the Austrian administration. In October, 1934, a further double assassination followed, that of the anti-Nazi French Foreign Minister, Louis Barthou, in Marseilles, along with King Alexander of Yugoslavia, whom he was welcoming on a visit to France. The murderers were Croat extremists who had links with Berlin, though not directly with official Nazism. Barthou's successor was to be Pierre Laval, who was to become an expert in two-faced diplomacy.

France, which lost the Saar by plebiscite to Germany in

January, 1935 – the first of Hitler's territorial gains – was represented in Berlin from 1933 to 1938 by André François-Poncet, whose memoirs concerning these years make dramatic reading. When he first met Hitler he was, he says, 'struck . . . by the vulgarity of his features and the insignificance of his face.' He found Hitler's celebrated eyes 'vague, dull and opaque, save when some violent urge possessed him'. He described his features as 'flabby', his mouth as 'mean', his expression 'set and dismal'. His eyes were 'globular and dull grey, coming to life only in anger or in a trance'. When angry he rolled his r's. Even his anger he considered more comical than frightening. In conversation, however, even as early as April, 1933, Hitler appeared easy, relaxed and frank. The following year, François-Poncet attended Hindenburg's state funeral and noticed with some concern Hitler's strange attitude when he gave the funeral speech: 'He was more nervous than ever, excited, spasmodic, flushed', entirely out of keeping with the mood of the occasion. He orated extravagantly, 'And now, o dead General, take your place in Valhalla!' This was Hitler exploiting a great public occasion at which ambassadors and other international representatives were captive spectators. François-Poncet, like the other diplomats, had to get used to the unexpected changes in Hitler's moods and performances, and guess at the reason for them. However, during private meetings with diplomats, Hitler was often relaxed and knowledgeable.

Another watchful observer on these occasions was the interpreter, Paul Schmidt, who from 1935 became the principal intermediary between Hitler and the senior diplomatic representatives. Hitler, who had no gift for languages, admired Schmidt's exceptional skill. Already a highly experienced interpreter, Schmidt first worked for Hitler when Sir John Simon and Anthony Eden visited Berlin in March, 1935. He was never a Nazi, rather a dutiful civil servant. Hitler naturally interested him; his friendliness to the British delegates was obviously due to the triumph their presence represented. Schmidt noted that Hitler 'expressed himself clearly and adroitly' and was 'very sure of his arguments'. He used no notes, but often paused to think before speaking.

Among the many colours recorded for Hitler's eyes, Schmidt chose the conventional blue. Hitler had, he says, 'clear blue eyes which gazed penetratingly at the person to whom he was speaking'. Yet 'his mind was busy with his own thoughts, and he was unaware of his surroundings'. His face seemed to gain expression when he spoke of something of special importance to him; 'his nostrils quivered as he described the danger of Bolshevism for Europe', and he emphasized his words with 'jerky, energetic gestures of the right hand, sometimes clenching his fist'. He spoke at unusual length, only stopping for translation at intervals of fifteen or even twenty minutes. Those of his listeners who did not understand him, found it difficult to retain interest. Only once did he show his capacity for rage, and this at the mention of Lithuania, which he claimed repressed the German minority in Memel. Then he immediately became a different person. Schmidt grew accustomed to these rapid transitions. 'He would suddenly fly into a rage; his voice could become hoarse, he would roll his r's and clench his fists, while his eyes blazed.' When he entertained his British guests in the evening he wore 'tails', which, says Schmidt, looked ill-fitting, as if they had been rented. Hitler never appeared at ease in formal dress, apart from uniform.

The occasion for the visit by Simon and Eden was to persuade Hitler to sign a pact securing the peace of Europe, both East and West, widening the effect of the Locarno Pact of 1925, which affected only Britain, France, Germany and Italy. German rearmament was by now no secret; indeed just before the visit, the establishment of an Air Force, the re-introduction of conscription, and the expansion of the army to over one-half million had been announced, in total defiance of the Versailles Treaty. Hitler's friendly welcome for his British visitors had therefore its own vein of irony. Eden, as we have seen, found him far more self-confident than in 1934. The response from France was to sign the Franco-Soviet Pact, supported by a similar pact with Czechoslovakia for mutual assistance in the event of aggression.

This came as a shock to Germany; according to François-Poncet, 'April 1935 marks the climax of European unity against the ambitions of the Reich.' But this cohesion was not to last.

Hitler replied in May with one of his great tactical speeches to the Reichstag, an oration against war, coupled with a plea for mutual security among the nations, and an attack on Soviet Russia as the universal threat to Europe. In preference to Locarno, or any form of multilateral agreement, he offered individual pacts of non-aggression with each country in turn. What he stood for was peace, he declared; 'Whoever lights the torch of war in Europe can wish for nothing but chaos.' Europe breathed her relief that the *enfant terrible* in their midst was a dove, after all. But that same day the Reich Defence Law was promulgated, which gave Schacht his supreme (if temporary) power to devise an economy geared to guns.

Hitler was cunning in the choice of gestures he made, designed to further, and not to injure, his interests. The naval pact he signed with Britain limited German naval power to a bare thirty-five per cent of Britain's surface fleet. Hitler felt little use for a navy on the grand scale, while Britain's readiness to make such an agreement without consultation with France, which was also a naval power, was very much resented. He was careful to exclude U-boats, in which he could reach parity with Britain.

Hitler chose this year, 1935, to enact the Nuremberg Race Laws on the occasion of the Nuremberg Party Rally in September. This was an affront to Jewish people as a whole, though the laws naturally applied at this stage to Germany alone. German Jews were deprived of their citizenship, and marriage beween Germans and Jews was forbidden.

Hitler was further encouraged by the division in Europe occasioned by Mussolini's invasion of Abyssinia. The British led the campaign against Mussolini in the League of Nations, insisting on the imposition of sanctions and finally driving Mussolini to Hitler for moral support. The sanctions proved completely ineffective, and met with no support from Laval in France. But as a result, the idea of the Berlin–Rome axis was born, bringing with it partnership rather than rivalry between the two dictators. At the same time Hitler himself was judging the appropriate moment to take his next step along the path towards dominance in Europe. The Franco-Soviet pact (which in any case had divided France itself) was as good an excuse as any for Hitler to pretend that the 1925 Locarno pact, to which Germany was a party, should be put in doubt, and that French duplicity in this matter demanded the reoccupation of the demilitarized Rhineland, a further flagrant breach of the Versailles Treaty. The Franco-Soviet pact was finally ratified on February 27th, 1936, and Hitler's men moved into the Rhineland on March 7th.

This action was Hitler's greatest gamble so far. The High Command was dead against him, knowing that if the French decided to move, Germany would lack the strength necessary to oppose them. This was the first major occasion when France and Britain could have combined, at small price, to oppose Hitler's aggressive policy. Hitler was later to boast that anyone other than himself would have lost his nerve at such a time. But his psychological assessment of his opponent's moral weakness was only too accurate. Schmidt has recorded Hitler's repeated comment on this event:

> More than once, even during the war, I heard Hitler say, 'The forty-eight hours after the march into the Rhineland were the most nerve-racking in my life . . . If the French had then marched into the Rhineland, we would have had to withdraw with our tails between our legs, for the military resources at our disposal would have been wholly inadequate for even a moderate resistance.'[2]

But the French did nothing, accepting their moral defeat.

Hitler made all the capital he could out of the Franco-Soviet pact. He spoke again before the Reichstag:

> You know . . . how hard was the road that I have had to travel since January 30th, 1933, in order to free the German people from the dishonourable position in which they found themselves, and to secure equality of rights . . . why should it not be possible to put an end to this useless

strife between France and Germany which has lasted for centuries? ... Why should it not be possible to lift the general problem of conflicting interests between the European States above the sphere of passion and unreason and consider it in the calm light of a higher vision?

The Reichstag rose and applauded Hitler as an inspired leader and yet again he resorted to a general vote by the German people to ratify his action. He held a token election to the Reichstag and, with no opponents allowed, won a ninety-nine per cent poll (45,001,489 votes from a total of 45,453,691 qualified voters!).

1936 became a year of celebration for Hitler. First, a non-intervention agreement was signed in July with the new Austrian Chancellor, Kurt von Schuschnigg, in which Austria was acknowledged to be a German State, though independent. Secondly, events followed which were to draw Mussolini closer to him. It was also in July that the League of Nations withdrew the abortive sanctions imposed on Italy, while the civil war in Spain, breaking out in the same month, afforded opportunities for Italian and German collaboration. Hitler was delighted at the emergence of this war and immediately agreed to give secret help to Franco, though not on the scale of Italy. Spain was to prove an ideal training ground for Hitler's soldiers and airmen, while the war itself was to be yet another violent cause of internal political dissension in France. Nothing could have been more opportune. At a conference held in Paris in April and attended by the French Ambassadors from Poland, Italy, Britain and Germany, François-Poncet declared that Hitler must be regarded as a pirate who 'observed neither the manners nor the morality of the regular navy', that is, the diplomatic corps. 'When Hitler spoke of peace,' he added 'it was German peace, *pax germanica*.' He used fair talk to cover his violation of agreements and treaties which no longer suited him.

Hitler's relationship with Mussolini became much warmer than before. He received Count Galeazzo Ciano, Mussolini's son-in-law and Italy's Foreign Minister, in Berchtesgaden, and set out to charm him. The first blue-print for an alliance was prepared, and it was Mussolini who used the term 'axis' the following November in reference to the common outlook of the regimes in Italy and Germany. The anti-Comintern pact, signed the following year, formed the initial basis of this alliance.

But it was the Olympic Games which were scheduled to take place during August, 1936, in Berlin which gave Hitler his finest opportunity to promote himself before the representatives of the world. Schmidt, the interpreter, was in a unique position to observe this:

> It would require a whole book to record the hundreds of conversations at which I interpreted for Hitler, Goering, Goebbels and other leaders as they conversed with foreign notabilities – Kings, heirs apparent, politicians, men of learning and men of the people from almost every country in the world . . . Many emphatically expressed their admiration for Hitler and his endeavours for peace, and for the achievements of National Socialist Germany. Those days seemed to me a vital apotheosis of Hitler and the Third Reich.[3]

François-Poncet uses almost exactly the same words, adding that Hitler had by now impressed himself upon the consciousness of Europe as an extraordinary personage. 'Crowned heads, princes and illustrious guests thronged to Berlin, eager to meet this prophetic being who apparently held the fate of Europe in his hand.' The organization of the games was handled impeccably; a great stadium holding 100,000 spectators was constructed in forest land to the West of Berlin, a kind of concrete Colosseum sunk into the earth. Hitler, however, disliked the idea of using concrete because it lacked durability; he would have preferred an edifice of stone. But, in any case, he was constructing what he held to be a far superior stadium in Nuremberg, where, he told Otto Dietrich, he intended one day to hold German Games which would oust the Olympiad. Leni Riefenstahl's film of the games in Berlin was to provide an unforgettable record, its long, impressionistic opening drew on the legendary mystique of the Games in order to give Hitler pride of place as the central figure inaugurating the event in modern times. A deep tolling bell, a hymn composed by Richard Strauss, a thousand doves released at the moment of initiation lent the games much the same aura as the Nuremberg Rally. The French, whose athletes might well have been withdrawn in protest at Hitler's breach of the Locarno Pact, decided to participate, and in the march gave Hitler and the Olympic dignitaries the Olympic salute, which was so like that of the Nazis that the great crowd roared with delight. In contrast, the American contingent merely removed their hats in a single simultaneous movement. Lavish receptions were given to the guests of honour by Hitler and the other Nazi leaders; Goebbels and Goering vying with each other in the extravagance of their displays. Champagne flowed. Although sport had little appeal for Hitler, he attended the games, observing the performances of his athletes, according to François-Poncet, with 'a passionate interest. When they won he beamed, slapping his thighs loudly and laughing as he looked at Goebbels, when they lost his expression hardened and he scowled.' His open disgust at the spectacular display put on by Jesse Owens, the black American athlete, drew much unfavourable comment.

Hitler played host to many notable visitors at this time, among them the former British Prime Minister, David Lloyd George, whom Hitler flattered by calling him 'the actual victor of the World War'. Hitler was in turn flattered by Lloyd George's obvious admiration for 'the man who has united the whole German people behind him'. He confirmed Hitler in his belief that multilateral undertakings with other nations were dangerous, and that mutual non-aggression pacts with neighbours were sufficient, since they could be discarded without causing a chain reaction. Hitler and Lloyd George parted in a glow of mutual admiration. 'He is a really great man,' said Lloyd George to Schmidt, who had interpreted for him. The Duke and Duchess of Windsor were also received at Berchtesgaden the following year; although the Duke was more circumspect in his compliments, Hitler took his presence in Germany as a sign of warm approval. Other visitors included the Aga Khan, Sir Oswald Mosley, Leader of the British Fascists, and a descendant of

Confucius, who happened also to be the brother-in-law of the Chinese Leader, Chiang Kai-Shek.

Indeed, Germany in 1936 put on all the airs and graces of international celebration. Tourists were welcomed with brassy music at the frontier stations, and the year was replete with festivals, all nationalistic in character. In March, there was the annual Festival of Heroes of the First World War; Hitler would lay a wreath on the tomb of the Unknown Soldier, and the ceremony was followed by a military parade. In April, Hitler's birthday was celebrated; the gifts he received were publicized, and the festivities were followed by another military parade. In May, Labour Day was celebrated as the feast of the workers, while in October came the Harvest Festival in honour of the peasants followed by the inevitable military parade. Greatest of all was the annual Party Rally at Nuremberg; this lasted a full week, and turned the ancient city into the 'pilgrim shrine' of Nazism. As François-Poncet put it, 'Many visitors, dazzled by Nazi display, were infected by the virus of Nazism . . . Heedless of the sinister realities lurking beneath the deceptive pomp of these prodigious shows, they were ripe for collaboration.'[4] Pretty blondes from abroad were assigned elegant SS officers as escorts. The air was filled with music, and the red streamers with their swastikas stirred in the wind.

The Rally was scheduled to devote a day to each major branch of the Nazi movement. There was the Inaugural Day, at which Hitler gave his opening speech, a Workers' Day (with carefully rehearsed manoeuvres carried out by tens of thousands), a Youth Day, a Party Officials' Day, a Brown Shirt Day for parades by the Party militia, a *Reichswehr* Day for Army displays, and the Closing Day, ending with fireworks and searchlights. Only with the arrival in 1937 of Sir Nevile Henderson, the new British Ambassador dedicated to the impossible task of developing friendly relations with Germany, did certain members of the diplomatic corps agree among themselves to attend the rally. Henderson forced the pace by deciding to go. François-Poncet went for a single day in prickly disapproval. But William Dodd, the American Ambassador, who was not a professional diplomat, refused to appear.

The principal social event in 1937 was the first visit to Germany by Mussolini in September. The ground was prepared by a succession of top level visits to Rome, led by that of Goering in January. Mussolini was by no means sure of his ground with Hitler. He did not favour Hitler's policy in Austria; he was technically committed to Austrian independence, and he did not want to share a common frontier with Germany. He was also anxious about Italy's prestige as a Mediterranean power. Hitler, in turn, was anxious to establish his own prestige with the Duce, which had suffered considerably at their Venice meeting in 1934. Mussolini arrived in a special ten-coach train with Ciano and a large retinue in uniform. Hitler received him in Munich, accompanied by *his* retinue in uniform, supported by massed bands, and crowds shouting '*Heil*' and '*Duce*'! Mussolini spoke adequate German, and Schmidt had little to do but watch Hitler during the ensuing conversation. He found Mussolini more open and volatile than Hitler. 'The differences in their laughs were also interesting. Hitler's always had a flavour of derision or sarcasm ... whereas Mussolini's laugh was free and whole-hearted, a liberating laugh.' The discussion was vague, but full of mutual agreement on general issues. Mussolini was subjected to a demanding programme of receptions and parades which were designed to impress him in Munich and elsewhere, culminating in a great public assembly in the Olympic Stadium in Berlin, the route to which was lined by giant banners with the emblems of Fascist Italy and Nazi Germany, and columns surmounted by golden eagles. A torrential outburst of rain and thunder accompanied Mussolini's bombastic address to an audience said to be some 800,000, but reduced and scattered by the rain. 'The greatest and most genuine democracies that the world knows today are Germany's and Italy's. Tomorrow all Europe will be fascist,' he bellowed in Italian-accented German. He returned wet through, driven in a car kept open by order. Mussolini's visit was essentially more social than political. Hitler felt the need to impress him with the sheer might of the new Germany.

Behind all these festivities Hitler was preparing for eventual war. In a speech to the Reichstag on January 30th he had openly and formally repudiated the Versailles Treaty. 1937 was the year in which Goering finally ousted Schacht as economic controller of a Germany solely dedicated to rearmament and military preparation. In November Hitler revealed his plans to an inner circle of ministers and Commanders-in-Chief – Blomberg, Fritsch (both soon be be discarded), Admiral Raeder, Neurath and Goering. The minutes of this meeting are preserved. Hitler spoke of the need for *lebensraum* (living space) for Germany in order that she might become self-sufficient and unite all racial Germans in a single great community. He saw Germany's present military power maturing by 1943, though her prime antagonists – Britain, France and Russia – should be engaged if possible before that year. He foresaw the need to overrun Austria and Czechoslovakia, gambling on the non-intervention of France and Britain on account of their internal weakness. The position, he said, was fluid, but he wanted his principal ministers and army commanders to keep in mind the broad strategy which lay ahead, so that no move he might make as opportunity arose would catch them unprepared. They were in charge of the preparations for ultimate action; he would choose the appropriate time and the nation to be disposed of.

A fortnight later in Berchtesgaden he received Lord Halifax. Halifax brought him greetings from the new British Prime Minister, Neville Chamberlain, a man dedicated to peacemaking. The meeting was scarcely a success; Hitler was in a bad temper because he considered that the British were opposed to the fulfilment of his will in Europe. Halifax remained phlegmatic. Hitler felt now fully prepared for the denouement of 1938 – the year in which he rid himself of Blomberg and Fritsch and became Supreme Commander of the Armed Forces, with Brauchitsch as his Army Commander-in-Chief. He also displaced Neurath in favour of Ribbentrop as his Foreign Minister.

1938 was the year of the *Anschluss* (union) of Germany with Austria and the year of the occupation of the Sudeten territory, the area of Czechoslovakia with a German-dominated population. The map of Europe was to begin its succession of changes in Hitler's favour. Hitler was holding the

Austrian Nazis in check, preferring if possible a peaceful take-over through a Nazi-controlled government under Kurt von Schuschnigg to a *coup d'état* by the hotheads, in other words an extension of his old policy of 'legality'. For Schuschnigg this represented an impasse. The Rome-Berlin axis had removed any likelihood of intervention by Mussolini, while the pressure of the Austrian Nazis made the internal situation dangerous. Papen was in an uneasy position as German Ambassador in Vienna, and in fact was recalled as a result of one of Hitler's impulses, following the ministerial changes occasioned by the Blomberg and Fritsch affairs.

Hitler invited Schuschnigg to Berchtesgaden in order to browbeat him. 'The whole history of Austria,' he said, 'is just one uninterrupted act of high treason.' He referred to himself as 'perhaps the greatest German in history,' and then demanded immediate agreement by the Austrian Chancellor to demands which, typically, he left undefined. This was instant diplomacy by personal onslaught, a technique Hitler was to use more than once after 1938. The nature of the demands were conveyed through Ribbentrop after an interval for lunch; the Nazis were to be given a free hand in Austria, their leader, Arthur Seyss-Inquart, made Minister of the Interior, while other Nazi Ministers were to be given charge of the Army and Finance. Hitler eventually reappeared, surrounded by senior officers of the High Command who were there to dress the stage. Schuschnigg's efforts to temporize were vain. Hitler proceeded to threats: 'You will either fulfil my demands within three days, or I will order the march into Austria.' Having blackmailed Schuschnigg, Hitler applied the brakes slightly for psychological effect by giving him three days to decide. Schuschnigg felt he had no alternative but to agree on the spot. Hitler's rage immediately disappeared; he invited his victim to supper. Schuschnigg declined. It was Papen who gave the *coup de grace*. 'Well now,' he said, 'you have seen what the Führer can be like at times. But the next time I'm sure it will be different. You know, the Führer can be absolutely charming.'

That was February 12th, 1938. Schuschnigg went back

determined to hold a plebiscite asking the Austrian people if they wanted to remain independent. When Hitler heard of this, it was too much for him. During the night of March 10th, the German forces moved up to the Austrian frontier. March 11th Goering took over where Hitler had left off, and the telephone became the medium for the final act of blackmail. Seyss-Inquart became Chancellor in place of Schuschnigg, and German forces responded to his 'appeal' and crossed into an unresisting Austria at dawn on March 12th.

Hitler's only real worry was the reaction of his ally, Mussolini. 'The Duce accepted the whole thing in a very friendly manner,' he was told on the telephone from Rome by Prince Philip of Hesse, his emissary to the Duce. Hitler gave way to an outburst of emotional gratitude. 'Tell Mussolini I will never forget him for this,' he said, 'never, never, never, whatever happens.' Henderson merely 'protested' on behalf of the British Government; the French, in the midst of a political crisis, did nothing. The Czechs hastened to assure Hitler that they accepted the *fait accompli* without anxiety. But the Führer no longer cared. He entered Austria in triumph, moving straight to Linz, where he had lived as a boy and had been registered as a deserter. He laid a wreath on his parents' tomb in Leonding. On March 14th he entered Vienna. He openly wept at the sight of the document recording the new law which declared 'Austria is a province of the German Reich.' Already the security arrests had begun; opponents were being taken into custody by the thousand. Back in Germany, another plebiscite was ordered for April in the form of a further nominal re-election of the Reichstag with its confirmation of Hitler as supreme ruler. In Germany he received a 99.08 per cent mandate, while in Austria, under new duress, the vote was given out to be 99·75 per cent. The Nazis did not tolerate things by halves.

While the wheels of fortune were turning in Hitler's favour, there was little time to lose. Chamberlain, in a speech of March 14th, even went so far as to refuse any guarantee of help to Czechoslovakia, to which France was bound under the Franco-Czech alliance. Eden, disgusted with the turn of events under Chamberlain, had already resigned in February, 1938. He had been replaced by Lord Halifax.

German readiness for military action doubled during 1938; between April and late autumn the number of Army divisions virtually doubled, from twenty-eight to fifty-five. This was necessary because Czechoslovakia, the next in line to receive the brunt of Hitler's demands, was a well defended nation. Moreover, their armies were equipped by the famous Skoda armaments plant. But their allies on paper, France and Russia, certainly did not want a military confrontation with Hitler. Britain, intent on securing peace in Europe, would be the last to encourage the Czechs to go to war.

The weakness of the Czech position was the peripheral territory of the Sudetenland with its German population of over three million, and its strong Nazi movement under Konrad Henlein, subsidized by the German Foreign Office. The Sudeten Germans had been stirred to further revolt following the Anschluss. While the Sudeten crisis was being fostered, Hitler paid a return visit in state to Italy, taking with him an entourage of five hundred, spread over three special trains, replete with every kind of uniform. In Rome the leaders were conveyed by horse-drawn coaches. The streets were bannered and floodlit at night. The constant change of costume presented difficulties, and the German *chef de protocole* lost his job because he allowed Hitler to inspect a guard of honour outside the San Carlo Theatre in Naples in evening dress when the King of Italy appeared in full-dress uniform. There was little time for serious political discussion, as had been the case when Mussolini visited Germany.

On his return to Berlin, Hitler was faced by a sudden, unpleasant situation. The Czech government, alarmed by the alleged massing of German troops along their frontiers, ordered partial mobilization. Unexpectedly, the European powers issued warnings to Germany, while both the French and the Russians reaffirmed their intent to help the Czechs. Hitler, angry as seldom before, was forced to withdraw such few forces as he had actually mustered, his plans, still incomplete, spiked by the Czech action and the support it had elicited. After a week of savage rumination in the Berghof, he returned to Berlin on May 28th to hold a conference of war with his Chief of Staff. 'It is my unalterable decision to smash Czechoslovakia by military action in the near future,' he declared. 'The execution of this directive must be assured by October 1st, 1938, at the latest.'

There followed a long, hot summer spent largely at the Berghof. Hitler sat back, and let the matter simmer. The Czechs, he knew, were under pressure from their friends to keep the peace. Geographically, they were isolated, surrounded by potential predators, since both Hungary and Poland had designs on areas of Czechoslovakian territory; Slovakia, after all, had once been part of Hungary. As for Russia, all Hitler could hope for was that the mutual distrust between France and Britain, on the one hand, and Moscow on the other would lead these uneasy allies to fall apart in any hour of crisis. Hitler watched and waited, building up his forces for the diplomatic putsch to come.

This was by far the biggest gamble yet, and the German High Command was deeply anxious about the risks their Supreme Commander appeared ready to undertake. Hitler for the first time engaged in a major dispute with his senior generals, as a result of which General Ludwig Beck, later to be the figurehead of the German resistance to Hitler, resigned as Chief of Staff. Brauchitsch, the Army Commander-in-Chief, although opposed to Hitler, bowed to his superior will, and so inaugurated that supine attitude which was to be characteristic of the High Command for the next seven years. By 1938 Hitler's supremacy was so assured he could override the most senior commanders, staging bouts of fury which made doyens of the army feel like schoolboys under the lash of a tyrannical and unpredictable headmaster. It is true that the first winds of serious opposition to Hitler began to stir faintly among a few high-ranking officers and dissident civilians, who felt Hitler was becoming paranoid and leading Germany to destruction. Their vague plan at this early stage was to arrest the Führer and form a military government which would bring him to trial. Their weakness was that they could never persuade enough members of the High Command to disregard their oaths of loyalty to Hitler and confront him at the height of his success with the German people. This was to become an only too familiar impasse for the small but influential group who from 1938 sought what few opportunities they could to incite a revolt against the Führer. In any case, they could only approach a few senior generals who they knew would not betray them.

Meanwhile, at the September rally in Nuremberg, Hitler unleashed the echoing rhetoric of hate against President Benes of Czechoslovakia. 'One will never reconcile so irreconcilable an enemy as are the Czechs,' he shouted into the bank of microphones which carried his voice to the farthest reaches of Germany, and made the world outside its boundaries shiver. His threatening behaviour was not without effect. Chamberlain, Prime Minister of Britain, offered to fly to Berchtesgaden to mediate with the furious dictator. This in itself was a diplomatic victory likely to encourage Hitler in his calculated aggression. At the same time, Chamberlain's sudden gesture of appeasement discouraged any attempt by those who sought to displace the tyrant inside Germany. Henlein and the Sudetens staged incidents in order to give Hitler the excuse to call them victims of a reign of terror, in spite of the fact that Benes had made offers to grant them their expressed demands. Hitler took every advantage of his position in the game. 'I am prepared to risk a world war rather than allow this to drag on,' he shouted at Chamberlain, whose one desire was to be the emissary of peace. Hitler, following a familiar pattern, had begun by talking quietly, and then let his voice rise to a crescendo as the heat grew in him. But when Chamberlain tried to challenge him – 'so you are determined to proceed against Czechoslovakia in any case . . . In the circumstances it is best for me to return at once' – Hitler immediately drew back. Then he played another card, demanding self-determination for the Sudetens. Chamberlain had no mandate to proceed further, and Hitler refused to let him have the transcript of their conversation.

Chamberlain returned to Germany on September 22nd to conduct the second stage of the negotiations, this time at Godesberg on the Rhine. He had succeeded in the meantime in winning the Czechs and their allies the French to the idea of ceding the Sudeten territories to Germany. But, to Chamberlain's indignation, Hitler now refused to accept the very thing he had previously demanded, with British guarantees on the proposed new frontiers. He wanted immediate occupation, and became excited and abusive. The meeting was broken off, and the leaders remained in their hotels on opposite sides of the river, their every movement watched by the assembled representatives of the international press. They resorted to sending each other letters. At the final session, Hitler demanded the withdrawal of all Czech forces, and the ceding of the Sudeten territory by September 28th. 'This is an ultimatum!' cried Chamberlain. At that moment a message arrived that Benes had ordered general mobilization. War seemed inevitable. But Hitler continued quietly, 'Despite this unheard of provocation, I shall, of course, keep my promise not to proceed against Czechoslovakia during the course of negotiation.' And, as a concession to Chamberlain, he advanced the date for action to October 1st – but he added for good measure that the territory he would seize by force would naturally be much greater than that he would occupy by agreement.

That was September 24th and Chamberlain returned to Britain, only to send a letter on September 26th to say Hitler's terms were wholly unacceptable both to the Czechs and to his government. The letter was brought personally by Sir Horace Wilson, and Hitler completely lost his temper, leaping up, shouting and rushing to the door, only to return in a mood of sulky defiance as the diplomats stood and watched him. His fury was unabated, though now under control. He maintained the threat of using force, and both in public and in private abused Benes as a warmonger. Wilson gave Hitler to understand before his departure that Britain would support France if she went to the help of Czechoslovakia. Hitler replied furiously, 'So – next week we'll all find ourselves at war with one another.'

During a notorious speech in the Sportpalast on September 26th, he claimed that the Sudenten problem was positively the last he had to solve, his final territorial demand in Europe. But in his heart he still shrank from outright war, and sent Chamberlain a letter on September 27th which left the door still open to further negotiation. When François-Poncet intervened, telling him he could get the essentials of what he wanted without war, he found Hitler 'brisk, nervous and tense', as well as 'perplexed' and 'disturbed'.

It was at this juncture that Mussolini offered his services as mediator, and Hitler eagerly accepted. This gave him the opportunity to pause on the brink of violence, prior to the Munich conference, which Mussolini, Chamberlain, Daladier all attended with their Ambassadors. But there was no Czech representative. Mussolini in effect conducted the proceedings, and according to François-Poncet, Hitler clung to him 'like his shadow', 'fascinated and hypnotized', and at a severe disadvantage through lack of languages. Hitler calmly took the territory he wanted and removed the threat of war, while the world's press and radio awaited the outcome of these sad deliberations. Hitler had shown what his teeth were like when fully bared; and now his generals could have another year to prepare for the war to come.

The Munich agreement was signed on the afternoon of September 30th, yet Hitler was 'pale and moody'. The victory was his, but at the cost of grave risk, and he felt baulked in his further objective of revenge on Czechoslovakia. He was, said Schmidt, 'changed and self-absorbed', realizing that Germany no less than France and Britain thought Chamberlain the hero of the hour, and not himself. Chamberlain returned to Britain overjoyed with another piece of paper signed by Hitler which he believed assured the peace of Europe in his time. But Czechoslovakia had been blackmailed by her 'friends' into a most painful capitulation, and Hitler's armies marched into the Sudetenland on October 1st. Within a month, Poland and Hungary had claimed their share, too, of Czech and Slovak territory.

Hitler had learned another lesson at Munich. The days of veiled 'legality' were finally over. It was better now to take the thing he wanted without resort to acrimonious negotiation, to outface the powers opposed to him by the speed of the *fait accompli.* If in 1938 Hitler had still felt it necessary to use the procedure of negotiation, in 1939 he finally committed himself to the demands of his own will and his own intuitive judgement. Yet when François-Poncet flew to Berchtesgaden to take his leave before quitting his post in Germany, Hitler appeared quite rational and ready quietly and reasonably to discuss any aspect of European politics. This was one Hitler, but the other was within, volcanic and 'possessed', determined now to take over the rest of Czechoslovakia, which was breaking up under the strain of successive phases of dismemberment.

In one of the cruelest individual acts of his career, Hitler allowed the aged President Hacha to come to Berlin on March 14th for a conference conducted in the small hours of the following morning after a prolonged period of waiting. The President, whose heart was weak, pleaded for the independence of his country. He was, says Schmidt, 'flushed with agitation'. Hitler coldly and quictly threatened him with instant invasion, and forced him to telephone Prague and urge immediate capitulation. When Goering threatened to bomb the capital, Hacha collapsed, only to be revived by Hitler's doctor, Morell, using a hypodermic needle provided hurriedly by Goering. Hacha recovered and capitulated. By four o'clock in the morning he had signed away his country; by 6.00 a.m. on March 15th Hitler's troops were on the move. That same day Hitler entered Prague to celebrate his 24 hour *coup d'état*. Europe was frozen into alarmed acceptance of this *fait accompli*. Even the Duce was unhappy. 'Every time Hitler occupies a country he sends me a message,' he grumbled to Ciano.

One week after Prague, Hitler occupied Memel, a part of Lithuania bordering on East Prussia with a predominantly German population. This was the last territory Hitler was to gain without the war his generals were still trying to prevent. Neither Britain nor France could tolerate any longer these continual breaches of good faith. Hostility to Hitler had been exacerbated still further by the hideous Nazi program against the German Jews and their property on the night of November 9th, 1938, ostensibly as the expression of racial outrage at the murder of a German diplomat in Paris by a young Jewish fanatic. Repercussions had been strongest in Britain and the United States, where so many German and Austrian Jews had taken refuge, exiled by Nazi terrorism. Indeed, by 1939 the scales could be said to have dropped from the eyes of the most hardened of appeasers. There was universal concern about Hitler's next aggression, and how he might be stopped.

Hitler was caught up by his own momentum. He was now at the head of a nation 80 million strong, with Czechoslovakia as his first major satellite. As success piled on success without the loss of a single German soldier, his ambition to fulfil his destiny as the greatest German in European history demanded still further spectacular achievements. Hitler was dazed by his own image; nothing that his intuition dictated seemed impossible. In 1939 the rearmament programme was trebled, with credit stretched to breaking point. Armaments taken over in Czechoslovakia added substantially to German military supplies. The prime target now, in the spring of 1939, became Poland. In the East, a treaty with Romania, signed in March, gave Germany preferential control over the country's resources.

Germany had a ready-made case against Poland – the existence of the Polish corridor to the sea and the free city of Danzig on the Baltic coast. The corridor, some fifty miles wide, separated Germany from her territory in East Prussia, while Danzig, with its substantial Nazi movement, was, in Hitler's view, a part of the German Reich. Hitler demanded immediate negotiations on these matters. But the Polish diplomats refused to be browbeaten by either Ribbentrop or Hitler, and their defiance was suddenly reinforced by Chamberlain's unexpected announcement on March 31st of unconditional British support for Poland, with which the French government concurred. Hitler behaved like a spoiled child, thumping the table and striding up and down in a rage as he uttered threats against the British for their unwarranted interference in the affairs of Eastern Europe. Forthwith he determined a date for the invasion of Poland and the 'liberation of Danzig' – September 1st, 1939. He kept it to the day.

It was at this stage that President Roosevelt intervened to urge, somewhat late, the cessation of Nazi and Fascist aggression in Europe. He became a sitting target for Hitler's sarcasm in a powerful speech to the Reichstag on April 28th, justifying his record as the saviour of an oppressed people living in a country which lacked the size and wealth of America, which had not hesitated to use force to resolve her own national destiny. After delivering this diatribe, Hitler retired to Berchtesgaden for the greater part of the summer, returning to Berlin only for the most pressing diplomatic or military conferences.

Nothing is stranger in this strange story than the well-meaning attempts of the wholly amateurish and self-appointed Swedish 'diplomat', Birger Dahlerus, to avert the coming war. Encouraged by Goering, who was his friend, he flew back and forth between Germany and Britain urging last-minute negotiations between the British government and Hitler. On August 26th Goering took him to see the Führer. He carried an official letter from Lord Halifax reiterating Britain's desire for peace. It was the middle of the night when he finally entered the Chancellery. He glimpsed the manic side of Hitler which, even if enacted for his benefit, showed a paranoic pressure in the manner chosen for display:

> Hitler . . . suddenly got up, and, becoming very excited and nervous, walked up and down saying, as though to himself, that Germany was irresistible . . . Suddenly he stopped in the middle of the room and stood there staring. His voice was blurred, and his behaviour that of a completely abnormal person. He spoke in staccato phrases: 'If there should be war, then I shall build U-boats, build U-boats, U-boats, U-boats.' His voice became more indistinct and finally one could not follow him at all. Then he . . . raised his voice as though addressing a large audience and shrieked: 'I shall build aeroplanes, aeroplanes, aeroplanes, and I shall annihilate my enemies.' He seemed more like a phantom from a story-book than a real person.[5]

The truth of the matter would appear to be that, as in the case of Czechoslovakia, Hitler would have been prepared to achieve his object by blackmail rather than by force of arms, but that he was by now prepared to risk an all-out war rather than hold back. His actions during the summer months all point to this: the 'Pact of Steel' signed on May 21st, the startling non-aggression pact with Russia signed finally on August 24th, after mutual hesitation, so that both these fundamentally opposing nations might play for a little time. Even Hitler's hours of lazing at the Berghof covered feverish preparations in Berlin. He was undoubtedly suffering from strain, and deeply embittered at Mussolini's defection, as he saw it, when the Duce wrote, on August 25th, that 'Italy is not ready for war.' He made a characteristic gesture to Chamberlain in Britain, a German guarantee of the continued existence of the British Empire in return for British non-interference in the Polish question. After all, he said to Henderson, 'he was by nature an artist, not a politician, and that once the Polish question was settled, he would end his life as an artist.'

The final order for the campaign against Poland, which continued to counter Hitler's threats in an unrealistic gesture of bravado, was laid down at the Berghof on August 22nd at a conference of the senior commanders. Notes taken of Hitler's address ended with this admonition:

> Close your hearts to pity. Act brutally. Eighty million people must obtain what is their right. Their existence must be made secure. The strongest man is right. The greatest harshness.

10

Hitler as War Strategist: The Period of Success, 1939-1942

Hitler embarked on war with an army of fifty-one divisions, five of which were Panzer equipped, representing in all over one-half million men, and an Air Force of twenty-one Squadrons, representing some 260,000 men. The policy was to attack Poland with paralysing suddenness, destroying her armed forces with lightning blows. This was the blitzkrieg, the lightning war, which Hitler used to claim was more humane than prolonged warfare.

Humanity was not in evidence on Friday, September 1st. A number of condemned prisoners were dressed in Polish uniforms, given fatal injections, and their bodies shot through with bullets at Gleiwitz, on the German side of the Polish border. This incident was staged for the purpose of providing an excuse for the attack on Poland, and press representatives were taken to view the bodies of the 'invading Poles'. 'I am wrongly judged if my love of peace and my patience are mistaken for weakness . . . bombs will be met with bombs,' declared Hitler to the Reichstag on the very day of the invasion. Hitler, and Hitler alone, declared war on Poland, and faked the cause.

After the speech, Dahlerus saw him a second time. He found Hitler 'nervous and upset inside'. He grew excited, shouting he would fight England for one year, two years, three years if they wanted it. His arms were flailing and his voice rose to a shrill scream. He brandished his fist, and bent down so that it almost touched the floor. Dahlerus, unused to Hitler's emotional displays, was deeply embarrassed.

Mussolini again offered to intervene, but on Sunday, September 3rd, Britain declared war, since Hitler had disregarded the British ultimatum that he should withdraw his troops from Poland. Hitler received the news, according to Schmidt, 'silent and unmoving'. The French declaration of war followed the same day. Hitler had never believed either country would actually come to the aid of Poland. He left Berlin for the front, his headquarters established in a special train. The war with Poland lasted three weeks; the Polish army, brave to the last, was swept aside by Hitler's Panzers and motorized divisions. The old-fashioned Polish Cavalry could not oppose the German tanks. The Polish air force was wiped out on the ground by the Luftwaffe's onslaught. Only Warsaw held out in the final days, and the war ended with the centre of the city a burned-out shell. Secret clauses in the German-Soviet pact had allowed for Russia's occupation of Eastern Poland; this began on September 17th. Stalin drove a hard bargain over the Polish territories, and Russia also took the opportunity to occupy the Baltic States of Estonia, Latvia, Lithuania. Hitler, after taking formal possession of Danzig on September 19th was back in Berlin by the end of the month, master of new terrain to the East, one third the size of Germany.

Hitler now gambled on the assumption that, with the sudden collapse of Poland, Britain and France would seek to make peace. That would be the logical thing to do, as Hitler understood logic. The Western powers had not fired a shot or dropped a bomb throughout the entire Polish campaign. Hitler had been too quick for them.

Ciano was able, on a visit to Berlin on October 1st, to observe Hitler in his hour of triumph. 'He seems absolutely sure of himself,' he wrote in his diary. 'I found Hitler very serene . . . his face bore traces of recent fatigue, but this was not reflected in the alertness of his mind . . . What most impressed me is his confidence in ultimate victory. Either he is bewitched, or he really is a genius.'[1] It appeared to Ciano that Hitler would make the offer of peace for the effect this might have both inside and outside Germany, but that his real desire was for further victories, this time over the Western Powers. Nevertheless, he must appear to put them in the wrong. After reviewing his forces in Warsaw, he issued his 'peace' challenge to France and Britain in a speech to the Reichstag on October 6th: 'I believe even today that there can only be real peace in Europe and throughout the world if Germany and England come to an understanding.' But he boasted of his victory in Poland – 'in all history there has scarcely been a comparable achievement' – and of the final renunciation of Versailles the disappearance of Poland represented. He claimed the pact with Russia was a further sign of the will to peace in Europe, each defining their respective spheres of influence. Britain and France were left as the only belligerents. This was Hitler speaking on stage; he spoke, according to eye witnesses, more calmly than usual. But behind the scenes he told his commanders this offer of peace was a propaganda device, 'necessary from a psychological point of view'; it did not alter his war aim – 'That is and remains the destruction of our Western enemies.' 'The attack should be carried out this Autumn,' he wrote in a memorandum of October 9th addressed to his General Staff. War directives were issued on October 9th and 18th and again on November 29th. Yet the campaign was continually postponed.

War in the West was really illogical in Hitler's ultimate view; his ambition for his country's expansion lay only in the East. As a first stage in his plan he divided his area of occupied Poland into two sectors; that to the West was incorporated with the Reich, that to the East was established as a territory called the Government-General. 1,500,000 Poles and Jews were deported East during the harsh winter months from the territory taken over by the Reich, which was then peopled by families of German stock. The barbarity of Nazi rule began to be experienced to the full when Himmler and the SS took over in Poland, while Hitler turned his attention to more important matters – a quick conclusion to the war in the West, and the ultimate campaign against Russia. This was what the High Command most feared, their overwhelming success in Poland was no indication, in their view, that a similar blow to the West would follow suit. They sought to dissuade Hitler from striking against the powerful French Army, aided by her ally, Britain. Behind the scenes, the small group of army and civilian dissidents, headed by General Beck, the retired Chief of Staff, tried once again to widen the circle of those who planned to displace Hitler, but as before they failed. Hitler was too powerful, and too obviously successful for them. They had to be content to issue treasonable warnings to those nations to the West which Hitler was planning to overrun. They were given little encouragement by the Allies, and their warnings were to be largely disregarded. Neither Holland nor Belgium wanted to know.

The winter stalemate of 1939–40 involved continual vacillation on Hitler's part. The fact that Britain and France failed to withdraw from the war, yet in fact did little or nothing about it, proved an embarrassment to Hitler, who had bought time from Russia in August, 1939, solely to build up his strength for the inevitable confrontation with his prime enemy, Stalin. He did not want to expend this precious period on a prolonged and wasteful war in the West, which could only act as an encouragement to Stalin to regard Germany's eastern frontiers (now contiguous with Russia) as the more vulnerable. Hitler certainly did not want Russia to be the initiator of the war in the East. That privilege must be his.

Franz Halder, in his post-war attack on Hitler written from the point of view of the German High Command (he was Chief of Staff from September, 1938 until his dismissal in September, 1942), maintains in *Hitler as War Lord* that the Führer's so-called genius as a military strategist is largely spurious. He sees him as impatient to realize his larger imperial ambitions, driven on by the brute force of his will and swayed always by political rather than military considerations. He was, Halder says, always 'bewitched by the magic of numbers' in his army, disregarding the need for 'the slow, organic growth' of a well-trained force. He refused to recognize the valid limitations of his armed forces, whether on land, sea, or in the air, or to take account of the internal weaknesses of an army which had been expanded too rapidly. As distinct from Napoleon, who watched over his men with almost paternal care, Hitler had no human feeling whatsoever for his armies, but deployed them as the agents of his will. Halder condemns him as a political, never a military strategist, an 'irresponsible gambler', his 'stubborn will guided by dark intuition'.

Hitler's concern during the winter of 1939–40 was how best to achieve a quick victory in the West so that he could be free to turn his full attention to the East. As directive followed directive through the winter, the range of the projected attack widened to include Holland and Belgium, followed in March by Norway and Denmark, in each case to anticipate potential invasion by Britain, seen to be 'the animator of the fighting spirit . . . and the leading enemy power.' 'The basic aim,' said Hitler, 'is to lend the operation the character of a *peaceful* occupation, designed to protect by force of arms the neutrality of the Northern countries,' but 'our operation should come as a surprise.' This it undoubtedly did. The invasion of Denmark and Norway on April 9th led directly to the fall of Chamberlain and his replacement by a real war lord, Winston Churchill, who became Prime Minister on May 10th when Hitler invaded Belgium and Holland. By now, the German Army had increased to one hundred and thirty-six divisions, eighty-nine of which took part in the invasion.

Halder exposes the vacillation of Hitler's strategy, and the counter moves by the General Staff to minimize the Führer's misjudgements, but concedes that the final plan was a good one, though he doubts if Hitler understood its full implication in military terms. 'Time and again he created difficulties for the operational Commander . . . At Dunkirk, he prevented the complete destruction of the British Army by withdrawing the German tanks which were already at their rear.' This was, apparently, in order to give Goering's Air Force the pleasure of victory, with the result that the British managed to withdraw substantial forces, some 338,000 men, who survived to fight another day. Goering nevertheless acclaimed Hitler a *Feldherr* (war Lord), giving no credit to the Commanders in the field whose actual operations won the war in France.

There is much to be said for this post-war assessment made out by the German Generals against Hitler's mismanagement of the army. The truth would appear to be that the *panache* of the moment was his; his was the energy and driving force behind all the campaigns. It was his war and his alone, and up to 1942 he won it, driving his unwilling staff before him. But for him, there would have been no German Army capable of these spectacular strikes, no full-scale development of the concepts of blitzkrieg, no Panzer divisions, no Luftwaffe with its appalling striking strength. Having driven his forces into premature action, Hitler could rightfully claim these successes in Poland and later in the North and West of Europe to be his, however much he may have vacillated and erred on points of detail in both planning and operation. Even Halder admits that Hitler's technical knowledge of the machinery of warfare was considerable; where he failed as a military strategist was in longer-term planning and making sure in terms of logistics that the feats he demanded of his armies were feasible. He covered his many tactical errors by means of the sheer brute force of his operations and his utter lack of humanity in the deployment of his men. He did not fight alongside his armed forces, like Napoleon; he merely used them. Nevertheless, it was he alone who foresaw the collapse of the formidable French Army, and collapse it did. The war which began on May 10th was over on June 20th. Only Britain remained obstinately unconquered. Hitler could not refrain from the momentary dance of delight and triumph before the signing of the French capitulation. He spent three hours viewing Paris, the only visit of his lifetime. Speer accompanied him in the fleet of staff cars. Their visit took in the Opera, the Eiffel Tower, and the Invalides, where Hitler stood for a long while in silence before Napoleon's tomb.

The relationship of Hitler and Mussolini is of great interest. While Hitler's respect for Mussolini and for Italy rapidly waned, his affection for the Duce survived the severest disappointments. According to Halder, it was typical of Hitler's mentality that he hoped to strengthen Mussolini's position by allowing him to participate in the splendour of his own military fame.

Mussolini was to prove a very indifferent ally. Hitler had accepted his neutrality during the Polish campaign, which he had held to be a wholly German matter. But war against the Western powers and Russia was a different and much larger undertaking. In March he had written to Mussolini stating plainly that when war started the place of Italy was at

Germany's side. Mussolini was in a dilemma; as Ciano put it, 'the Duce is fascinated by Hitler, a fascination which involves something deeply rooted in his make-up . . . His military success – the only successe that Mussolini really values and desires – is the cause of this.'[2] The two dictators had met at the Brenner Pass on March 18th. Hitler was friendly, talked most of the time to his admiring listener, and, according to Ciano, was 'less agitated than usual'. Mussolini confirmed that, at a time convenient to him, he would 'move with Germany'. Schmidt, who was present, says Hitler spoke of his preparations for the coming war. 'Numbers and figures piled up' as a result of Hitler's 'amazing ability to carry in his head troop strengths, casualty figures and the state of reserves, as well as technical details about guns, tanks and infantry weapons.' But he gave him no details of what was to happen, or when. 'Hitler had no confidence in the Italians,' adds Schmidt. Three weeks later he invaded Denmark and Norway.

This meeting was complicated by the presence in Europe of Roosevelt's peace envoy, Sumner Welles, who was in Rome at the time, having arrived there from Berlin after seeing Hitler on March 2nd. His purpose included an attempt to persuade Mussolini to remain neutral. The conversation he had had with Hitler was cool on both sides, and he was treated to one of Hitler's usual political tirades. According to Ciano, Mussolini, in private, blew hot and cold about Italian involvement in the coming war. Mussolini had his own ambition in the Balkans, more particularly in Yugoslavia, following his occupation of Albania in April, 1939. He held the Balkans and the Mediterranean to be his proper sphere of interest. Friendly exchanges had followed Hitler's Scandinavian ventures, and Hitler had sent a special communication by envoy to Rome to time with his invasion of Belgium and Holland. Mussolini's attitude was ambivalent concerning Italian involvement in Hitler's forthcoming war. He would enter it only when there was a quasi-mathematical certainty of winning it, yet he coveted a share in military glory and in the fruits of victory. By the end of May he was calculating when to intervene in the attack on France. 'He wants to create enough claims to be entitled to his share of the spoils,' writes Ciano. Italy finally entered the war on June 10th. This was barely in time; by June 17th the French were asking for an armistice, and the Italian Army had done precisely nothing.

Hitler and Mussolini met again at Munich on June 18th and 19th. As Ciano put it, 'Mussolini is very humiliated because our troops have not made a step forward.' Hitler had wanted a quick peace settlement, and the Italians were virtually excluded from its formulation. According to Schmidt, Hitler was in a conciliatory mood as far as the West was concerned. 'He suddenly wondered whether it really could be a good thing to destroy the British Empire. "It is, after all, a force for order in the world," he said to a rather nonplussed Mussolini.' On June 20th the armistice documents were drawn up and translated overnight by candlelight, under Hitler's supervision, in a small French church near Hitler's headquarters, prior to signing at Compiègne the following day.

Speer has described Hitler's strange but somehow characteristic action at the moment, 1.35 a.m. on June 25th, when the armistice was to take effect. Hitler and his entourage were sitting in a peasant house in the evacuated village of Bruly le Peche, near Sedan. Hitler ordered the lights to be put out and the windows to be opened. They sat in darkness, waiting for the note of the bugler sounding the traditional signal for the cessation of hostilities. Heat lightning lit the sky in flashes. After the bugle notes had died away, Hitler was heard to murmur, scarcely audibly, 'This responsibility . . .' Then he ordered the lights to be put on again, and the conversation returned to normal. Hitler was indulging in the mystique of greatness.

On July 19th, Hitler, in a speech to the Reichstag, made a final calculated attempt to obtain peace with Britain:

> I feel it to be my duty before my own conscience to appeal once more to reason and common-sense in Great Britain as much as elsewhere. I consider myself in a position to make this appeal because I am not the vanquished beg-

ging favours, but the victor speaking in the name of reason. I can see no reason why this war must go on.[8]

According to Ciano, who was present, 'Hitler speaks simply and, I should say also, in an unusually humane tone.' Ciano found the German hierarchy only too anxious for peace with Britain, which would free them to turn their attention to the East. But Britain, unaccountably, in the face of bombing, invasion, and what Hitler held to be certain defeat, refused to give way. Hitler concentrated during midsummer on breaking the British will through bombing, a task assigned to the ever-willing Goering, and the destruction of supplies to the island through U-boat action at sea. A directive of July 16th outlines the plan for invasion – Operation Sea Lion – following Goering's anticipated successes in bombing, and the annihilation of the British Air Force on the ground. Hitler's instinctive fear of the sea, and the depleted state of the German navy following the losses of the Norwegian campaign, encouraged him to rely on bombing to soften Britain up for invasion. But the High Command was in continual dispute as to the best method of invading the island. Indefinite postponement of the invasion took place at the end of July, 1940, but Goering was given the order to carry out the devastation of Britain from the air. From mid-August, 1940, to mid-May, 1941, the battle of the Spitfires versus the Messerschmitts and Stukas raged day and night over Britain, with only a brief lull from mid-January to early March. It became increasingly plain that Britain could hit back and defend her shores. The cost in aircraft and crews was prodigious, but Hitler had never taken notice of such costs provided the turnover of new men and machines was assured. According to Halder, the German Air force never completely recovered from the severity of its losses.

Although Hitler's prime concern continued to be Russia, the expansion of his conquests elsewhere brought increasing obligations. The French and British spheres of influence in North Africa could not be neglected. Raeder was urging collaboration with the Italians in order to cripple the British presence in the Mediterranean (Suez, Malta, Gibraltar) and prevent the French from becoming a springboard for a British attack on the Axis powers in Europe. In August, French Equatorial Africa declared for General de Gaulle, and Free French forces were being set up in Britain. Spain might be brought in as a further ally. Hitler saw the force of these arguments, mastery of Asia Minor could follow, with invasion of the Balkans, Turkey and even the Ukraine to follow. This gave Hitler much food for thought, but so did the growing strength of Russia in the East.

Much depended now on Mussolini and Franco. After the fall of France, Britain made the Mediterranean her centre of conflict in order to keep her bases there supplied, and maintain a clearway to the Suez and the Middle East. On land, the confrontation came at the frontier of Italian Libya and British Egypt. Hitler lectured Mussolini during a brief meeting of the dictators on October 4th at the Brenner, about the Italian naval, air, and land offensive against the British in North Africa. Mussolini was in a good mood because of Hitler's apparent interest, at last, in the Mediterranean theatre of war.

Franco, however, practised both evasion and greed in his dealings with Hitler, demanding as the price of entry territory in Africa and massive aid in supplies and equipment which Germany could not afford. Hitler, who had behaved like a child when Franco sent him a present in September, travelled to meet Franco on October 23rd, on the Spanish frontier at Hendaye. Franco, though three years younger than Hitler, failed to respond to the special act of impressive self-display and cajolery which Hitler put on for the occasion. Gibraltar for Spain was the immediate bait he offered. Franco's reaction to Hitler's high claims was a quiet scepticism. Hitler, according to the ever-present Schmidt, became 'more and more restless', and the meeting concluded with nothing agreed. Franco was never to enter the war. Hitler went on to see Petain in France, and was equally unsuccessful in his attempts to persuade him to become an active ally in the war, particularly to secure the French possessions in Africa. Hitler, said Schmidt, 'seemed profoundly disappointed'.

The next shock came from Mussolini, who, with only a day's warning to Hitler, decided to attack Greece on October 28th. The blitzkrieg, in the German style, was to fail completely, partly through unexpected bad weather during the first days. Graziani's minor gains in Egypt had failed to mature into a major strike, and Mussolini, humiliated in Africa, was in vain seeking compensation in the Balkans. Hitler's temper was strained to the limit when he heard of Mussolini's intention. His train was hastily rerouted to Italy, but he arrived on the day the campaign opened, too late to stop this foolhardy venture. Out of affection for the Duce, he controlled himself and only gave expression to his friendship for Mussolini, whom he would soon have to rescue, not only in Greece, but in Africa as well. Each dictator was trying to out-do the other. Hitler had, in effect, just occupied Rumania for the sake of its oil early in the month, his spheres of interest drawing ever closer to Mussolini's. Nevertheless, public solidarity had to be maintained. A Tripartite Pact between Germany, Italy and Japan had been signed in September.

The nearest to meeting Stalin that Hitler ever came was a meeting with Molotov, Stalin's Foreign Minister, who visited Berlin on November 12th. Molotov waited coldly for Hitler to finish one of his impassioned speeches on the future of nations led by men of destiny, and then cross-questioned him on German intentions in Finland, Rumania and the Balkans, and on the real significance of the Tripartite Pact. Hitler hated direct questions of this kind, and parried them with generalities which Molotov refused to accept. Hitler claimed he had no permanent interest either in Finland or the Balkans – only temporary needs for supplies. Molotov was patently unimpressed. Twice, discussions were interrupted by air-raid warnings; during the second of these he shared a shelter with Ribbentrop, who claimed, like Hitler, that the British were finished. Molotov made his celebrated reply, 'if that is so, why are we in this shelter and whose are those bombs that fall?' Relations with the Soviet Union finally foundered as a result of this meeting, and Hitler was to state later, in his final Table-Talk, recorded in the Bunker, that following his meeting with

Molotov he knew he must launch his attack on Russia.

By December, 1940, British power had been built up in the Mediterranean. Severe damage had been inflicted by the British on the Italian fleet at Taranto in November, and on December 9th Wavell began the swift and brilliant campaign in which his 30,000 men drove the Italians out of Egypt. Within two months he had advanced 500 miles into Italian Libya, destroying ten divisions of Italian troops and taking 130,000 prisoners. By then Hitler was forced to intervene. German units under Rommel began to arrive in February, 1941, to establish the Afrika Korps, but the centre of immediate attention was Greece and the Balkans. Plans for a German invasion of Greece in the Spring, launched through Rumania and Bulgaria, were already in hand by December.

Hitler's tenderness for Mussolini was no doubt enhanced by his failures. It appealed to Hitler's ego to come to the rescue of the senior dictator with manifestations of German generosity. On December 31st he sent him a letter of good wishes 'from the bottom of my heart' in this period when 'recent events have perhaps lost you the support of many people'. He was, he says, 'a man who feels bound to you alike in good times and in bad'. When Mussolini, embarrassed and ill-tempered, met the Führer in the Berghof on January 18th, 1941, Hitler's friendliness and assurance over the coming campaign in Greece impressed the Italians, and, says Ciano, Mussolini returned 'elated, as he always is after a meeting with Hitler'.

But Hitler's main objective remained Russia, though the seeds of his ultimate failure were already being sown by the scale of diversions he was increasingly prepared to accept, at this stage in the Balkans and the Mediterranean. The massive complications involved can already be foreseen in Hitler's directives of November 12th and December 10th and 13th, 1940, covering the whole field of operation, though many of these proposals (such as the capture of Gibraltar) were never to be put into effect. Twenty-four divisions alone were earmarked for the invasion of Greece, where in February the British had started to give aid. But on December 18th the celebrated directive twenty-one for Barbarossa warned that, 'The German Armed Forces must be prepared to crush Soviet Russia in a rapid campaign . . . the ultimate objective of the operation is to establish a defence line against Asiatic Russia from a line running approximately from the Volga River to Archangel.' The blitzkrieg strategy had the Hitlerian ring: 'The bulk of the Russian army stationed in Western Russia will be destroyed by daring operations . . . It will be the duty of the Air Force to paralyse and eliminate the effectiveness of the Russian Air Force.' No date for the actual invasion appears in the directive, but Hitler intended all preparations to be complete by May 15th, 1941.

In March, the situation changed yet again, with the revolution in Yugoslavia. The new government was anti-German and Hitler was both shocked and angry at the emergence of a new potential enemy in this sensitive area. 'To treat the German Reich in this way is impossible' he was to declare in a speech to the Reichstag. On March 27th, the day after the revolution became known, he summoned the High Command and ordered the destruction of Yugoslavia 'militarily and as a national unit . . . with merciless brutality . . . in a lightning operation'. A detailed plan was issued the same day. Rumanian, Bulgarian and Hungarian participation was brought about by Nazi diplomatic pressure, though the Hungarian Prime Minister, Count Teleki, shot himself rather than agree in person. Bulgaria and Hungary were bribed with the promise of Yugoslav territory. Belgrade was bombarded on April 6th and the country was taken over by the German 12th Army by April 17th, only three weeks after the new government had been proclaimed. Yugoslavia was dismembered as Hitler, and Hitler alone, determined.[4]

It was essential also that Greece be occupied and the British driven out of this area of Europe. Again the blitzkrieg worked; the Greek Government capitulated on April 24th and the British were forced to evacuate the mainland and finally Crete by the end of May. This was Hitler at his most ruthless when time was all that mattered. The launch of the Barbarossa operation was severely threatened by these unwelcome diversions. Other operations against the British were the encouragements Hitler held out to the Arabs in the Middle East to harass the British, and to the Japanese to open a second front in the Far East by capturing Singapore.

On May 10th Hitler received one of the most profound personal shocks of his life when Hess, his oldest and closest comrade among the Nazi hierarchy, stole a test plane and flew to Scotland, ostensibly to intercede with the British for peace with Germany. Insofar as his motives are clear, he could not bear the thought of Germany going to war with Russia while at the same time in dangerous conflict with the British. It has been claimed this was a collusive act, and that Hitler knew and approved the mission. All the evidence points the other way. Every eyewitness testifies to the devastating effect the news had upon him. Dietrich says it was like 'a blow in the face'; Schmidt said, 'Hitler was as appalled as though a bomb had struck the Berghof.' Jodl said, 'I never in my life saw a man in such a fury . . . He was afraid the Italians would think he was negotiating peace behind their backs.' Speer, who was there to discuss advance plans for victory parades, heard from an adjoining room 'an inarticulate, almost animal outcry' as Hitler roared for Bormann. He claims Hitler 'never got over this "disloyalty" '.

Hitler's much delayed invasion of Russia came with a suddenness that took the Russians by surprise. 'When Barbarossa begins, the world will hold its breath,' Hitler had said. Some 170 Russian divisions, many not up to strength but including 34 tanks divisions, opposed 154 German divisions, with some 50 Panzer units, supported by some 2,700 aircraft of the Luftwaffe, as well as a small number of Rumanian, Hungarian, Finnish and, later, Italian divisions. Again, the pretence was that Russia was about to attack Germany, if Germany did not first attack Russia. 'I cannot undertake the responsibility of waiting longer,' Hitler wrote to Mussolini on June 21st. The bluff that the massing of troops was connected with the war in the Balkans and the Mediterranean had lulled the suspicions of the Russians, and timely warnings from Stalin's spies, from the British and even from the Russian Embassy in Berlin, had all gone unheeded.

Soviet forces spread along what was their Western front

represented about one half of the entire Red Army as it was constituted at the time of the invasion. It was in a weakened condition, and morale was relatively low following the savage purge of officers that began in 1936. More senior Russian officers were lost through the purge than during the entire war with Germany. As a result, the Germans faced an army led largely by new and untried officers, and a High Command inexperienced in leadership and more fearful of Stalin than they were of the Germans. Much of their equipment was obsolete, which meant they were no match for the German Panzers and collapsed before their onslaught and that of the Luftwaffe. Moreover, they were deployed in echelons – fifty-three divisions spread up to 50 kilometres from the frontier, and the rest in the second and third echelons, respectively 100 kilometres and up to 400 kilometres in depth from the frontier.

It could be said that the Russian forces, from Stalin downwards, suffered, like their allies in the West, from wishful disbelief in Hitler's bad faith. Stalin failed in the first instance even to grasp what was happening. He made no public pronouncement until July 3rd, and only took over formal command a month after the invasion. He was then nervous and depressed. Later he took toll of the Commanders who had failed. Like Hitler, he conceived his ultimate strategy in political rather than strictly military terms; like Hitler, he tended to interfere in points of detail in the operations, making wrong assumptions and committing grave errors. But, unlike Hitler, he proved capable of learning from experience and trusting those Generals, notably Marshal Zhukov, Russia's greatest operational strategist, to work unimpeded in the field. Whatever his grave faults, both as supreme commander and political tyrant, Stalin gave the people of the Soviet Union remarkable leadership during the final phases of the war. He was at his best in the mobilization of manpower and the ultimate organization of the vast Soviet war machine. This, combined with his capacity in the end to rely on the initiative of his ablest generals, finally turned the war in Russia's favour.

At the start, Hitler's immediate, as distinct from his long-term, strategy worked miraculously, though his final version of Barbarossa was adopted against the better judgement of the High Command. The three-pronged attack, in the north towards Leningrad, in the centre towards Moscow, and in the south towards Kiev and distant Stalingrad through the Ukraine, was modified by Hitler, who showed decreasing interest in capturing Moscow, where there was a concentration of Russian forces as well as Russia's greatest centre for communications and armaments. If the aim was to defeat the Soviet Army before the winter, it was, in the view of the High Command, essential to take Moscow. Halder remarks that, in deflecting forces from the centre to the north to occupy the Baltic States and increase pressure on Leningrad while at the same time stepping up the weight of the drive in the south, Hitler was playing the politician rather than acting as a good strategist. Leningrad and Stalingrad must fall. Hitler spoke in characteristically insulting terms to his Commander-in-Chief: 'Only completely ossified brains, absorbed in the ideas of past centuries, could see any worthwhile objective in taking the capital.' In the outcome, the initial staggering successes – one third of the Russian Army killed or captured in the south-west campaign alone, while in the centre, Smolensk and in the north, the outskirts of Leningrad were reached by September – masked the fact that Hitler never gained his principal objectives; Leningrad (which he endeavoured to surround and starve into submission rather than directly attack), Moscow and ultimately Stalingrad did not fall, nor was the Russian Army ever annihilated. The Ukraine however, fell temporarily into Hitler's outstretched hands. The price Hitler paid for his deflections to the north and south was that Leningrad and Moscow were able to hold out until the winter came to bog down the German armour and freeze Hitler's inadequately clothed soldiers. Nevertheless, the German Panzers at one point reached within twenty-five miles of Moscow. But Hitler had started too late and attempted too much. Only after the most strenuous arguments did he recommence his deferred attack on Moscow; the attack was initiated finally at the end of September. On December 5th, damaging counterattacks were launched by Soviet forces.

Hitler's strategy in this most complex of campaigns was a matter of impulse, not of long-term and careful calculation. He cared nothing for the sufferings of his troops, and indeed had refused to consider supplying them with appropriate clothing on the grounds that they would by then have returned to Germany victorious to spend Christmas in their homes. The temperature fell to 40° below zero, and they were still there; many died of the cold. Hitler's method of covering up his own tragic blunders was to dismiss some of his ablest commanders, including Rundstedt, Hoepner, and even Guderian. But Brauchitsch was the principal scapegoat. Hitler said to Goebbels that he held Brauchitsch to be 'a vain, cowardly wretch' who had let him down. Goebbels comments that Hitler's plan of campaign had 'crystal clarity: ... Had Brauchitsch done what he ought to have done, our position in the east today would be entirely different.'

Hitler involved himself more and more in the detailed conduct of war. On December 19th, according to Halder, he said to the Chief of the General Staff: 'This little affair of operational command is something that anybody can do. The Commander-in-Chief's job is to train the Army in the National Socialist idea and I knew of no General who could do that as I want it done. For that reason I've decided to take over command of the Army myself.' The dismissed generals had to bear the brunt of criticism; they were the men who were alleged to have let Hitler's grand strategy down. 'It is essential that the Commanders in the field should be given clear, long-term orders to provide them with a basis for independent action within the framework of a unified plan,' wrote Halder after the war. Yet, if any general proposed strategic withdrawal to preserve his men and strengthen his position, Hitler opposed it with 'fanatical fury', ordering the Army 'to fight to the last man'. Officers in the field were 'ignominiously cashiered' for making local withdrawals to save their troops. Fear of Hitler's revenge became, says Halder, the guiding force for holding officers and men in impossible positions. Hitler would telephone personally even to junior officers in the field, demanding no retreat.

On December 7th, the day following the Russian counter-attack, the Japanese conducted their blitzkrieg on the American fleet in Pearl Harbor. Hitler, although taken by surprise as he had so far always taken others, seems to have accepted the action by the Japanese as a *fait accompli.* 'This method is the only proper one,' he said to the Japanese Ambassador, 'one should strike as hard as possible and not waste time declaring war.' However, he took the step of declaring war on the United States, whose position, on account of the aid she had been giving to Britain, had long been clear. In a speech of December 11th, in which he declared war on the United States, he abused President Roosevelt as a Jew-dominated capitalist.

The year 1942 was to see a further phase in Hitler's gradual withdrawal from the real world in which he was conducting his war at so much cost to Germany as well as to his opponents. He spent increasing time in the Wolf's Lair near Rastenburg as he called his general headquarters for the Russian campaign. The Wolf's Lair was set deep in the forests of East Prussia. Here, remote from the actual fighting, he led an abnormal life in which human relationships played almost no part. It was punctuated by sudden excursions to Berlin or the Berghof, or to his other wartime centres, such as his southern headquarters near Cracow or in the Ukraine. The 'Wolf's Lair mentality' took possession of him, and he of it, his routine dominated by the daily war situation conferences when he pored over large-scale maps with the staff of the High Command, who had little or no influence over the decisions he took. The Wolf's Lair was in a gloomy forest region which reminded Schmidt of 'the fairy tale of the wicked witch'. It was miles from any other human habitation; in Hitler's rooms the lights had to be on most of the day, and Hitler at this stage seldom went out. Surrounded by protective wire fencing, it was like a prison camp to which the sun could scarcely penetrate. The hutments were built of stone; later bomb-proof bunkers had to be built with walls of reinforced concrete camouflaged grey and green.

Hitler gradually grew more pale, more unhealthy in appearance as the year wore on. As Speer points out, he became obsessed by the need for self-preservation, which led him to have bunkers of ever increasing thickness built for himself and his staff. Those at Rastenburg had walls fifteen feet thick.

Life at the Wolf's Lair reflected life at the Chancellery or the Berghof. He could not bear to be alone, and postponed retiring until the latest possible hour. This meant a late morning start, with adjutants queuing up outside his quarters with urgent messages. He was not even available for appointments; he would see only those he wished, when he wished, issuing peremptory demands for men he felt the need to consult, whether they were near or far. He ate at Headquarters with his immediate staff officers after the midday situation conference, keeping them at table with his interminable talk until late in the afternoon, however pressing their duties might be. A later situation conference took place at night, and the evening meal, followed by talk until three or four in the morning, tolled heavily on those he kept around him. He talked about almost everything but the war, and his monologues of the period were recorded in the form of *Table-Talk* by Bormann's order. He was obsessed by the foreign press, long resumés of which had to be prepared for him day and night. With such a person probing into the details of the conduct of the war on every front, the nervous state of his staff officers, both senior and junior, can be imagined.

Concern about Hitler's health began to manifest itself again in 1942. His favourite physician, Dr Morell, gave him vitamin injections. But from 1942 on the strain began to tell on him. He was fifty-three, and he never relaxed except through incessant talk. When Ciano saw him in Salzburg in April, he wrote, 'Hitler looks tired. He is strong, determined, and talkative; but he is tired . . . I see for the first time that he has many grey hairs.' To Otto Dietrich, who had known him well through the 1930s, he had no serious physical disease, but his capacity for anger increased with the burdens he undertook and the frustrations he brought upon himself through his impossible demands and his refusal to face brute facts in wartime. Dietrich has described his rages, the real as distinct from the enacted, more lucidly than most:

> They represented the revolt of his demonic energies against the world of crude reality, this emotion being vented against some human object. They were the thunder of a hard will being shattered by the still harder reality of things. Hitler's mind stirred up his heart; his blood in turn inflamed his brain. The fury raged itself out in a hurricane of words that contradiction only lashed to greater intensity. At such times he would crush all objections simply by raising his voice ... In none of these rages, however, did Hitler ever let himself be carried away to the point of inflicting physical abuse ... I do not believe his states of violent agitation were the symptoms or the consequences of some acute physical illness. On the contrary, these outbursts of emotion were the cause of his frequent physical distress; they were his disease. These explosive blasts of an overcharged brain, which left him in a state of exhaustion, affected the nerves of his stomach.[5]

He did nothing to help himself or those gathered round to serve him. His private life merged with his public duties, day and night. He gave up seeing films. His sole pleasure was talking in company, and occasional visits to the Berghof. Apart from Eva, whom he saw little, his only real companion was his dog. 'His whole heart belongs to that dog,' wrote Goebbels at the time. Goebbels did his best to cheer him with clever conversation during his monthly visits to headquarters or when they met in Berlin. Speer wrote:

> Goebbels knew how to entertain Hitler ... with irony at the right place and admiration where Hitler expected it, with sentimentality when the moment and subject required it, with gossip and love affairs. He mixed everything in a masterly brew; theatre, movies and old times. But Hitler also listened with eager interest – as always – to

a detailed account of the children of the Goebbels family ... Goebbels contrived to strengthen Hitler's self-assurance and to flatter his vanity.[6]

But Goebbels himself, in his diaries for 1942 which in part survive, is constantly concerned about Hitler's health. On March 20th he notes: 'The Führer, thank God, appears in good health. He has been through exceedingly difficult days, and his whole bearing shows it ... He must take the entire burden of the war on his shoulders ... It is really touching to hear him complain about the winter that has caused him such terrific worries and difficulties ... He has already become quite grey ... to have aged very much.' On April 27th he wrote: 'The Führer told me that the condition of his health was such that he simply must take three months' leave some time.'[7]

At the beginning of the year Hitler had been sufficiently confident to leave his headquarters and make a speech in Berlin on January 30th in which he claimed he had 'unbounded confidence' in himself; Goebbels in turn claimed in his diary that in this speech, 'The Führer has charged the entire nation as though it were a storage battery.' In March, Hitler declared again in public, 'A world is being forged anew,' and on April 26th, in pointed reference to Napoleon, he said, 'We have mastered a destiny which broke another man one hundred and thirty years ago.'

The winter had taken its toll in Russia; German casualties exceeded a million, and the heavy armour was in bad shape for the spring hostilities. Hitler did one wise thing; he appointed Albert Speer Minister for Armaments. A brilliant organizer, Speer was to achieve wonders even though he was totally inexperienced for the work and had to contend with the thousand bomber raids which were to inflict such devastation on Germany's industrial front. On the other hand, Martin Bormann, who in certain respects had succeeded Hess after the latter's flight to Scotland, became Hitler's secretary and began to hedge the Führer in, making access to him for all but the service chiefs, Himmler and Goebbels, virtually impossible without his knowledge and consent.

Bormann was to act as a further barrier between Hitler and the world outside the confines of his military headquarters or the Chancellery.

On the war front Hitler enjoyed his last successes during the summer. In Africa, Rommel succeeded in capturing Tobruk and driving the British back over the Egyptian frontier to El Alamein, seventy miles west of Alexandria. However, in October, Generals Alexander and Montgomery led the Eighth Army in their spectacular counterattack which broke Rommel's line. Again, Hitler interfered, insisting Rommel stand his ground and be defeated instead of making the full and orderly retreat he planned. By the end of the year only Rommel's picked troops were left intact, and by then withdrawn some 700 miles west of El Alamein. In November, there had been Allied landings on the Atlantic and Mediterranean African coasts. In Russia, Hitler made spectacular gains in the south, penetrating deep in the direction of Stalingrad on the Volga, a thousand miles east from Warsaw, and pushing down from Kiev to Rostov, the Crimea and the Black Sea. Hitler moved his headquarters to the Ukraine. By September the battle for Stalingrad had begun. Once again, Hitler had deflected his forces, this time to the south, at a period when Stalingrad would have been far easier to take. When winter came, Stalingrad was to be the turning point of Hitler's campaign in Russia.

General Halder is bitter about the way Hitler recklessly extended his lines of advance, even at one point sending the Crimean Army north to help in the campaign against Leningrad instead of taking Stalingrad. When the General Staff tried to oppose the excesses of his 'greedy imagination', he said repeatedly that the Russians were 'dead'. Halder wrote:

> When he was read a statement ... that in 1942 Stalin would still be able to muster another one and one-fourth million men in the region north of Stalingrad and west of the Volga and at least half-a-million more in the eastern Caucasus and the region to the north, and which proved moreover that the Russian output of first-line tanks amounted to at least 1,200 a month, Hitler flew, with clenched fists and foam in the corner of his mouth, at the

one who was reading this statement, and forbade such idiotic twaddle.[8]

Speer reinforces this severe criticism. 'Hitler, by a succession of wrong-headed decisions, helped to speed the end of a war already lost.' Even allowing for the bitterness of those who had suffered so much frustration and humiliation at the hands of their Führer, it is plain by now that Hitler's political genius foundered on the battlefield.

11

Hitler's Europe: Master Race, Slave Labour and Genocide, 1941-1945

> Never consider the Reich secure unless, for centuries to come, it is in a position to give every descendant of our race a piece of ground and soil that he can call his own. Never forget that the most sacred of all rights in this world is man's right to the earth which he wishes to cultivate for himself and that the holiest of all sacrifices is that of the blood poured out for it.

This was Hitler writing during 1925 in Landsberg. Fifteen years later the dream of power was becoming a reality. The expansion of the Nazi Empire to the East was opening up new territory, living space for an ever-increasing number of 'Aryan' German people. The artificial frontiers were falling against the inevitable pressure of Europe's master-race, while other areas not directly occupied were being earmarked as 'spheres of influence' of importance to Germany for the service they could render in men and resources, such as Hungary and Rumania. Eastern territories actually incorporated into the German Reich, notably Western Poland, were 'germanized', that is, families of pure 'Aryan' German blood replaced those of inferior stock, who were ruthlessly dispossessed and driven East.

The occupied countries to the north and west of Germany were each placed under the authority of a Reich Commissioner (for example, Denmark) or a Military Commandant, if the area was vulnerable (for example, Belgium, Northern France, Yugoslavia). In certain territories, Hitler established puppet governments using local collaborators (such as Vidkun Quisling in Norway) or figureheads held to be 'responsive' to German control, such as Marshal Petain in Vichy France, the area of France left unoccupied until 1942. A country such as Belgium retained its normal governmental administration, but under strict German control. 'Aryan' countries, such as Denmark, Hitler hoped would live as 'normal' a life as possible under the wing of Germany. But behind the whole German administration lurked the teeth of the SS and Gestapo, often detested by the German military, but present to ensure 'security' and act if there should be the slightest sign of resistance among the civilian population. The most vicious control was always that established in the East: Hans Frank's repressive administration of the Government-General (formerly central Poland), or Reinhard Heydrich's administration of the so-called 'Protectorate' of Bohemia-Moravia.

Hitler established varied degrees of citizenship in territory incorporated into the Reich. German nationality itself was accorded only to people of proven German stock. 'Associate citizenship' was given to loyalists who could not claim German origin, though they remained in the Reich. They might, for example, be Flemish. The rest became stateless, if not actively driven out. Second-class citizenship or statelessness affected people, for example, in Luxembourg, Alsace-Lorraine, or Danzig. Rule by decree and the imposition of a police state 'secured' German authority everywhere in Hitler's New Europe, whether inside or outside the Reich itself. The black-uniformed SS began to incorporate local national 'loyalists' in their ranks; the SS in fact recruited a kind of German-controlled Foreign Legion; the Gestapo, also under the control of Himmler, acted as secret police, and operated very often in civilian clothes. The most fearful of the decrees under which they acted was the notorious *Nacht und Nebel* (Night and Mist) decree of December, 1941, which empowered the secret police to spirit away anyone they deemed to be endangering German security; they disappeared without trace, and their families never heard of them again. Arrests were normally made in the small hours of the morning.

A further control of all occupied territories came through the economy. The money of the area became 'germanized'; dispossession of property or take-overs at knock-down price were common; firms were placed in the hands of pro-German managements. Jews were totally dispossessed without compensation. Gradually, slave-labouring was introduced; workers in occupied countries were controlled, and liable to conscription. In Poland all workers were in any case conscripted, while in the West, the younger workers were subjected to 'pressure' to go and work 'voluntarily' in Germany. By 1944, almost five million foreign workers were labouring in the Reich, including almost two million Russians, almost one million Poles, and three-quarters of a million French.

The record remains, in the form of notes made by Bormann, of Hitler's personal statements about the treatment of the Poles. These statements were made during a meeting at the Chancellery on October 2nd, 1940, when Hans Frank, their new Governor, was being given his orders. Hitler said:

> The Poles, in direct contrast to our German workmen, are especially born for hard labour ... It is necessary to keep the standard of life low in Poland ... The Government-General should be used by us merely as a source of unskilled labour ... There should be one master only for the Poles – the Germans ... Therefore all representatives of the Polish intelligentsia are to be exterminated. This sounds cruel, but such is the law of life ... The task of the priest is to keep the Poles quiet, stupid and dull-witted.[1]

When it came to the invasion of Russia, Hitler stated at a conference held on July 16th, 1941:

> On principle we have now to face the task of cutting up the giant cake according to our needs, in order to be able: first, to dominate it; second, to administer it; and third, to exploit it. The Russians have now ordered partisan warfare behind our lines. This partisan war again has some advantages for us; it enables us to eradicate everyone who opposes us.[2]

It was the invasion of Poland in 1939 and of Russia in

1941 which confronted Hitler with the most dire of the social problems the Nazis had to solve: how to get rid of the large numbers of people whom they simply did not want. First of all, this meant the Jews, of whom there were some three and a quarter million in Poland, mostly impoverished. Those who had escaped into the Russian sector of Poland in September, 1939, were only to fall into German hands in 1941, along with further Jewish populations in the area of Russia occupied by the Germans. Russia had some five million Jews, mostly concentrated in the West and in the Ukraine. The concept of racial extermination, genocide, beginning first with the unwanted Jews and extending later to the unwanted Slavs, gypsies and other peoples caught in the path of the German advance, originated during 1940–41. Since this policy was strictly secret, and full knowledge was as far as possible limited to those who carried it out, namely the SS, the orders remained mostly verbal. Nevertheless, more than enough evidence survives to show that the original orders came from Hitler, and that Himmler, and through him Heydrich, were put in charge of this hideous task.

Two genocide operations ran parallel from 1941. The first, relatively limited, action was that of the so-called SS Action Groups, working in close association with the Army during the initial phase of the invasion of Russia. No more than 3,000 men were involved, recruited from the SS, and formed into units to follow the army and mop up resistance. This took the form of mass killings of Jews (automatically classed as Partisan) along with all who could be classed as Communist government agents, or resistance workers. These Action Groups, though at times sickened by their task and kept going with alcohol, succeeded in exterminating one million people, largely Jews, within about one year. The order for this action, signed by Heydrich and dated July 17th, 1941 survives.

The second genocide operation was that which led to the establishment of the extermination centres based on concentration camps in the Government-General, that is, outside the Reich itself and inside Polish territory. The notorious, veiled order for this was given in writing to

Heydrich by Goering, acting on Hitler's behalf. It was dated July 31st, 1941:

> Supplementing the task that was assigned to you on January 24th, 1939, to solve the Jewish problem by means of emigration and evacuation in the best possible way according to present conditions, I herewith instruct you to make all necessary preparations as regards organizational, financial and material matters for a total solution (*Gesamtlösung*) of the Jewish question within the area of German influence in Europe ... I instruct you further to submit to me as soon as possible a general plan showing the measures for organization and for action necessary to carry out the desired final solution (*Endlösung*) of the Jewish question.[3]

The orders for genocide were normally expressed in ambiguous terms, such as 'final solution'.

Parallel with this order, indeed integrated with it, was the meeting in Berlin to which Himmler summoned Rudolf Hoess, commandant of Auschwitz concentration camp near Cracow in the Government-General. Speaking as a witness at the International Military Tribunal in Nuremberg in April, 1946, Hoess said of Himmler:

> He told me ... that the Führer had given the order for a definite solution of the Jewish question. We, the SS, were to carry out that order ... We had chosen Auschwitz because of the easy access by rail and also because the extensive site could readily be isolated ... About 20,000 acres of the surrounding country had been cleared of all inhabitants ... The actual compound called Birkenau, where later on the extermination camp was constructed, was situated two kilometres from the Auschwitz camp.[4]

Hoess claimed that he personally was responsible as commandant for the deaths of some two million prisoners. He showed no sign of remorse, he had been obeying valid orders. Auschwitz was to become the principal centre for extermination, growing in efficiency as its mechanized plant (gas chambers combined with banks of ovens for the destruction of bodies) improved radically in 1943. The Auchwitz-Birkenau complex was intended to accommodate up to 230,000 prisoners, who were to be worked to death in special war factories set up to exploit this turnover of slave labour by I.G. Farben Industrie, Siemens, Krupp, and the like. 'One day Himmler will be our biggest industrialist,' said Hitler in November, 1941. The large number of prisoners brought in by rail from all over the Nazi empire were lined up and arbitrarily divided at sight into those condemned to immediate death and those allowed temporary survival as labourers.

Hitler himself made two public statements which hinted at his genocide of the Jews. The first was during a speech made in January, 1939:

> If international-finance Jewry inside and outside of Europe should succeed once more in plunging nations into another world war, the consequence will not be the Bolshevization of the earth and thereby the victory of Jewry, but the annihilation (*Vernichtung*) of the Jewish race in Europe.[5]

The second occasion was in a speech made in September, 1942, when Auschwitz was in full operation:

> I have spoken of two things: first, now that the war has been forced upon us, no array of weapons and no passage of time will bring us to defeat; and second, that if Jewry should plot another world war in order to exterminate the Aryan peoples of Europe, it would not be the Aryan peoples which would be exterminated, but Jewry.

Death came to the Jews in many ways, through starvation and disease in the ghettoes of the Government-General. In the Warsaw ghetto, which housed nearly half a million Jews, nearly 50,000 died in 1941 alone. Half a million died in the ghettoes and labour camps as a whole. In addition to Auschwitz, other extermination centres, notably Chelmno,

Treblinka, Belsec and Maidanek collectively equalled Auschwitz in the total of human destruction. In so far as the numbers involved can be calculated, it would appear that 5,100,000 Jews died out of the 8·3 million in German-occupied Europe, including the USSR. But the Slavs, and especially Russian prisoners of war, were massacred on an equal scale; some three and a half million died in captivity. Poland lost six million, at least half of whom were not Jewish. Stalin was to claim in 1946 that some seven million Russian civilians died as a result of the war, many deliberately allowed to starve to death. 'If today you do harm to the Russians, it is so as to avoid giving them the opportunity of doing harm to us,' said Hitler, in September, 1941. 'The stronger asserts his will; it's the law of nature ... The Slavs are a mass of born slaves, who feel the need of a master.'

The fact that Hitler delegated the task of racial extermination to Himmler and Heydrich does not mean that he put the matter out of his mind, or was unaware of what was happening in the secret camps, as Goering tried to maintain at the Nuremberg trial. Goebbels's diaries for 1942 are quite uncompromising, as entries for February and March show:

> The Führer once more expressed his determination to clean up the Jews in Europe pitilessly. There must be no more squeamish sentimentalism about it ... Their destruction will go hand in hand with the destruction of our enemies. We must hasten this process with cold ruthlessness ... Not much will remain of the Jews. About sixty per cent of them will have to be liquidated; only about forty per cent can be used for forced labour ... It's a life and death struggle between the Aryan race and the Jewish bacillus. No other government and no other regime would have the strength for such a global solution as this.

With the Jewish and Slav extermination centres situated in the East, the concentration camps in Germany and in the occupied countries to the West specialized in political prisoners, treating them with increasing harshness. Their treatment led to deaths by the hundreds of thousands in such centres as Bergen-Belsen, Ravensbruck and Sachsenhausen in the North, Buchenwald in central Germany, and Dachau and Mauthausen in the South. In the end, not far short of a million prisoners were to die in the camps in Germany itself. Himmler, Heydrich and Eichmann became names synonymous with the bureaucracy of extermination, the absolute elimination of the racially unwanted or the politically recalcitrant. Hitler's attitude to the German people, with whom he was so closely identified, was no less ruthless, once they opposed him. Human beings, whether civilian or members of the armed forces, became mere units to Hitler, units who were for him, or units who were against him. He deployed them one against the other, with death, either glorious or dishonourable, as the inevitable outcome for millions.

The megalomania of destruction was expressed in Hitler's orders on the war front itself, such as that of September 29th, 1941, on the future of Leningrad, in which he demanded to have it 'wiped from the face of earth'. His orders were 'to close in on the city and blast it to the ground'. As for the people: 'In this war for existence we have no interest in keeping even part of this great city's population.' But neither Leningrad nor Moscow, which he equally willed to have destroyed, yielded to the repeated pressure of the German armed forces.

From July, 1941, to September, 1942, Bormann obtained Hitler's permission to have what came to be called his Table-Talk recorded in shorthand by two officials, first Heinrich Heim and later Henry Picker, at mealtimes or during the late night sessions over tea and cakes. Bormann acted as editor, checking, annotating and filing the resulting typescripts, which he marked as 'Notes of fundamental interest for the future. To be preserved with the greatest care.'

The Table-Talk is the most illuminating introduction there is to both Hitler the man and the thinker. His audience at these monologues was largely male, with special guests, such as Himmler frequently indicated. By far the greatest part was recorded during a period of the war when Hitler could still feel confident of success. His 'thoughts' covered everything in which he was interested: his autobiographical allusions, and his views on religion. His deep-rooted racial prejudices, directed largely against the Jews and the Slavs, appear throughout. He conceived of man as existing on various evolutionary levels, with the Nordic peoples representing the highest plane ('the ancient Greeks ... were Germanics'). 'Aryan' supremacy is absolute, and once all peoples belonging to this highest level band together, there is nothing to prevent them from dominating the rest of the world's inhabitants, as Britain (which Hitler so much admired) all but achieved from an island which at the time had less than fifty million inhabitants. 'Only the man who knows how to give orders has pride,' he said, and pride was the great quality of the British. From the absolute premise of 'Aryan' superiority most of the rest of his philosophy was generated – the spread east for *lebensraum*, his concept of colonialism ('it is an imperative obligation for the white man, in the colonies, to keep the native at a distance'), the development of large areas where people of inferior race exist only to serve the higher representatives of the species, who are the only ones to possess armies, weapons and power. He believed in the subjugation of women to the same ultimate purpose, assiduously breeding superior stock and leaving the rest to their men ('I detest women who dabble in politics'). The right women should have children with or without the benefits of marriage; this was an imperative order of Nature, which does not care about priest or registrar. The few lyrical passages in the whole of Hitler's Table-Talk concern the beauty of women. But in other respects they were inferior. 'Man's universe is vast compared with that of women.' In education, he was against what he called 'scholastic slime'; education should, he thought, be aimed at developing the brain and talent of the child towards fulfilling his natural bent, not at the production of an intellectual monster! Naturally, there would be little or no education for second- or third-class citizens.[6]

Hitler claimed that the basic guide to life is science; while science seeks out the truth and progresses, religion is retrograde and given to maintaining illusions. Science demands the evolution of the highest in the species at the expense of the rest, such as the Jews. 'When I realize that the species is in danger, then in my case sentiment gives way to the coldest reason'; 'the Jews must clear out of Europe . . . if they refuse to go voluntarily, I see no other solution but extermination.' But even the highest must make their sacrifice in war, and must be utterly subject to the State: 'Organized life offers the spectacle of a perpetual renunciation by individuals of a part of their liberty.' Also, 'the idea of solidarity was imposed on men by force, and can be maintained only by the same means.' Hence, for Hitler, the highest species must forever maintain their supremacy in a world where they are vastly outnumbered by the lower grades in the human scale, and this means war, which at once subjugates the inferior while maintaining the morale and solidarity of the superior, preventing them from relapsing into the comfort-loving mediocrity of the bourgeoisie. 'For the good of the German people, we must wish for a war every fifteen or twenty years.' 'It fills me with shame when I think that I have lost more blood shaving than in the field of battle'; 'a people cannot lay claim to mastery of the world unless it's ready to pay with its blood.'

Behind all this lies his evaluation of himself. 'It's a great time,' he said, 'when an entirely unknown man can set out to conquer a nation, and when after fifteen years of struggle he can become, in effect, the head of his people.' 'I couldn't say whether my feeling that I am indispensable has been strengthened during this war. One thing is certain, that without me the decisions to which we today owe our existence would not have been taken.'

However successful Hitler may have appeared to be, by the autumn of 1941 he was building up a strong head of opposition both to himself and to the cruel form of police state his regime now represented. There had been, before the war, a weak front of opposition within the armed forces, the only powerful organization in the State which Hitler could not afford to lose. He had, to a considerable degree, overcome the initial independence of the army by making himself the Supreme Commander on the death of Hindenburg. But the army represented a long-established, tradition-laden hierarchy in the State, and there was bound to be resistance to Hitler's autocratic and ill-tempered methods of dealing with the personalities of the High Command, although he was constantly re-casting its personnel to rid himself of malcontents and consolidate his authority.

The story of Hitler's relationship to the military hierarchy is therefore a strange one. Nonentities like Keitel regarded themselves as the agents of Hitler's directives, and they contributed nothing to his strategy. Others, such as Halder, chafed rather than rebelled, advising where they could, but never ultimately standing up for what they believed to be right. Guderian, however, whose personality was perhaps the toughest of all, was prepared to face dismissal by telling Hitler to his face what he felt should or should not be done, and so he was often out of Hitler's favour. Hitler could not do without a High Command, however much he took upon his own shoulders; he was forced to employ Guderian because of the latter's obvious ability, strength and pertinacity. But Hitler undoubtedly hastened his own downfall by his inability to work with his senior staff, whose morale sank lower and lower as their advice was summarily rejected, while tasks were foisted upon them which were impossible to fulfil. Rommel, the most dashing of Hitler's generals and the one adopted by the British as their enemy favourite, remained loyal to Hitler during his days of success on the African front, but finally became identified with the growing resistance to the Führer which grew from 1938 to the end of the war.

This organized resistance movement in Germany centred round a few strong, idealistic personalities, whose religious faith was largely responsible for their defection. They conceived Hitler to be anti-Christ, though they appeared, like so many Germans, to be unaware of the worst that was being done in the name of Germany in the extermination camps. Mostly they belonged to a relatively right-wing, upper-class segment in German military and diplomatic circles. Gradually they were drawn together round the figure of General Beck, the former Chief of Staff who had resigned in 1938 rather than be party to Hitler's acts of bluff and aggression. He had been succeeded by General Halder who, without joining the inner circle of the Movement, gave useful information from time to time. Prominent among the older generation with whom Beck was in touch was Carl Goerdeler, who had resigned from a senior position in Hitler's administration before the war; Ulrich von Hassell, former German Ambassador in Rome; Field-Marshal von Witzleben; General Olbricht, an excellent administrator and a staff officer at the War Office; and General Stülpnagel, Military Governor of France. Prominent among the younger generation of senior officers who turned against Hitler and advocated his assassination were Major-General von Tresckow, his friend Major Fabian von Schlabrendorff, and Colonel Count von Stauffenberg.

Another centre of disaffection was Military Intelligence, headed by the somewhat enigmatic figure of Admiral Canaris. Both Canaris and his deputy, General Oster, were anti-Hitler, and were primarily responsible for leaking information to the nations of the West that a German attack was on its way, only to be frustrated by the determinedly wishful disbelief in Hitler's aggressive plans which seems to have possessed the Führer's victims. As soon as war began, Canaris enlisted a number of prominent but secret anti-Nazis into his ranks, including the eminent pastor, Dietrich Bonhoeffer. Outside these two circles, but known to them, was a third, the so-called Kreisau Circle, headed by Count Helmuth von Moltke, a group of intellectuals and, in some cases, Anglophiles, who were mainly opposed to Hitler's assassination or any violent action. They were idealists and philosophers. In addition, there were considerable anti-Hitler stirrings among working-class groups, both Socialist and Communist, which had suffered martyrdom by the thousands but failed to form an organized resistance movement.[7]

The fact that virtually all these men of the right were good Christians and aristocrats or gentlemen brought up within a strict ethical code made the decision to strike Hitler down more difficult for them. Many, those with a military background, were bound by an oath of personal loyalty to Hitler, but this, they recognized, had been imposed upon them, and one by one they resolved the matter with their consciences. The problem then was threefold: First, how to reach Hitler in order to assassinate him; second, how to sound out a sufficient number of highly placed generals and prepare them to accept and support a military *coup d'état* when it happened, and not betray or oppose them; third, how to form a kind of 'shadow' government to stand ready to assume power the moment Hitler was dead. The weakness of their numbers, coupled with Beck's ill-health (he had an operation for cancer in 1943) meant that they were dogged by difficulties. Nonetheless, they were to make two serious attempts on Hitler's life, in 1943 and 1944, while supporting a number of wholly abortive suicidal attempts at assassination during the same period.

Hitler, of course, was well aware that he was a constant target of assassination. His dual fear was that his health would collapse, or that he would be the victim of assassination before his mission was accomplished. This, since 1938, was what had driven him to expand his conquests in the shortest possible time. His health was watched over by the ever-present Dr Morell; his safety was the province of the SS, who guarded him day and night wherever he might be. No one could enter his presence bearing arms; briefcases were normally searched. Even his waiters were SS men. His food was specially prepared by his trusted Viennese vegetarian cook, Konstanza Manzialy, who accompanied him everywhere. When he moved from the Chancellery to the Berghof, or to his various headquarters, he travelled at times and by routes which were never pre-announced. His few public, or semi-public appearances, were wholly erratic; he never did the expected thing. The only practical way to assassinate him was either to undertake a suicide mission and get close to him (and several young men offered their lives to achieve this, but never had the final opportunity to get near him), or to have a highly placed and trusted staff officer belonging to the inner circle of the resistance smuggle a bomb into Hitler's presence on the occasion of a military conference or one of his daily situation sessions. Where was such a man to be found? Nevertheless, two separate attempts of this sort were to be made: one in 1943, when a time bomb was placed on Hitler's aircraft after a military conference on the Eastern front, and the other in July, 1944, when a time bomb was introduced by Stauffenberg into

Hitler's situation conference at his headquarters in Rastenburg.

Strangest of all, perhaps, is the case of a special attempt on Hitler's life early in the war. On November 8th, 1939, Hitler attended, as usual, the annual assembly of old Nazi supporters at the Bürgerbräukeller in Munich, the place where the 1923 putsch had been initiated. Usually this was a lengthy, nostalgic occasion, but this time Hitler spoke only briefly and then hurried away with the other Nazi leaders. Twelve minutes after his departure a bomb went off near the rostrum, killing seven people. Immediately, extravagant efforts were made to connect this attempt with the British Secret Service, even to the extent of kidnapping two known members of it. Captain S. Payne Best and Major R. H. Stevens, had been making contact with an 'anti-Nazi' German officer in Holland, a member of SS Intelligence. The reason for associating the British with the attempt was to stir the German people to an increased hatred of Britain. Just as in the Reichstag fire, the Gestapo discovered the agent, a Communist called George Elser in Dachau, who confessed to manufacturing and placing the bomb; under pressure from the Gestapo, he implicated Best and Stevens, who, like Elser, stayed in captivity until the end of the war. Elser was kept as a relatively privileged prisoner until April, 1945, when the Gestapo finally killed him. Presumably, he knew too much.

For many years it had been assumed that the Nazi leadership had organized this attempt in order to incriminate the British. More recent research, however, has proved conclusively that Elser was indeed the only originator of the attempt.

Hitler, however, was not fated to die as the result of assassination. He was to reserve to the end his right to kill himself.

12

Downfall, 1943-1945

The fuel which drove Hitler to his downfall was, in the end, his blind will. As he said to his staff officers at a situation conference in May, 1943, 'The decisive thing is the will.' This was his criticism of the Italian forces in the Mediterranean and the Rumanian division on the Eastern front. They lacked the vital will he ascribed to the German forces. The verbatim transcriptions of his situation conferences which have survived the war show his distrust of the Italians. 'We succeeded with the Germans,' he said in December, 1942, 'but not with the Italians, and we don't succeed with the Italians anywhere.'

Nor did he succeed with the Germans when they were placed in an impossible situation, as the 6th Army was at Stalingrad. Friedrich von Paulus, the Commander in the field who, to spur him on at the last moment was created a Field Marshal, finally surrendered when he was cut off, besieged and battered into submission by the Russians at the end of January, 1943. German forces outside could not break the Russian stranglehold, and Paulus was not permitted to fight his way out of Stalingrad. In spite of Goering's boasts, the Luftwaffe was powerless to fly in the 750 tons of supplies required daily. Paulus's troops were in the end starving, sick and suffering from the cold, but Hitler's attitude remained adamant: 'The Sixth Army will do its historic duty at Stalingrad to the last man.' It was a test case for the Führer's implacable authority, and it resulted in the loss of twenty German Divisions, killed or captured, and the first German Field Marshal to fall into enemy hands. Hitler was appalled. 'When the nerves break down, there is nothing left but to admit that one can't handle the situation and to shoot oneself,' he said, prophetically. 'This hurts me so much because the heroism of so many soldiers is nullified by one single characterless weakling.' The shame was concealed by the wording of the communique issued on February 3rd: 'True to their oath to fight to the last breath, the Sixth Army under the exemplary leadership of Field Marshal von Paulus has been overcome by the superiority of the enemy.' Read to the roll of drums over the German radio, the catastrophe was emphasized by four days of national mourning.

With the parallel collapse of the German front in North Africa, Hitler became obsessed by two problems: holding his ground on the 1,200 mile Russian front, and preserving a strong defensive position in the Balkans. Allied strength in North Africa represented the ultimate threat to his southern flank in Russia, launched through the Balkans. Writing to Mussolini in February, 1943, Hitler said, 'I regard the situation in the Balkan peninsula with the gravest concern.' He feared also the threat represented by the growing number of organized partisans, whose presence everywhere in the occupied territories, and especially in Russia and the Balkans, constituted a growing hazard to the Germans. The previous month he had summoned Marshal Antonescu to his headquarters to press for increased Rumanian participation in the war. A report of this meeting, as experienced by Antonescu, revealed that Hitler was 'obsessed with the Russian question ... we had the impression of a man tortured by grave preoccupations. He spoke to us at length of his past, of his loneliness, of his revolution ... He seemed to draw strength from the great memories of his past to neutralize the bitterness of the present hour.' The theme of the lonely 'man of destiny' was reiterated in his letter to Mussolini:

> You can hardly imagine how much I want to spend a couple of days personally with you ... For what I am to Germany, Duce, you are to Italy ... No episode on any front can be considered ... in isolation, since they are all part of a vast chain of events which will ultimately be decisive for the destiny of the whole of Europe ... But I can assure you that I am happy to be alive at such a time

> and to be able to fight in defence of these immortal values . . . It does not therefore sadden me that I was chosen to bear this destiny, but I am proud and happy it should be so.[1]

These immortal values, however, had to be fought for brutally, especially in dealing with partisans. 'If someone is faced by an emergency he can only deal with in the most brutal way, he's entitled to use any measure that promises success,' Hitler said to his Staff Commander in December, 1942.

Hitler's only relief lay in incessant talk. Ciano was quite brutal about this as early as April, 1942, when he had accompanied Mussolini to the meeting at Salzburg:

> Hitler talks, talks, talks, talks. Mussolini suffers . . . On the second day, after lunch, when everything had been said, Hitler talked uninterruptedly for an hour and forty minutes. He omitted absolutely no argument: war and peace, religion and philosophy, art and history.[2]

Later he wrote, 'I believe that at heart Hitler is glad to be Hitler, because this permits him to talk all the time.' The verbatim transcription of the situation conferences, often called twice a day, shows Hitler's capacity to digress on side issues, until military discussion degenerated into gossip. Sometimes his excessive talking, like his outbursts of anger, were tactical, as Speer suggests when he refers to Hitler's 'habit of killing opposition by long, exhaustive and numbing speeches'. Only Goebbels appears to have enjoyed his prolonged, heart to heart talks with the Führer, as his diaries for 1943 show. 'The Führer invited me into his air-raid shelter where we had a four-hour discussion in private'; 'These four hours with the Führer were very beautiful and engendered much confidence'; 'our conferences lasted far beyond midnight'. Goebbels realized the therapeutic value of talk for Hitler.

1943 was a bitter year. Rommel was driven out of Africa, losing a quarter of a million men, Sicily was occupied by the Allies, and Mussolini fell. The Badoglio government defected, the Allies landed in southern Italy, and, in Russia, the Red Army began the great drive which put the Germans in retreat from the area west of Moscow south to the Black Sea. Between July and September, Smolensk, Kursk, Orel, Kharhov and Rhostov had all returned to Russian hands. By January, 1944, virtually half the conquered Soviet territory of the south, including large areas of the Ukraine, had been recovered. With the U.S. Army Air Force bombing Germany by day and the R.A.F. bombing by night, the industrial areas were suffering heavy damage throughout the year. The Luftwaffe took a heavy toll on the bombers, but its capacity to attack was severely restricted, with heavy commitments in Italy and the Mediterranean as well as the Eastern front. The top echelon was torn over policy. Adolf Galland, as General of Fighters, was demanding a four-to-one ratio of fighters to bombers from Goering for service in Germany, but Hitler preferred to have his fighter strength in action on the fighting fronts. Goering lapsed into apathy; he was in any case under the influence of his addiction to paracodeine, a derivative of morphine. He retired as often as he could to his great mansion in the forest north of Berlin, or to his chalet near Berchtesgaden, on the excuse of ill-health. The failure of the Luftwaffe to meet the impossible demands made by Hitler led to a severe decline of his prestige. Goering thrived on success; failure drove him into a state of lethargy.

One of Hitler's most serious misjudgements was to insist on modifying the first German jet-fighter, the ME 262, into a 'mini-bomber' because he could not accept the idea of defensive, as against aggressive, warfare. This even led to suicide among senior officers in the Luftwaffe, and to the complete moral collapse of Goering, who was unable to stand up to Hitler on this matter of principle.[3]

It was Goebbels who kept the most enthusiastic contact with the Führer during this difficult time. In March, 1943, Goering told him, 'the Führer has aged fifteen years during the three and a half years of war.' Goebbels was worried that Hitler had 'become such a recluse' and that he was leading such an 'unhealthy life'.

He never gets out into the fresh air. He does not relax. He sits in his bunker, worries and broods. If one could only transfer him to other surroundings. But he has made up his mind to conduct this war in his own Spartan manner, and I suppose nothing can be done about it.[4]

Goebbels noted, perhaps with some satisfaction, the decline of Goering's prestige with Hitler. The Führer in March 'was very suspicious of Goering, claiming that he did not appreciate the decisive importance of air warfare . . . Nevertheless, he believes, as I do, that Goering's authority is indispensable to the supreme leadership of the Reich.'

If Goering was 'rather ill', Hitler himself, says Goebbels, had 'stomach trouble' which Morell was trying to relieve. Goebbels too felt overstrained and sought the help of Morell. In April, Hitler retired to rest at the Berghof, where he celebrated his fifty-fourth birthday. In May, he was back in Berlin for a national conference of Party officials, another occasion for expansive talk, extending to the churches, the Jews, the 'liquidation' of the 'rubbish of small nations' (*Kleinstaaten-Gerümpel*) still existing in Europe, the supremacy of the German Herrenvolk, and Charlemagne. Afterwards, Goebbels enjoyed some private discussions with Hitler. 'He is still the old Führer, though fatigued and a little shaky.' Nevertheless, 'within him there glows a fiery spirit'. He indulged in a favourite topic, the ineptitude of the senior officers in the Army: 'He is absolutely sick of the generals.' Even Goebbels thinks that at times his opinion 'is so caustic as to seem prejudiced or unjust . . . All generals lie, he says. All generals are disloyal. All generals are opposed to National Socialism.' Unable to bear the sight of them, he told Goebbels he no longer ate in the generals' mess at Headquarters. Indeed, towards the end of May he returned to the Berghof.

Goebbels also worried about Hitler's withdrawal from the public. Goebbels himself liked to keep in the public eye, even in time of trouble. 'One cannot neglect the people too long,' he writes in the diary. People 'keep asking why the Führer does not visit the bombed areas . . . why the Führer doesn't talk to the German people and explain the present situation.' The question of Hitler's public silence came to a head with the fall of Mussolini.

During 1943 the two dictators had met twice; in April and July. Mussolini came to the April Conference at the Castle of Klessheim near Salzburg with the intention of pressing Hitler to end the war with Russia and consolidate the Axis sphere of influence in central Europe and the Mediterranean. He was, in a sense, to be spokesman for the nations providing aid to Hitler on the Eastern front, Italy, Rumania and Hungary. As usual, he had been hypnotized by Hitler, and as a result, said little. Sepp Dietrich had told Goebbels that the Duce 'looked sick and frail, and gave the impression of being tired and washed out.' He was, in fact, suffering from severe stomach cramps. Mussolini's doctor had written in his diary: 'He looks tired, his face is pale, he has great pockets under his eyes.' 'The Axis must face the fact that it is saddled with Italy,' said Hitler to Admiral Doenitz in May.

In July Mussolini was summoned yet again to meet the Führer and hear his views on the catastrophic situation in Italy. Hitler was determined by now to take over effective command in Italy, leaving the Duce only nominally in charge. They met in Feltre on July 19th, arriving in separate planes. Hitler gave Mussolini a two hour lecture, reviewing the total situation. He emphasized pointedly that he personally was 'sacrificing the whole of his time and personal comfort to the task of bringing about a settlement in his own lifetime', and that 'this was a question of willpower'. Mussolini, under the strongest pressure to stand up to Hitler, even to the point of withdrawing Italy from the Axis, and from the war, was only able to reiterate former appeals for increased help.

He had less than a week left in power. Following an overnight meeting of the Grand Council, Mussolini was given an audience by the King on Sunday, July 25th, told he must resign and, on leaving the palace, placed under arrest. Marshal Badoglio succeeded him as head of the government.

The effect of the fall of Mussolini on Hitler was one of profound shock rather than actual surprise. His initial reaction was extravagant, to use a parachute division to occupy Rome, arrest the King and Badoglio, and seize the Vatican. 'I'll go right into the Vatican,' he declared. 'Do you think the Vatican embarrasses me? . . . That rabble [the diplomatic corps] is in there. We'll get that bunch of swine . . .' Goebbels and Ribbentrop more prudently opposed direct action against the Vatican. Rommel, now Commander-in-Chief in Italy, thought nothing should be done without deliberation.

Goebbels was in a bind over what he could say to the press. Rumour was rife in Germany. He had to be content with announcing that Hitler had sent Mussolini an edition of Nietzsche's works for his birthday on July 29th. With German forces already present in Italy, the situation was not hopeless, and Badoglio played for time by pretending to maintain the alliance with Germany. 'I am extremely happy over the equanimity with which the Führer judges the situation,' wrote Goebbels before leaving Rastenburg for Berlin.

In any event, no precipitate action was taken during the next few weeks: Hitler merely watched the situation and built up his forces in Italy. On September 8th the Badoglio government suddenly declared an armistice, following the allied landings in Salerno, south of Naples. Hitler, although preoccupied at the time in the Ukraine, experienced 'a queer feeling of unrest' and hurried back to Rastenburg in time to hear the news from Italy. He was joined by Goebbels, who found him looking 'exceptionally well'. 'It is always to be noted,' he added, 'that in times of crisis the Führer rises above himself physically and spiritually.'

On September 10th he broadcast to the nation his first public speech since March. It was transcribed on magnetophone band in Berlin from Rastenburg. Unlike the speech in March, he read it well, to Goebbel's great relief. After paying tribute to Mussolini, he made it clear that the fight in Italy had 'for months been carried on mainly by German forces'. Then, he added, in fair warning to likely traitors in Germany:

Hope of finding traitors here rests on complete ignorance

of the character of the National Socialist State; a belief that they can bring about a July 25th in Germany rests on a fundamental illusion as to my personal position, as well as about the attitude of my political collaborators and my Field Marshals, Admirals and Generals.[5]

Hitler immediately undertook the action he had originally planned in July. On September 12th an SS unit under the command of Otto Skorzeny landed by glider in the area in the Abruzzi mountains where Mussolini was being held, rescued him and flew him to Vienna. Hitler wanted him to act as political figurehead to re-establish the Fascist regime in northern Italy. Nevertheless, Hitler was unalterable in his determination that the administration of Italy should be German-controlled. However, although only sixty years old, Mussolini was a spent man. He was prepared to act as Hitler required, but he showed little real interest in the political rehabilitation designed for him. According to Goebbels, Hitler was shocked that Mussolini showed no inclination to wreak vengeance on those who had brought about his downfall. This, Hitler felt, 'showed his real limitations. He is not a revolutionary like the Führer or Stalin.' He was too preoccupied with purely domestic problems to please his Nazi champions. He was in good health, however, as was Hitler after his period of rest at Berchtesgaden where he started taking regular walks, his Alsatian dog Blondi accompanying him.

Speer has given us a close portrait of Hitler as he was in the later months of 1943. In spite of his frequent moods of despondency, he always 'displayed confidence in ultimate victory . . . The more inexorably events moved towards catastrophe, the more inflexible he became, the more rigidly convinced that everything he decided on was right.' At the same time he became less accessible, using Bormann and Keitel as his principal shields against intrusion. But, in Speer's view, he was under no illusion about the grim significance of the joint demand for the unconditional surrender of Germany promulgated by the Allied leaders in January, 1943. Goebbels records in his diary that they talked openly about the possibilities of peace negotiations with either Stalin or

Churchill. Hitler preferred to deal with Stalin, whom he had always admired as a 'practical politician', than with Churchill, whom he held to be a 'romantic adventurer' who over-indulged in alcohol.

Speer was astonished to find how hard Hitler disciplined himself, how hard he applied himself to work, how much detail he was able to absorb. When sheer exhaustion set in, he would retire to the Berghof to recover. (He spent fifty-seven days there in all between July, 1941, and March, 1943, a period of twenty months; he was also at the Berghof for three months following April, 1943, after which he returned for nine months to his headquarters. Then he spent four months away from headquarters from mid-March, 1944.) But even at the Berghof he naturally had to follow the course of the war closely; the daily situation conferences moved to Berchtesgaden. 'Overwork and isolation,' says Speer, 'led to a peculiar state of petrification and rigour. He suffered from spells of mental torpor, and was permanently caustic and irritable.'[6] Decisions had to be forced out of an exhausted brain. Contrary to popular belief, Hitler encouraged his military staff not to be servile; the discussions were loose and informal, even gossipy. But the prolonged conferences, lasting for hours by day and night, did not alter Hitler's real decisions. He treated them solely as advisory. His insomnia and lack of companionship at night made him keep his personal staff and visitors up until the small hours. 'He spoke of the agony of lying awake if he went to bed earlier.' The talk became discursive and banal, though Hitler would try to be human, and even gallant to his female secretaries. Triviality relaxed him. He would contemplate what he would do once peace came, and he could change the field-grey uniform he had assumed for the period of the war for his old peacetime jacket. If he talked, it was, on the whole, a good sign, but often he let the company lapse into long, deadly silences.

He began the morning late, with information about the world's press and reports on the air-raid damage in Germany. He used a magnifying glass now as his eyesight since 1942 was too poor to read print or maps. (Since he did not want to reveal any sign of failing sight in public, he had his scripts typed on special machines set with very large type.) In studying the reports, he seemed far more concerned at the loss of public buildings than at civilian casualties. Then would follow the first mid-day situation conference with its numbing effect on the staff. 'In the stupefying world of the headquarters,' writes Speer, 'we remained unmoved by what Hitler's decisions might mean at the front, where men were fighting and dying.' Hitler worked from maps, and never visited his front line troops or saw battle being waged. While the technical communications with the battlefronts were excellent, the human communications were nil. Hitler could not stand retreats and forced his exhausted troops to thrust themselves against the enemy. When they failed, his anger would vent itself on any representative from the battlefront involved who happened to be at headquarters. 'In his talk Hitler seemed to me to be betraying an obsession,' says Speer.

Another close observer was the historian, Professor Ernst Schramm, who was assigned to Hitler's headquarters in January, 1943, to keep the official diary of the Army High Command. Like Speer, Schramm adopts an objective, sophisticated attitude towards Hitler, describing him exactly as he found him, and dispelling some of the erroneous suppositions which have gathered round his name. For example, in Schramm's view, Hitler was not superstitious (though prepared to exploit superstition in others), nor had he much use for Himmler's solemn exploitation of German mythology, with its attempt to revive pagan ritual. Schramm considers he was, after a fashion, cultured, though in a wholly disorganized way, allowing himself to become prejudiced and arrogant in the application of his knowledge. He had a marked sense of humour, which he preferred to exercise in private, a ready response to music and a wholly bourgeois taste in the arts. He could be a shrewd judge of character, though his interest in people was confined to their potential usefulness. However, he had a peculiar vein of loyalty once he had adopted a person in his scheme of things. He did not like discarding anyone who had been genuinely helpful to him, which accounts for his reluctance to act against Roehm, and his profound embarrassment at the time action was taken. His innate, personal conservatism narrowed his intimate circle, and made it difficult for him to vary his routine of life, or acquire friends. Friendship, in any real sense, was unknown to him.

His principal weapon in dealing with his generals and Party officials was his phenomenal memory for facts and statistics. As Speer says, 'Hitler's memory for figures was the terror of his entourage.' But he respected people who had a genuine specialized knowledge he could make use of, and Speer learned to counter Hitler by making use of staff with specialist skills as his allies at conferences. Schramm, however, maintains that it was 'very difficult to come to grips with what Hitler really thought and perceived, difficult to clarify the extent to which he was motivated by logic or impelled by instinct.' Only his anti-semitism seemed deep and real. He felt Hitler was a kind of strategic actor, his rages often simulated to instill fear and impose his will on his reluctant senior staff.

Although he regarded himself as highly rational, with a capacity to be 'ice-cold', as he liked to put it, he depended for his decisions, once he reached them, on his 'intuition', a kind of innate shrewdness. Once he lost, he did not cry over spilt blood; the failures of the past were left to bury themselves. He was, says Schramm, 'morally uninhibited', without any human feeling for people as a whole, soldiers or civilians. He gave the millions he consigned to death no further thought once the decision was reached to sacrifice them. As for the Germans, the Herrenvolk, he said, 'If the German people are not prepared to give everything for the sake of their self-preservation, very well! Then let them disappear!' Schramm, like Speer, would not underestimate the significance of Hitler's personality or the hold he was able to exercise over all but the very few, the rare, exceptional people who found the strength and the courage to oppose him.

At the beginning of 1944, Hitler anticipated the full onslaught to come in the West with a special order demanding of all German forces 'a fanatical will to end this battle victoriously . . . The fight must be hard and merciless, not only against the enemy, but against all officers and units who fail in this decisive hour.' It must become 'a hazardous enterprise which will be drowned in the blood of Anglo-Saxon soldiers'. The battle in Italy was one of the hardest in the war; the Allies only reached Rome on June 4th. On June 6th, the D-day landings began in Normandy; in the East 'fortresses' had been established to stay the Russian advances (the so-called 'wavebreak' principle), but by July they had reached the frontier of East Prussia and advanced through Poland to the Vistula. The territory of the Reich itself was now threatened.

On July 20th came the major attempt on Hitler's life by the dissident army officers. It was the second attempt of its kind; the first had been on March 13th, 1943, when Baron Henning von Tresckow, a staff officer on the Eastern front, aged forty-two, and his close friend and adjutant, Dr Fabian von Schlabrendorff, working in association with General Beck's group in Berlin, prepared a delayed-action bomb disguised to look like a parcel containing two bottles of Cointreau. The package was entrusted to a member of Hitler's entourage at the moment he was stepping into the Führer's plane when it was due to take off for Rastenburg, following a visit Hitler had made to General Kluge's headquarters at Smolensk; it was passed off as a gift for a fellow officer in Rastenburg. But the bomb failed to function, and Schlabrendorff had the nerve-wracking task of flying immediately to Rastenburg and recovering the package before it was delivered and opened. While Hitler had been in Kluge's office, Schlabrendorff had picked up his military-style cap, and found it to be heavy with protective metal plate. He also watched Hitler eat, his face close to the plate as he devoured the mixture of vegetables prepared by the cook he had brought with him and pre-tasted in his presence by Dr Morell.

Secondary attempts, in the form of suicide missions undertaken in turn by Colonel von Gersdorff, Axel von dem Bussche, and Ewald Heinrich von Kleist, young officers who were members of the German Resistance, were all abortive. The officers' lives were fortunately not sacrificed. Then, in June, 1944, Colonel Count Claus Schenk von Stauffenberg, aged thirty-seven, was appointed Chief of Staff to General

Fromm, Commander of the Reserve Army, whose headquarters were at the War Office in the *Bendlerstrasse* in Berlin. From this date, Stauffenberg had direct access to Hitler, since he had to attend certain of Hitler's situation conferences representing Fromm. He was a war hero of considerable repute, who had insisted on continuing to serve although he had lost, in action, his right forearm, two fingers of his left hand and his left eye. Such disabilities spared him the normal search to which all those entering Hitler's presence were subjected. He volunteered to carry a bomb into Hitler's conference, finally placing a briefcase containing a time bomb near Hitler's feet at the mid-day conference on July 20th, 1944.

Stauffenberg bluffed his way out of the compound of Rastenburg and was on his way back to Berlin by air before the staff realized how the explosion had come about. But Hitler was spared, since another officer had, by chance, moved the briefcase after Stauffenberg had left, and a large plinth under the table had sheltered Hitler from the worst of the blast. Stauffenberg arrived in Berlin sometime before five o'clock convinced of his success; he had heard the explosion. But Hitler, badly shaken, had been helped out of the wreckage of the hut where the conference had been held, and closed down all communications with the outside world. In consequence, the conspirators waiting in the War Office were unable to receive the prearranged signal to commence the operation for the take-over of Berlin.[7]

The whole business became hopelessly tangled. Stauffenberg was identified as the officer responsible; Hitler communicated with Goebbels, who was in Berlin, and before the night was out, Stauffenberg and his closest associates had been shot as traitors, while Beck had been forced to commit suicide. The whole network of conspirators began to be rounded up for the great public trial Hitler in his wrath determined to stage as a major act of recrimination. His voice hoarse and broken, he went on the air at one o'clock in the morning, vowing vengeance on this 'very small gang of criminal elements who will now be ruthlessly exterminated'.

Eva Braun had gone swimming when news of the attempt

reached the Berghof. She was fetched back in a state of panic, although she had been told that Hitler was only slightly hurt. She tried to telephone Rastenburg, but could not get through, and finally she collapsed with a nervous breakdown. When Hitler telephoned her himself to assure her little had happened to him, all she said was, 'I love you. God protect you.' When Hitler sent her his blood-stained uniform as a souvenir, she almost fainted; then she locked herself in her bedroom with the tattered garments. Hitler wrote to her, typing the letter himself:

> My dear Tschapperl, (Little One)
>
> I am quite well. Don't worry about me. I'm just a little tired. I hope to come home soon and to have some rest in your arms. I have a craving for rest, but my duty to the German people surpasses everything. Don't forget that my personal danger bears no comparison with that of the soldiers at the front . . . I have sent you the uniform of that wretched day. Proof that Providence protects me and that we no longer have to fear our enemies. With all my heart.[8]
>
> A.H.

Eva replied urging him to come home as soon as possible. 'Ever since our first meeting I have sworn to follow you everywhere, even unto death. You know that I live only for your love.'

Hitler was both angry and elated. He had been spared by a miracle which showed the hand of Providence was in his favour. Mussolini had been due to visit Rastenburg that very afternoon and had been received by Hitler and shown in triumph round the wreckage of the map room. 'It is not the first time I have escaped death miraculously,' Hitler said to the Duce. 'I am now more than ever convinced that the great cause which I serve will survive its present perils, and everything will be brought to a good end.' Only at the crowded tea party held late in the afternoon, did a sudden onrush of rage seize him, and he rose suddenly and shouted, 'I will crush and destroy the criminals who have dared to oppose themselves to Providence and me.' During August and

September the fearful inquisition of officers and civilians held to be involved was carried out by Roland Freisler, President of the Nazi People's Court in Berlin. The victims were bullied and humiliated, and many were cruelly executed, their hanging filmed so that Hitler might see that his vengeance had been fully exacted.

Hitler's injuries were in the end more psychological than physical. His hair had been singed, his right arm partially paralysed, his right leg burned, his eardrums damaged and his buttocks bruised so that he had, as he put it himself, a 'backside like a baboon'. His trousers had been ripped down as if with a knife. Four officers had been killed, and two severely injured. He was fortunate to have escaped so lightly. But the shock had a lasting effect on his nervous system. The gravest moral shock was the revelation that Rommel had been linked with the conspirators. Rommel was told to commit suicide to avoid the disgrace of a trial, and, to save his family, he obeyed this final order from the Führer.

The defensive walls with which Hitler had surrounded Germany, in the East, in the South, in the West, and finally inside the Reich itself, now began to crumble, though the bravery of the German soldiers made the advances as hard as possible. Paris fell on August 25th, the day Finland asked for an armistice, and Brussels fell on September 3rd. Rumania reversed sides, displacing Antonescu and declaring war on Germany, Bucharest had to be evacuated. On September 12th the American Army reached the Western frontier of Germany. Hitler demanded 'fanatical determination' from every able-bodied man, and the Allies had temporary set-backs, notably at Arnhem, and in northern Italy. But Hungary, Yugoslavia and Greece were lost in October, while by December the Russians were in Budapest.

On November 25th, Hitler issued a further general directive to his forces:

> The war will decide whether the German people shall continue to exist or perish. It demands selfless exertion from every individual. Situations which have seemed hopeless have been redeemed by the courage of soldiers

contemptuous of death, by the steadfast perseverance of all ranks, and by inflexible, exalted leadership.

Should a Commander, left to his own resources, think that he must give up the struggle, he will first ask his officers, then his non-commissioned officers, and finally his troops, if one of them is ready to carry on the task and continue the fight. If one of them will, he will hand over command to that man – regardless of his rank – and himself fall in. The new leader will then assume the command, with all its rights and duties.

Signed Adolf Hitler.[9]

The surprise attack launched for Hitler by Rundstedt in the Ardennes in mid-December was contained and rubbed out by mid-January. When Hitler met his commanders on December 12th to lecture them as they sat with watchful SS guards, he was described by one general as 'a stooped figure with a pale and puffy face, hunched in his chair, his hands trembling, his left arm subject to a violent twitching . . . When he walked, he dragged one leg behind him.' But the record of the speech he made to them on December 28th, in which he claimed that an offensive strategy is always less costly than a defensive one, is firm and lucid. By the end of December, the Russians had overrun East Prussia, and were entering Silesia.

On January 21st Hitler sent out a directive insisting he be told the truth; all officers from the Commander-in-Chief downwards

are responsible to me that every report made to me either directly, or through the normal channels, should contain nothing but the unvarnished truth. In future, I shall impose draconian punishment on any attempt at concealment, whether deliberate or arising from carelessness or oversight.[10]

However, on January 30th, the twelfth anniversary of Hitler's coming to power, Speer handed Hitler a memorandum declaring that 'the war was over in the area of heavy industry and armaments'; food and household needs, he said, should now have priority. He ended his statement:

> After the loss of Upper Silesia, the German armaments industry will no longer be able even approximately to cover the requirements of the front for ammunition, ordnance and tanks ... From now on the material preponderance of the enemy can no longer be compensated for the bravery of our soldiers.[11]

Hitler turned on Speer after receiving this memorandum and said in a cold, cutting voice: 'You cannot write that sort of thing to me. You might have spared yourself the trouble of such conclusions. You are to leave to me the conclusions I draw from the armaments situation.'

13

Aspiration in Death

By March, 1945, Allied forces in the West had reached the Rhine; in the East, Soviet forces were in East Prussia, Silesia and Hungary. Hitler's only method of combating the collapse of his forces was by issuing terror-orders against any soldiers who deserted or surrendered while still unharmed; the threats included the penalization of their relatives. On March 20th, he issued his notorious scorched-earth directive; everything 'which could in any way be used by the enemy immediately or in the foreseeable future for the prosecution of the war will be *destroyed*'.[1] The Armed Forces were responsible for the destruction of military material and installations in the immediate path of the enemy advance, while Speer was responsible for the destruction of civil resources, without regard to the effect this might have on the welfare of the German people. All communications, railways, waterways, electrical installations, were to be destroyed beyond repair. 'We can no longer afford to concern ourselves with the population,' Hitler said in Speer's presence in March.

Hitler presented a signed photograph of himself to Speer on the latter's fortieth birthday. When he tried to sign it, he said, 'Lately it's been hard for me to write even a few words in my own hand. You know how it shakes.' Then he added, 'If the war is lost, the people will be lost also. It is not necessary to worry about what the German people will need for elemental survival. On the contrary, it is best for us to destroy even these things. For the nation has proved to be the weaker, and the future belongs wholly to the stronger eastern nation.' The good will have been killed, he added, so the rest don't matter. We now know, from the lengthy 'testament' he dictated during February, that Hitler was gradually, inevitably, resigning himself to defeat.

Speer had already begun to plot with Guderian to prevent the wholesale destruction of bridges. His disillusion with Hitler had set in the previous year, finding him impossible to deal with in rational terms and resenting the abuse heaped on him when he presented truthful reports. He had even contemplated introducing poison gas into the ventilation system of the Bunker at a time when Hitler was in it; but he had found this in the end impossible to realize. Preservation of the German people now ranked uppermost in Speer's mind. He found most people regarded the war as over, and were thinking of how best to look after themselves.

The two men in high places who persistently opposed Hitler's destructive policy were Guderian and Speer. On March 28th Guderian refused to allow Hitler to abuse General Busse, whose assault on the Küstrin bridgehead had failed through no fault of his own. Gerhard Boldt, a young officer in Army Intelligence who became one of Guderian's adjutants, was present, and has described how Guderian in great agitation cut Hitler short and in a loud, forceful voice rejected outright his interpretation of the action. Hitler slumped down in his chair, and turned pale. After a moment's silence, he suddenly sprang to his feet with an agility which seemed impossible. His pallid face was marked by 'large, red blotches'. His left arm, the whole left side of his body, shook and he appeared to be about to throw himself at Guderian, who 'stood rooted to the spot like the rest of those present'. Only the heavy breathing of the two men could be heard. 'Then Hitler poured out a stream of invective, accusation and loathing' against the whole Officer Corps. Guderian, roused and angry, answered back, criticizing Hitler's leadership, and his abandonment of the German population in the East. Then the other officers present recovered their senses. Fearing Guderian's arrest, they tried to calm the situation. Guderian was called to the telephone, and when he returned, the atmosphere was tense, oppressive, but quiet. The conference continued; Guderian was merely dismissed, and sent on sick leave. He was succeeded as Chief of the General Staff by General Krebs.

Guderian has himself described what this confrontation was like:

> His fists raised, his cheeks flushed with rage, his whole body trembling, the man stood there in front of me ... having lost all self-control. After each outburst of rage Hitler would stride up and down the carpet-edge, then suddenly stop immediately before me and hurl his next accusation in my face.[2]

Speer's own confrontation with Hitler, which followed on March 29th, took an entirely different form. Hitler was cold but calm, and challenged Speer, accusing him of disobeying his order for destruction. Speer says that he replied quietly, in a tone of resignation, saying, 'Take the measure you think necessary, and grant no consideration to me as an individual.' He felt, however, that Hitler had already made up his mind. 'You are overworked and ill. I have therefore decided you are to go on leave at once,' he said in a friendly voice. Speer did not favour this solution. He asked to be dismissed since he had lost his powerful ally, Guderian. Hitler insisted he could not spare him, and then added, very quietly, 'Speer, if you can convince yourself that the war is not lost, you can continue to run your office.' It was an insight into Hitler's capacity for self-delusion, or his attempt to overcome his despair through an illusory optimism.[3]

A compromise was reached the following day. Speer placed himself 'unreservedly behind' Hitler. He was immediately met with a rush of grateful emotion, the Führer's eyes filling with tears, 'as they so often did nowadays'. But Speer insisted the destruction orders should remain in his hands, that is, at his discretion, and not delegated through him to the local *gauleiters*. Hitler signed an order to this effect. Speer then ended his war, preventing the destruction of Germany's economic life to the best of his ability. He had as good relations with General Krebs as he had had with Guderian, and influential *gauleiters*, such as Kaufmann in Hamburg, sided with him. Even Hitler was prepared to modify his orders for the destruction of bridges in order to facilitate the counterattacks his imaginary forces were to inflict on the surrounding enemy.

Boldt has given us an invaluable picture of this final phase of Hitler's life. He had first seen the Führer face to face in February: 'All his movements were those of a sick, almost senile old man. His face, especially around the eyes, spoke of total weariness and exhaustion. Only in his eyes was there an indescribable, flickering brightness which had an alarming, totally unnatural effect.'[4] In spite of Guderian's tough, soldierly realism and Speer's carefully worded reports emphasizing the need to concede defeat, Hitler succumbed to the delusion that he still had the resources to fight back. 'He could not tolerate the idea that anything should influence his free and inspired masterminding of vast, tactical plans.' He neglected the carefully prepared reports and analyses presented by his military staff; he reached his decisions intuitively, and refused to be addressed 'in such a one-sided and biased way'. He called conferences day and night without thought that this overburdened the generals who were trying to hold the last remaining fragments of the front together. He turned his back on the overwhelming strength of the Russian forces driving resolutely on towards Berlin, of which he was provided with ample evidence. Hitler would stare blankly at these maps and statistics. Boldt writes:

> I held my breath while the fate of the German East was being decided. Hitler stood up slowly, limped a few paces and stared into space. Suddenly he stopped still and dismissed us quickly and coldly, without passing a single word of comment on the urgent plea he had heard.

The strain on Hitler was reaching its limit. The rages characterized by the appearance of red blotches on his face, the clenched fists, the biting of his lower lip, the use of insulting language, reflected the seeds of an inner despair. His 'decisiveness and intellectual energy' were replaced by many signs of physical and mental breakdown; the shaking of his hand and arm increased. He took what comfort he could from reading continually from Carlyle's study of Frederick the Great. Hitler had always seen Frederick II as his symbolic ancestor. Frederick had been at loggerheads with his father, had been a great reader in his youth, had been interested in literature, science and the arts, especially music; he had developed into an absolute ruler with an ostensibly enlightened attitude towards his subjects when he became King of Prussia in 1740. For a quarter century he had conducted campaigns intended to expand Prussian territory. What appealed now to Hitler was the period when Frederick, during the Seven Years War, had been hemmed in by French, Austrian and Russian forces and driven to despair and the brink of suicide. He had been saved only by his unbending will and the sudden death, in 1762, of the Russian Empress, Elizabeth, who was succeeded by Peter III. Peter admired him and formed a new alliance which enabled him to rescue his country from ruin, regain Silesia, and make Prussia once more a great power in Europe. When Hitler was tired, Goebbels would read Carlyle's words aloud to him, describing Frederick's Job-like isolation, disaster upon disaster piling upon his head. 'But for my books,' wrote Frederick, 'I think hypochondria would have had me in bedlam before now . . . We live in troublous times and in desperate situations – I have all the properties of a Stage-hero; always in danger, always on the point of perishing.' Hitler seized on these words with desperate relish, and awaited the miracle to come which would turn at least one of his enemies into an ally. He had always hoped it would be Britain.

The messages of tribulation continued to pour in. Model's Army Group was encircled in the Ruhr on April 1st; Model committed suicide; the number of German prisoners in the West since D-day now totalled two million. On April 9th, Königsberg, the last stronghold in East Prussia fell, while on April 12th, the U.S. Ninth Army crossed the Elbe. On April 13th the Russians took Vienna.

But President Roosevelt died on April 12th and the rejoicing in the Chancellery knew no bounds. Roosevelt's sudden death was somehow equated with the death of the Empress Elizabeth in 1762. Speer was summoned immediately to Hitler's Bunker in the Chancellery; Hitler held the news-clip in his hand, exclaiming, 'Here we have the miracle

I always predicted! Who was right? The war isn't lost!' Hitler sat down, at once dazed and liberated. The Americans, he was certain, would soon declare a truce.

On April 15th, Hitler issued an hysterical Order of the Day:

> For the last time our deadly enemies, the Jewish Bolsheviks, have launched their massive forces to attack. Their aim is to reduce Germany to ruins and to exterminate our people . . . While the old men and children will be murdered, the women and girls will be reduced to barrack-room whores . . . This time the Bolshevist will meet the ancient fate of Asia – he must and shall bleed to death before the capital of the German Reich. Whoever fails in his duty at this moment behaves as a traitor to our people . . . Form yourselves into a sworn brotherhood to defend, not the empty conception of a Fatherland, but your homes, your wives, your children . . . At this moment, when Fate has removed from earth the greatest war criminal of all time, the turning-point of this war will be decided.
>
> ADOLF HITLER.[5]

But it would seem that Hitler was already resigned to defeat. Between April 15th and 20th, which was his fifty-sixth birthday, the Russians broke through Krebs's defences and began the process of encircling Berlin with a two-pronged movement directed north and south of the city. They completed their encirclement by April 25th, when they began to close in on the Chancellery.

Hitler's birthday celebrations were a melancholy affair. They were preceded by Goebbels's last broadcast to the nation:

> I have shared joy and sorrow with the Führer, the unparalleled victories and the terrible set-backs of the crowded years from 1939 to today, and I still stand at his side and am convinced that fate will, after the last hard test, award the laurel wreath to him and to his people. I

can only say that these times, with all their sombre and painful majesty, have found their only worthy representative in the Führer.[6]

Hitler's ministers gathered for this last festive meeting with their Führer, held in the half-ruined Chancellery. Himmler, Ribbentrop, Goebbels, Goering, Speer, Keitel, Doenitz and Jodl were all there, with Bormann hovering watchfully at their side. Hitler was shaken by the hand and congratulated no more. Goering, in a new olive-coloured uniform which made him look like an American general, had a fleet of cars waiting outside. He was in a hurry to leave for Berchtesgaden after the situation conference; his great possessions in art and furniture had already travelled south by rail. Now he was anxious to leave before the Russians cut off the last remaining route to the south. 'You go,' said Hitler curtly. Their final leave-taking was a cold one. Himmler, the Nazi ascetic who had no rich possessions, had tried his hand as a commander in the field, and failed miserably; with the extraordinary diffidence characteristic of his nature when he was in doubt, he had been for some while on the verge of conducting peace negotiations with the enemy, entirely behind Hitler's back. He, too, said goodbye to the Führer, and hurried away to the north to conduct further furtive meetings, one of them with Norbert Masur, director of the Swedish section of the World Jewish Congress of New York. Negotiations for the liberation of Jews from the remaining German concentration camps were in progress, but without Hitler's knowledge. Speer flew immediately to Hamburg to continue safeguarding industrial plants and other resources in the Ruhr. He was, however, drawn to return once more to Berlin out of a kind of irresistible sympathy for Hitler, deserted as he now was except for the Service Chiefs, Goebbels and Bormann. Hitler received him on April 23rd; he appeared listless, and asked his advice about remaining in Berlin. Speer told him he should do so. Hitler then declared he would commit suicide. They parted finally in the small hours of the night, Speer filled with emotion, but Hitler taking his departure for granted, showing only indifference.

The previous day, Sunday, April 22nd, Hitler had had a

nervous relapse during the situation conference. He had leapt up, raving, and sworn he would not leave Berlin. The others could go if they wished. But he would stay. He would command the final battle. Then, in Boldt's words:

> Hitler slowly sank back into his chair ... his outburst ended in complete collapse ... He sobbed like a small child, and continuing to sob, he admitted ... 'It is all over. The war is lost. I shall shoot myself.'[7]

Led by Jodl, attempts were made by the generals to comfort him, and remind him he must still take command. They pleaded with him to move to Berchtesgaden, but he refused. His question put to Speer the following day was therefore, probably, only rhetorical. But at the situation conference on April 23rd, he was once again trying to initiate offensives against the enemy.

On April 22nd, Goebbels, his wife, and their family of six young children moved into the Bunker to spend their last days with the Führer. Eva Braun was already with him. She had arrived in Berlin from Berchtesgaden around April 13th, travelling without permission. There is no record whether Hitler was glad or sorry to see her, but from the moment of her arrival she set out to establish a tone of cheerfulness in the gloom of the Bunker. According to Speer, Magda Goebbels suffered from a heart attack after her arrival, and on April 23rd he visited her in her room in the Bunker to say goodbye; she was in very low spirits. But Eva, in her room, which was tastefully furnished, 'radiated an almost gay serenity', and she was, unlike anyone else in the Bunker, thoughtful about others. She gave Speer champagne and cake, and she talked with him until three in the morning.

On April 19th she had written to her friend and biographer, Herta Ostermayr:

> We can hear the Eastern front artillery, and of course there are air-raids every day. From East as well as West. I spend most of the time in the Bunker, and there isn't much sleep. But I am very happy to be near *him* just now.

He asks me every day to seek safety in the Berghof, but I have always resisted it.[8]

On April 20th, after the birthday party, Ribbentrop had said to her: 'You're the only one who has some influence over him. If you tell him you would like to go south, he'll go.' But Eva had replied, 'He has to make the decisions, not I.'

On April 22nd, the fateful day he finally decided to die in Berlin, Hitler called together the remaining women on his staff – Gerda Christian and Traudl Junge, his secretaries, and his cook, Konstanza Manzialy.[9] In Eva's presence he told them all that there was a plane ready to fly them south. They refused, and Eva, putting her face close to his, said, 'You know I am staying with you. Why do you want to send me away?' Hitler then did what he had never done before in front of any other person; he kissed her on the mouth.

On April 23rd, Eva wrote to her sister:

Any day or hour now may be the end . . . The Führer has lost every hope. We others don't give up hope so long as he is alive . . . One thing is certain, we shall never let them catch us alive.

She then adds instructions about paying bills and giving farewell gifts. She had sent her jewellery away south with Dr Morell, who was among those who had left the Bunker. This was her last letter. Boldt saw her for the first time as late as April 26th, and he says she was 'making lively conversation'. She was very elegantly dressed in a close-fitting suit which emphasized her excellent figure. 'Undoubtedly an attractive woman,' says Boldt, 'but rather affected and theatrical.'

On April 23rd, Hitler was faced with what he held to be a personal betrayal. This time it was Goering, whose actions, largely well meant, were misunderstood by Hitler and exploited by the malevolence of Bormann. Goering held that, by the decree of June 29th, 1941, he was Hitler's appointed successor. He radioed two messages to Hitler asking whether he should assume the leadership in the Reich since the Führer had decided to stay in 'Fortress Berlin'. Unless that is, Hitler should change his mind and fly south. Incited by Bormann, Hitler lashed out at Goering, and then lapsed into apathy. It was Bormann who sent the message back rescinding the decree of 1941 in Hitler's name; this was then followed by a second message accusing Goering of high treason and demanding, according to the usual formula, that he resign all his offices of State on the grounds of ill-health. Bormann finally ensured Goering's humiliation by ordering his arrest by the SS. Hitler then ordered General Ritter von Greim to fly to him in Berlin; the purpose was not explained, but he intended to make him Head of the Luftwaffe in Goering's place.

Greim arrived on April 24th, brought in a light training aircraft at her insistence by his close friend, the intrepid airwoman, Hanna Reitsch, who had an hysterical devotion to Hitler. According to her, Hitler called the telegram from Goering 'a crass ultimatum'. All Goering was fit for, he declared, was to negotiate the capitulation. Greim, who had been severely wounded in the right foot during the dangerous flight into Berlin, was astounded at being told of his promotion, while Hanna Reitsch swore they would both atone with their lives, if need be, for Goering's defection.

A second 'betrayal' did not come to Hitler's attention until April 28th, by which time Berlin was wholly surrounded by the Russians. The Chancellery itself was coming under attack by Russian artillery. Himmler was now in direct contact with Count Folke Bernadotte, of the International Red Cross, and through him was attempting to offer capitulation by Germany to the Western Allies, in order to prevent Germany from being overrun by the Russians. Himmler, of course, had no authority even to explore this, but after resort to the astrologers, he was in no doubt that he would be declared Hitler's successor. He wanted to be in a favourable position with the Allies at the end of the war. However, news of these discussions was leaked to the allied press; the story broke on April 28th, and reached Hitler when the BBC broadcast it on the evening newscast. The news affected Hitler far worse than the messages from Goering. According to Boldt, he 'succumbed to a helpless paroxysm of rage, full of hate and contempt, such as few human beings can have experienced'. He fell on a helpless victim,

Eva Braun's brother-in-law, Hermann Fegelein, who had been caught trying to escape from the Bunker; Fegelein was Himmler's representative in Berlin. He was shot out of hand, and Boldt says Hitler 'received the news of Fegelein's execution in a state of pathological excitement'. He ordered von Greim and his companion, Hanna Reitsch, to fly north at once and arrest Himmler. A Luftwaffe pilot managed to take off during the small hours from the broad East-West axis near the Chancellery. Greim was hobbling on crutches, while Hanna Reitsch was hysterical at leaving the Führer, with whom she wanted to die. Hitler gave both her and Greim phials of poison as a parting gift.

Hitler's ever diminishing circle in the Bunker was spending its last days in an atmosphere which combined hallucination with despair. The hallucinations now were that General Wenck, with imaginary forces at his disposal, would break the Russian ring around Berlin. The despair grew out of the fact that defeat was real, actual, in the face of Russian tanks closing in on the Bunker itself. The troops defending Berlin fell back under the inexorable weight of the Russian armour.

Hitler summoned the members of his remaining circle and married Eva Braun. The image of the Führer could in his last moments be safely extended to take in the concept of marriage. It was Hitler's final gesture of gratitude for so many years of loyalty and devotion. A bewildered Berlin official was hurried in to conduct the ceremony; Goebbels and Bormann acted as the witnesses. Once again, hands were shaken in melancholy congratulation; bottles of champagne were produced; reminiscences were recalled, but Hitler finally reverted to the theme of defeat and impending suicide. He took Traudl Junge aside and dictated his will; according to Frau Junge, it was most unusual for him to require her to use shorthand. He had always preferred to dictate straight on to the typewriter.

By four o'clock in the morning the typescript was ready for signature. The personal section of the will bequeathed his properties to the Party or to the State, if the Party no longer existed. He referred to his last-minute marriage in strange terms: 'This will compensate us for what we both lost through my work in the service of my people.' He asked his executor, Martin Bormann, to look after the welfare of his wife's relatives, and that of his own kindred and immediate staff. Then he added: 'My wife and I choose to die in order to escape the shame of overthrow or capitulation. It is our wish that our bodies be burnt immediately.'

The political section of the will offered a summary of this situation as he saw it, a war thrust upon him by international Judaism, the heroic resistance of the German armies to evil pressure from all sides and his determination to die: 'I will not fall into the hands of an enemy who requires a new spectacle, exhibited by the Jews, to divert his hysterical masses.' He rebuked those members of the armed forces who had surrendered instead of dying in battle; he confirmed the expulsion of Goering and Himmler, and he appointed Doenitz as Reich President and Supreme Commander of the Armed Forces, as Hindenburg had once been. Goebbels was to become Reich Chancellor and Bormann Party Chancellor. They were enjoined 'to uphold the racial laws in all their severity'. Neither Speer nor Ribbentrop were bequeathed offices of state.

It was Hitler's intention that both Goebbels and Bormann should now leave Berlin. Goebbels, however, added his own personal appendix to Hitler's testament, refusing on behalf of himself, his wife and his six children, to desert the Führer. They preferred, he declared, to share death with him. Three separate copies of Hitler's testament were sent out of Berlin by three different messengers. Goebbels's appendix was attached to one of these.

By the time these messengers left around noon on Sunday, April 29th, the Bunker was entirely cut off from communication with the outside world. Hitler, waking from his sleep, held a situation conference after which he permitted many of the military staff to leave and escape as best they could. The Russians, it was estimated, would reach the Chancellery in forty-eight hours. Hitler was calm now, as a direct result of having made all the necessary decisions. He ordered his Alsatian dog, Blondi, to be poisoned. A second conference was held at ten o'clock that night, and Hitler sent out by hand a last message to his armed forces, paying tribute to those who had been brave, but once again blaming the General Staff, and in particular Goering, for their alleged betrayal. It was during that day that what must have seemed to him a symbolic item of news reached him over the radio – the assassination of Mussolini and his mistress.

The morale of those left guarding and staffing the Chancellery outpost had sunk to its lowest ebb. Men and women who might well be dead or in the hands of the Russians in twenty-four hours drank deep and became noisy and unrestrained in their behaviour. Hitler, oblivious alike to these alien sounds and the thunder of the Russian bombardment, summoned the women of his intimate staff to come and say goodbye during the small hours of Monday, April 30th. Once more, the small line of silent people assembled in the oppressive atmosphere; there were more solemn handshakes, more murmured words of farewell, and sudden outbursts of sobbing from the women who could not restrain their grief.

With Russian units less than a mile away, Hitler took lunch with his secretaries while Eva stayed in her room. He was quiet, and said nothing about his suicide. But after yet another farewell ceremony, Hitler and his wife finally retired to their apartments in the Bunker and took their lives at half-past three in the afternoon of Monday, April 30th. Their bodies were carried up into the gardens by SS men and, to the roar of the Russian guns, were soaked in petrol and burned. The bodies were not wholly consumed; what remained of them was finally buried in the Chancellery gardens late that night.

On May 2nd, when a Russian unit penetrated the Chancellery and went into the garden, they found the charred remains of Goebbels and his wife, whose joint suicide had followed Hitler's on May 1st. Inside the Bunker were the bodies of the six Goebbels children, who had been poisoned with cyanide by their parents, and the corpse of General Krebs, who had poisoned himself. After twenty-five years of speculation, it can be definitely asserted that Bormann died while making his escape from the Bunker.

The Russians had all the bodies they found examined and identified. The evidence of German prisoners caught while escaping from the Chancellery finally led to the exhumation of the remains of Hitler and his wife on May 5th. The autopsy declared death to have occurred through cyanide poisoning in both cases. Hitler was identified more particularly through his teeth. No mention is made in the Russian autopsy of Hitler's having been shot, yet the evidence of those who had carried the bodies up into the garden was that his head was smashed and bleeding. It would seem that Eva, under instructions from Hitler, had shot him through the head after he had taken the poison. Following this final duty, she had taken poison herself.

In the world of those still living, the Third Reich came to an ignominious end with the German capitulation of May 7th, 1945. Himmler was captured by the British, but managed to poison himself with cyanide. Goering gave himself up to the Americans, and poisoned himself in his prison cell two hours before he was due to be hanged, following the Nuremberg Trial. The momentum of death caught up with those who had survived their Führer. Only Hess, among the original Nazi hierarchy, still lives on, a dispirited old man awaiting death after over thirty years of incarceration in Spandau jail in the British sector of Berlin. The Western Allies have made frequent requests to the Soviet authorities that Hess be released on compassionate grounds, but this has always been adamantly rejected. Had they had their way, Hess would have been hanged in the first place, but their right to be present periodically in the Western sector of Berlin while taking their turn to supervise Hess's imprisonment remains of some diplomatic value to the Soviet government. So Hess, the last of Hitler's closest colleagues, is likely to remain in Spandau for the remainder of his days.

14

Aftermath

Hitler left behind his own final assessment of himself in the so-called 'Testament' dictated largely during February, 1945. It was finally discovered in the vaults of a bank in Bad Gastein, where it had been deposited by a Nazi official to whom it had been entrusted by Hitler and Bormann when he left the Bunker on April 22nd, 1945. It was first published in 1959.

Hitler's concept of what went wrong is naturally of the greatest interest. Although he admits to several personal errors, his mind was so closed to objective judgement that, like a skilful advocate, he rationalizes the events of the war in a form which makes him appear the victim of unhappy circumstances, the great man destroyed as much by the follies of his friends as by the machinations of his foes. He puts prior blame for the annihilation of Germany on Churchill ('This Jew-ridden, half-American drunkard', 'this senile clown'), who, because Britain was dominated by Jews, refused to free Germany to make war on the prime enemy of all, the Soviet Union: 'The ambition of my life and the *raison d'être* of National Socialism – the destruction of Bolshevism.' He blames Chamberlain for giving way to his full demands over Czechoslovakia, and so robbing him of the opportunity to settle the matter by force, starting the war in 1938, not 1939. 'However, you can hardly blame me if the British and the French accepted at Munich every demand I made of them!' He regards the elimination of Churchill, rather than that of Roosevelt (the 'Jew-ridden madman' at the head of 'that monster which calls itself the United States'), as the desired equivalent to the miracle which saved Frederick the Great. The United States he says can only be saved by her Germans, the valuable emigrants now lost to the Reich. As for the Axis, his fondness for Mussolini ('my equal ... perhaps even my superior') blinded him to the 'irremediable decadence of the Latin countries'.

> I must admit my unshakeable friendship for Italy and the Duce may well be held to be an error on my part ... I do blame myself for not having listened to the voice of reason, which bade me to be ruthless in my friendship for Italy.[1]

'Life,' he adds, 'does not forgive weakness.'

Italy, Spain, France collectively let him down. He claims he backed the wrong horse in Spain, he should have supported the working-class, who were not real Reds. He should also, he says, have captured Gibraltar. He should have been ruthless with Italy, refusing to pull her chestnuts out of the fire and so delay the vital war with Russia, which should have been won decisively in the summer of 1941.

> The trouble with us Germans is that we never have enough time ... The Russians with their vast expansion can afford the luxury of refusing to be hurried.

As for Russia, 'it was absolutely certain that one day or other she would attack us.' He finally realized this, he says, after Molotov's visit in 1940. 'Throughout the winter of 1940, and even more so in the spring of 1941, I was haunted by the obsession that the Russians might take the offensive.'

Again, he blames himself for not making better use of Islam. These people were free of the Jewish taint, as were the Japanese. Alliance with the Arabs could have turned the scales in the Mediterranean. The Italians prevented this ('Ah! If only the Italians had remained aloof from this war!'). As for Japan, he regrets they did not enter the war with Russia at the same time as he did. In spite of his paranoic hatred of the Jews, who are portrayed as the ultimate villains behind everything – in Britain, in the United States, in the Soviet Union – he claims, 'I am quite free of all racial hatred.' What he has done, he says, is to open the eyes of the

Germans to their 'inherent greatness' and 'the significance of the struggle they are waging for their very existence.' 'I have been Europe's last hope. She proved incapable of refashioning herself by means of voluntary reform. She showed herself impervious to charm and persuasion. To take her I had to use violence.' He claims, however, that National Socialist doctrine was 'not for export'. It applied only to Germany.

He foresees the world of the future as a confrontation between the two great powers, the United States and the Soviet Union, and there is little doubt which one he thinks will win. The United States, he says, has feet of clay. The power that will win is the one which most effectively eliminates Jewish contamination. As for Germany, she must keep herself racially pure and avoid becoming a pawn in the rivalry between the two great powers of the world.

Among those who have written most lucidly about the mind of Adolf Hitler is Professor Trevor-Roper. He has always emphasized that Hitler was in danger of being underrated because of the hideous nature of so much of what he said, or did, or caused to be done. As early as 1947 he wrote, 'In the early days of Nazism, Hitler showed a political genius which we are in danger now of forgetting.'[8] Condemned by unthinking people as a monster, a cheat, an agitator, a man lusting for personal power, a political adventurer, a sadist, or a madman, Hitler, who is one of the most notable and extraordinary figures in the whole of European history, can be far too conveniently discarded like an ugly memory. Using more picturesque language, Churchill spoke of him as the originator of 'a new Dark Age made more sinister, and perhaps more protracted, by the lights of perverted science.'

Trevor-Roper, introducing *Table Talk*, says that the quality, or capacity, of Hitler's mind has been underestimated merely because it is repellant. 'It had,' he wrote, 'nothing to recommend it but its power'. Rauschning's pre-war exposition of Hitler's 'thoughts' was regarded at first as largely fictitious; only later, and to their cost, did people come to realize Hitler meant what he said, and had set about massing the force to achieve it. He conceived the situation in Europe in terms of a universal crisis which he had been chosen by

Providence to put right. Exploiting entirely new techniques of propaganda, he placed himself at the head of 'his' people, proclaiming to them precisely what he conceived they ought to do. Exploiting an idea derived primarily from Nietzsche, he propounded a philosophy of the will. As Trevor-Roper puts it with appropriate force, 'With his coarse, powerful mind he raked and combed the centuries of human history and forced the reluctant facts into a brutal, uncritical, systematic philosophy for the fulfilment of his vast designs.' He accepted the barbarous because of its violent vigour, its rejection of debilitating bourgeois comfort, its reliance on brute leadership. He was, in all respects, without human feeling or moral restraint. For him, the only moral was that no conventional morality should inhibit the fulfilment of his purpose. Thus his philosophy was never a philosophy in any proper sense; rather it was a collection of ideas fashioned to justify and motivate his compulsive acts of will. Trevor-Roper regards *Table Talk* as the revelation of the mind of 'the most systematic . . . and yet the coarsest, cruellest, least magnanimous conqueror the world has ever known'.[3]

Furthermore, Hitler became a psychological enigma to his contemporaries. There were those who wanted to have him certified as insane. In 1938, certain responsible members of the German resistance approached the distinguished neurologist, Professor Karl Bonhoeffer, father of the celebrated Pastor Bonhoeffer, bringing with them a report describing every illness from which Hitler was known to have suffered compiled from reports made by military doctors. All Bonhoeffer would say is, 'From this it would seem very probably that the man is not quite sane.' But he refused, very correctly, to give them any kind of paper declaring Hitler was insane. It was necessary, he said, to analyse the patient through direct contact. Then, in 1942, as we have seen, Dr Walter C. Langer compiled for the American authorities all the evidence he could muster concerning Hitler's mind and character, and made such assessment of him as he could. Commenting on Dr Langer's compilations, the American historian, Robert G. L. Waite, feels that neither Bullock, nor Trevor-Roper, nor Schramm, in their various studies of Hitler's personality, face up to its pathological nature. It is for this reason that the importance of his youth and family background must be stressed; his character was very largely formed during his early youth and prolonged, semi-isolated adolescence. This is particularly revealed in his various relationships with women – his mother, his female relatives, his women friends.

A third, even more clandestine medical report on Hitler came into Himmler's hands from an unidentified medical source and was kept by him locked in his safe. We know of it only through the memories which Felix Kersten, Himmler's masseur, kept during the war. Kersten records that the twenty-six page report covered Hitler's medical record going back to the time of the temporary blinding he experienced at the end of the First World War. This is the report which gave rise to the unproven allegation that Hitler acquired syphilis while serving in the army, and that this was never cured; symptoms of the disease (the report claimed) had recurred during 1937 and again in 1942, revealing that Hitler was suffering from progressive paralysis. Himmler, deeply concerned, claimed that Morell was treating Hitler for the disease, and that the fate of Germany hung upon Morell's ability to keep the symptoms at bay. Kersten, who had had no medical training other than as a masseur, claims, 'I explained to Himmler that the illness might affect the mind by weakening the judgement and impairing the critical faculty, by producing delusions and especially megalomania; it might afflict the patient physically in the form of headaches, insomnia, loss of muscular force, trembling of the hands, confusion of speech, convulsions and paralysis of the limbs.'[4] However, a proper medical examination of Hitler was impossible; Hitler refused to undergo even the simplest physical examination. Himmler let the matter rest, since there was nothing else he could do. It is on the basis of this report, received at second hand through Kersten, that studies of Hitler such as that by Alan Wykes depend for their thesis that his abnormal behaviour was dictated by the tertiary effects of syphilis. However, the distinguished German medical authority, Dr Recktenwald, has gone on record that there is no evidence for this.

Speer, who was with Hitler to the last, has said that he

would not regard Hitler as insane. He was sane to the end in that he was completely responsible for his judgements and actions even if, at moments, the balance of his mind was disturbed. Much that he said and did, however, was irrational, as irrational as his concepts. But few, if any people, are entirely rational in their concepts and judgements and Hitler was not insane to the point that he could not be held responsible for what he did. Hitler must bear the full responsibility for his actions right up to the moment of his death.

Released from the charisma of the Führer's presence, Germany accepted her defeat and the prolonged process of 'de-Nazification'. Reactions among the leading Nazis, as was shown during the Nuremberg Trials, varied from hysterical remorse to phlegmatic stone-walling. If active resistance was minimal among Germany's millions, few claimed to have been ardent Nazis once the regime had disappeared. A few men, like Hoess of Auschwitz and Professor Ohlendorff of the SS Action Groups, freely admitted their crimes against humanity, but showed, especially in the case of Hoess, no actual remorse. Orders were orders and, emanating from Hitler, could never be questioned. Nazism at its worst depended on the loyal services of men with no more conscience or humanity in practice than Hitler possessed himself.

There remains the arguments put forward by A. J. P. Taylor, in his book *The Origins of the Second World War*, that Hitler is not (as usually represented) the classical villain of the piece, the Macbeth of Europe, but a brilliant, conscienceless improviser who was on the whole more capable of outwitting the other European statesmen than they were of outwitting him. Taylor claims that Hitler, without forethought or long-term planning, improvised his foreign policy as he went along, and that what happened in Europe was as much the doing of the other principal leaders in Europe as it was of Hitler. Taylor argues that Hitler was prompted into war by Chamberlain, Halifax, Daladier and the like. Of the Anschluss, for example, he says, 'It was sprung on him by surprise, and he took a chance, as always. There was here no planned aggression, only hasty improvisation.' The final stage of crisis was, says Taylor, produced by Schuschnigg. Hitler gambled, won, and found his self-confidence increased until, not long after, he jumped into an unintended war with Western Europe. 'Though many were guilty, none was innocent,' writes Taylor. 'This is a story without heroes; and perhaps even without villains.' This argument disregards Hitler's long-term commitment to his 'destiny', which dates back to his youth and was determined by his persistent will-power.

In some aspects of his life Hitler was ordinary, petty bourgeois, philistine. His attitude towards women was deficient, and perhaps, in the case of his niece Geli, to some extent perverse. And, as an authoritarian administrator and strategist, he worked through fear, resorting without warning to abuse and simulated rage, or, as frustration built up in him, giving way to a tornado of pent-up rage with no attempt at self-control while the torrent lasted.

But it is the charisma, not the crimes, which gives him his unique, if negative stature. He could hold vast crowds spellbound more by the manner of his speech and the exhibition of his personality than by the sense or quality of what he said. He used speech-making as a part of his political strategy, and there can be little doubt that it was here that he exercised his real genius. He must remain in history as a genius in the sphere of political manoeuvre, achieving many stages in his ambitious plan for Europe within the span of a mere five years, between 1938 and 1942. This genius, however, does not appear to extend to military strategy, at least as evidenced after the fall of France. As he admitted, he allowed the deployment of his military might to be diversified and stretched over too wide a field, and he expended it both wastefully and cruelly on too many fronts.

Like some men who achieve much, he was egocentric to the point of megalomania. He was the chosen one, the Messiah. Providence seemed to shine its light upon him, and to be on the point of granting him the ultimate ambition in his heart. He enjoyed twelve years of supremacy in Germany, and five years supremacy in Europe. How did he manage it? He has answered this himself:

> Genius is a will-o'-the-wisp if it lacks a solid foundation of perseverence and fanatical tenacity. That is the most important thing in all human life. People who only have ideas and thoughts and so forth, but possess neither firmness of character nor tenacity and perseverance, will nevertheless not amount to anything. They are mere soldiers of fortune . . . One can only make world history if one can back up an acute faculty of reason, an active conscience, and eternal vigilance with the fanatical perseverance that makes a man a fighter to the core.

Schramm goes back to Goethe to find a description of such a man as Hitler:

> The most fearful manifestation of the demonic, however, is seen when it dominates an individual human being . . . They are not always the finest persons, in terms of either mind or talent, nor do they commend themselves by goodness of heart, but they emanate a monstrous force and exercise incredible power over all creatures, and indeed even over the elements, and who can say how far such influence may extend? All moral powers combined are impotent against them. In vain do the more enlightened among men attempt to discredit them as deluded or deceptive – the masses will be drawn to them. Seldom or never will contemporaries find their equal, and they can be overcome only by the universe itself, against which they have taken up arms.[5]

The enigma of Hitler, therefore, and the endless curiosity he excites, is due to this dichotomy in his nature – the self-professed Messiah who in private life never outgrew the habits of the petty bourgeois, the implacable perpetrator of the greatest crimes against humanity who kissed the hands of pretty women in nervous anxiety to be thought correct, the man who electrified great audiences with the studied arts of a great actor and the insomniac who could not bear to be left alone, the implacable leader and the man who raged and wept in private when his follies and delusions recoiled upon his head.

Yet there is another, more romantic reason for the appeal Hitler makes to every generation. His is a Cinderella story, the story of the most unlikely lad to make good, the story of the ugly duckling. It has, behind it, the ultimate mystique of power. Hitler's greatness has all the qualities of legend. It has the pattern of a great rise followed by an equally momentous fall, the pattern of a dark Renaissance tragedy. It is a case of 'vaulting ambition which o'erleaps itself'. It has the primordial attraction of melodrama, the Machiavellian quality of evil incarnate in the actor-figures of Gloucester, Iago and Macbeth. Hitler remains in the public imagination a wholly romantic figure of evil contrasted, for example, with the solidity of Stalin or even of Mussolini. He is capable of being successfully caricatured by Chaplin, satirized by Brecht, and turned into the melodramatic centrepiece for innumerable films. One thing alone seems certain, interest in him and curiosity about his phenomenal character and career is likely to last as long as human history is studied.

Appendix

The recent publication of David Irving's book, *Hitler's War*, first in 1975 in Germany (where he suppressed it shortly after publication because of alleged editorial doctoring) and later in 1977 in the United States and Britain, excited considerable controversy, like others among this author's work – for example, *The Destruction of Convoy PQ 17* and *Accident – the Death of General Sikorski*. David Irving is an assiduous researcher who likes to use his findings to achieve dispute, turning the tables on the established point of view. It was therefore to be expected that he would attempt in this book, which he claims took some twelve years to prepare, to set the cat among the pigeons. It is good that he wishes to deflate the principal Hitler myth – that the Führer was some kind of authoritarian psychopath who mesmerized his subordinates into undertaking unparalleled enormities. However, it seems odd that he should feel the need to substitute for this another, as it were opposite myth – that the worst of these enormities were perpetrated in his name without either his knowledge or approval.

This new book deals only with Hitler's career from 1939, and is presented entirely from his personal viewpoint ('from behind his desk', as Mr Irving puts it) – the last five to six years of his life covering not only the final conflagration of the European War, but the 'final solution' of the European Jews who fell into Nazi hands. In structure this study of Hitler becomes a massive anthology of documents, individual recollections, statements of various kinds, and especially first-hand accounts of the councils of war between Hitler and his general staff. The author supports Hitler's own contention that it was indeed the German generals, and not the Führer's miscalculations, that lost the war for Germany.

But the real controversy the book occasioned sprang from

David Irving's attempt to exonerate Hitler from active responsibility for the genocide of the Jews – this on the ground that the author's years of rummaging among the thousands of documents preserved in the archives of the Third Reich and persistent interviewing of his surviving aides has led to the discovery of no kind of hard record that connects Hitler directly with this, the most massive of German war crimes. Our surprise lies in the fact that any historian of David Irving's prolonged experience should expect such a document to exist, in the first place, or, in the second place, to be left around to be discovered. The Nazi administration became past-masters in the art of circumlocution, and few if any in supreme authority (apart from Himmler and the SS), let alone Hitler himself, made any direct reference to the planned massacre of the Jewish people that started in 1941 following the conquest of Poland. Thus Goering was able to act evasively under cross-examination at the Nuremberg trial concerning the exact meaning of his written order addressed to Heydrich about the 'final solution' which the SS was required to devise for the Jews. It was left to Himmler and his SS staff to carry the full burden of a crime for which the other sub-leaders were equally responsible, however tacitly. How could they escape knowledge of a holocaust conducted on this scale and involving the connivance of thousands of camp staff, railway and other officials in every land from which the Jews were being transported?[1]

Mr Irving proclaims his book to be unique because he has relied on primary documentation throughout, and 'eschewed published sources', though it is difficult in the welter of material available in the archives and the number of lengthy studies of Hitler that now exist, to distinguish what is really new, as well as of primary importance in modifying one's view of Hitler, from what has in fact been drawn upon by Mr Irving's numerous predecessors. Lord Bullock, surely one of the most authoritative of Hitler's biographers, while reviewing the book at length in the *New York Review* (May 26th, 1977) came to the conclusion that 'the basis of Mr Irving's account remains evidence known to and used by other historians before him'. 'I suspect,' he adds, 'that quite a lot of additional material which he has gathered does not add substantially to what was known before.' The fact, too, that the many published memoirs and diaries of those who worked in proximity to Hitler have been substantially revised by their authors or editorialized by other hands for publication was already well-known – what matters is that the gist was not substantially changed in the process of reducing vast masses of material to a readable and publishable dimension. In any case, one is forced to weigh statement against statement, judgement against judgement, every time one draws on such material (published or unpublished) before reaching a reasonable understanding. The authors inevitably set out, almost to a man, to lay the blame for their misdeeds at the dead Führer's door but this was only to be expected. What in general David Irving wants to do is cut Hitler down to size. 'My central conclusion,' he writes in his Introduction on page xv, 'is that Hitler was a less than omnipotent Führer and that his grip on his immediate subordinates weakened as the war progressed.' As for the massacre of the Jews, 'for thirty years, our knowledge of Hitler's part in this atrocity has rested on inter-historian incest.'

After some twenty years of research, innumerable interviews with people either in direct contact with Hitler or closely concerned with those who were (see the Introductions and lists of Acknowledgements in our books on Goebbels, Goering, Himmler and Hess, as well as *The Hundred Days to Hitler*) this seems to us a very irresponsible conclusion to be reached in the process of de-mythologizing Hitler. It has always been common knowledge that he hated day-to-day routine administration, and left the donkey-work to the donkeys among his subordinates. But among his closest aides, none had spirit enough to act with absolute independence, except Hess on the one, rare and quixotic occasion of his flight to Scotland. That they, like the generals of the High Command, often concealed unwelcome information from him goes without saying – Goering could be reduced to tears by Hitler's rages, and Himmler, executive-in-chief of the genocide programme, was far too diffident and irresolute a man ever to have nerved himself to undertake entirely on his own initiative so monstrous and loathsome a task as the genocide of millions of Jews and Slavs had he not accepted it to be his bounden duty in the face of the Führer's demands.

But to try to exonerate Hitler entirely from primary blame for the holocaust is surely to misconstrue the whole nature of the man and the regime. Everything involving a major decision of policy emanated from Hitler, and Himmler would never have acted, or because of his very diffidence of nature desired to initiate the drastic policy of genocide with its vast administrative involvement and commitment in manpower, without heavy pressure from above. Did not Himmler expressly say so when passing on the order to effect the extermination of the Jews to Hoess, commandant of Auschwitz? (See page 180.) Did not Hitler himself directly refer to it in public in January 1939? (See page 181.) And did not Goebbels confirm this in his diary entries for February and March 1942? (See page 182.)

Notes

Chapter 1 (no Notes)

Chapter 2 Youth and Young Manhood, 1889–1918

1 *Mein Kampf* (edition 1939), pp. 20–21.

2 It was Hans Frank who was primarily responsible for initiating the myth that Hitler had a Jewish grandfather. Frank was one of Hitler's legal advisers in the pre-power years, and presided over occupied Poland from 1939. He was among those hanged after the Nuremberg Trial in 1946. During the last year of his life he was converted to the Catholic faith, made great play with what he termed 'easing his conscience', and with the help of the Franciscan monk and American Army padre Sixtus O'Connor, set out in writing certain notes and confessions. It was seven years before the papers were published: *Im Angesicht des Galgens* (*Facing the Gallows*; Munich, 1953). Frank recalls that around 1930–31 Hitler was angered at malicious rumours about his alleged Jewish grandfather, and instructed him (Frank) to use his legal expertise to clear the matter up. Frank's researches produced alleged documentary evidence that Hitler's grandmother, Maria Anna Schicklgruber, when working as a maid for the Frankenberger family in Graz, gave birth to a boy who became Hitler's father, Alois, who forty years later changed his family name to Hitler. It was further alleged that the Frankenbergers paid Maria alimony for 14 years. The story went that it was young Frankenberger, aged nineteen or twenty at the time, who had been responsible for the pregnancy. Another source was to give the family's name as Frankenreither – this was supposed to be as Jewish a name as Frankenberger. Franz Jetzinger, a former Catholic priest, who had been slightly acquainted with Hitler in the early years, produced a book which contained some interesting points, but also many obvious inventions – *Hitler's Jugend – Fantasien, Lügen und die Wahrheit* (*Hitler's Youth – Fancies, Lies and the Truth*; Vienna, 1956). Jetzinger quotes from an article published in *Paris-Soir* on August 5th, 1939 written by Hitler's nephew, Patrick,

stating that his uncle was the grandson of a Jew in Graz called Frankenreither. The article in fact contains the names of neither Frankenberger nor Frankenreither, nor for that matter does it mention Maria Anna Schicklgruber. No hint is given concerning Hitler's real or alleged ancestry. Patrick, the son of Hitler's half-brother, Alois and an Englishwoman was a notorious ne'er-do-well who constantly tried to gain some advantage from his uncle's fame. There is evidence Hitler gave him a hundred marks on one occasion, and on another a further five hundred, but otherwise he did all he could to disassociate himself from this unwanted relative. More recent research has proved that the young Jewish boy who was alleged to have caused the girl's pregnancy was in fact only 5 or 6 years old at the time, and that in any case the Frankenbergers were not Jewish. There is indeed no record that a single Jew lived in Graz at the time. Most of the more recent research on this subject is recorded by Werner Maser in *Adolf Hitler – Legende, Mythos, Wirklichkeit* (Munich, 1971). See also Jetzinger, *Hitler's Youth*, p. 10 et seq.

3 *Hitler's Table Talk* (edition 1973), p. 359.
4 *Mein Kampf* (edition 1939), pp. 22, 26.
5 *Table Talk*, pp. 188, 676.
6 *Mein Kampf*, p. 19.
7 *Mein Kampf*, p. 22.
8 Franz Jetzinger, *Hitler's Youth*, p. 85
9 *Mein Kampf*, pp. 30, 31, 17.
10 *Mein Kampf*, p. 20.
11 For researches into Hitler's financial position at this time, see Bradley F. Smith, *Adolf Hitler: His Family, Childhood, and Youth*, pp. 111–112.
12 *Mein Kampf*, p. 32.
13 August Kubizek, *Young Hitler*, p. 191.
14 Idem, p. 169.
15 Idem, p. 15.
16 See Maser, *Hitler*, p. 71.
17 See Kubizek, op. cit., p. 65.

Chapter 3 Munich, 1919–1923

1 Ludendorff had told the Government that the Front would collapse within a matter of days unless an Armistice was secured forthwith. This was kept from the public. The armistice was negotiated by the incoming Socialist Government; the Kaiser deserted to Holland and Ludendorff fled to

Sweden. But allegations were soon being made by nationalistic spokesmen that the Army had been 'stabbed in the back' when on the verge of victory by a Government controlled by Jews and Communists. They even appeared plausible to gullible people, since only a few months before the surrender the German army had stood poised within what appeared to be striking distance of Paris. But in fact the German army was quite incapable of making further headway, with British and American armour growing from week to week. As for the *Dolchstoss-Legende*, the myth of the victorious army stabbed in the back, this developed early in 1919 and through the period of the treaty discussions at Versailles. It was a boon to all the emerging reactionary movements, and of vital importance to Hitler's embryonic party. Every one of Hitler's innumerable speeches during this early period started with a fiery condemnation of the *November-Verbrecher*, meaning the 'criminals' who had betrayed the Fatherland in November, 1918.

2 *Mein Kampf* (edition 1969), p. 185.
3 Idem, Introduction by D. C. Watts, p. xxvii.
4 *Mein Kampf* (edition 1969), p. 203.
5 See Manvell and Fraenkel, *Hess*, p. 23.
6 Kurt G. W. Lüdecke, *I Knew Hitler*, p. 21.
7 See Manvell and Fraenkel, *Goering*, p. 25.
8 See *Hitler's Table Talk* (edition 1973), pp. 266, 107, 108.
9 Lüdecke, op. cit., p. 24.
10 Ernst ('Putzi') Hanfstaengl belonged to a prosperous Bavarian family of prominent music publishers. He had studied at Harvard, a contemporary of Franklin D. Roosevelt. More important in those days he had access to dollars which in the circumstances of galloping inflation in 1922–23 proved most useful in helping Hitler to purchase the *Völkische Beobachter*, the Nazi national newspaper. Later Hanfstaengl was to publish his own account of these days, *Hitler: the Missing Years* (1957).
11 Hanfstaengl, *Hitler, the Missing Years*, p. 35.
12 See Bullock, *Hitler*, p. 81.
13 See Shirer, *The Rise and Fall of the Third Reich*, pp. 76–78 for quotations from Hitler's challenging defence.

Chapter 4 Landsberg, 1924

1 Lüdecke, op. cit., p. 60.
2 To understand what shaped the irrational racial theories of the regime, with its contention of the superiority of the

'Aryan' *Herrenmensch* (Master-race), one must go back to the naïve assertions of 'Social Darwinism', which influenced the thinking of Rosenberg, Darré, Himmler and of course, Hitler himself. The very term 'Aryan' in this context, of course, is a misnomer; it never referred to race as such, but to the family of languages. In *Utopien der Menschenzüchtung: der Sozialdarwinismus und seine Folgen* (*Utopias of Human Breeding: Social Darwinism and its Consequences*), Dr Hedwig Conrad-Martius demonstrates the significant if eccentric development of 'Social Darwinism' since the late nineteenth century, primarily within the orbit of German thought. The creed advocated selective breeding and the elimination of the weak or undesirable from mankind; the society of the future can only be secured, it was alleged, by the survival of the fittest. One of the first of these advocates was the anthropologist Otto Amman. The theory was also advanced in the 1890s with sufficient seriousness by Wilhelm Schallmayer for him to receive an award from Baron Krupp in 1900. In the same period Alfred Ploetz advocated selective breeding together with the 'mercy-killing' of the 'illegally conceived', the sick and all racially undesirable people. Ploetz was not an anti-Semite, but like most Social Darwinists he considered that the new-fangled social welfare in civilized countries favoured the survival of the unfit. Fritz Lenz, a follower of Ploetz, advocated sterilization of those considered unfit to breed. Outside Germany, Count Gobineau in France and Houston Stewart Chamberlain, Francis Galton and Professor John Berry Haycraft in Britain, as well as Hiram Stanley of America also advocated selective breeding, while Charles Grant Allen, the nineteenth century novelist, favoured temporary marriages between racially and intellectually desirable partners. These ideas were supported by Darwin's contemporary, the zoologist A. R. Wallace and others.

Back in Germany, Baron Ehrenfels argued for polygamy and artificial insemination in order to ensure that the best breed in the species should reproduce itself on the widest possible scale. With Dr Hentschel of Dresden he advocated the establishment of *Menschengärten* as breeding centres in rustic surroundings in each of which 1,000 girls and 100 men, all carefully selected, could help secure quality for the future of the race. Walter Darré, Himmler's initial adviser and teacher, particularly admired Hentschel. In all the writers mentioned above lay the seeds of what was to become either actual practice or near-practice by the more extreme of the Nazis. 'There is no such thing as equal right for all,' Hitler said. 'Only those who rule by brute force are successful. It is the strong who need protection from the weak.' Himmler's *Lebensborn* homes, supported by the SS for unmarried mothers, though never actually centres for selective breeding, were deeply indoctrinated ideologically and exclusively devoted to the rearing of children of 'racially desirable' stock. They were, in fact confinement homes entirely reserved for the SS, and the ratio of married and non-married women admitted was in the end about equal.

3 *Mein Kampf* (edition 1969), pp. 59, 63.

4 Idem, p. 166.

5 See idem, pp. 63, 98.

Chapter 5 Reconstruction of the Party, 1925–1930

1 The catastrophic climax to the galloping inflation in Germany of 1922–23 coincided with Hitler's unsuccessful putsch in November, 1923, when he wrongly felt himself strong enough at least to challenge the Bavarian authorities. There is considerable significance to be attached to the relationship between the rise and fall in the Party's struggle for power and the economic situation in Germany during the 1920s and the early 1930s. Success for Hitler was invariably in inverse ratio to the prosperity of the nation. In the mid-1920s American loans were poured into the German economy, and with 'prosperity round the corner', the Nazi party was in a bad way. The then British ambassador considered Hitler had fallen 'into oblivion'. Hitler began to creep out of this oblivion only at the close of the 1920s, when the second economic crisis occurred. NSDAP representation in the Reichstag suddenly shot up from a mere dozen to over a hundred. As the crisis mounted during the early 1930s, with unemployment increasing from a million to some eight million, the Party's strength rose proportionately. It was the July elections of 1932 which marked what might be called the 'legitimate' climax of the Party's fortunes, as recorded in elections which were still free. Mid-1932 proved to be the high point of the economic crisis and in the number of unemployed. Four months later, in the elections of November, 1932, Hitler lost some two million voters and in consequence 32 seats in the Reichstag. This

was largely because the period of crisis was abating; by November there were in fact a million or so less in the dole queues than the previous July.

2 See Bullock, op. cit., p. 130.
3 See Manvell and Fraenkel, *Goebbels*, p. 65.
4 See *The Speeches of Adolf Hitler 1922–39*, Vol. I, p. 188.
5 See Bullock, op. cit., p. 166.

Chapter 6 Seizure of Power, 1931–1933

1 See Albert Speer, *Inside the Third Reich*, p. 93.
2 Hermann Rauschning, *Hitler Speaks*, p. 259.
3 See Walter Langer, *The Mind of Adolf Hitler*, p. 168.
4 Franz von Papen, *Memoirs*, p. 162.
5 See Bullock, op. cit., p. 232.
6 Joseph Goebbels, *My Part in Germany's Fight*, p. 207.
7 Papen, op. cit., p. 256.
8 During the 1960s a considerable controversy was started by F. Tobias's book, *Der Reichstagsbrand: Legende oder Wirklichkeit?* (1962), in which it was claimed that Marinus van der Lubbe caused the Reichstag fire on his own, without any assistance by the Nazis. There has been much well-documented evidence, however, that it was technically impossible for the young Dutchman, who was almost blind, to start so great a conflagration alone within such a short space of time. What matters historically, of course, is the fact that the fire afforded the new regime the excuse to introduce the Enabling Law which gave Hitler his dictatorial powers, the right to rule by decree from the end of March, 1933 until the end of the War. However, the figures for the preceding election on March 5th, following intense campaigning by the NSDAP and violent attacks on the opposition, resulted in less than a 50 per cent vote for the Nazis, leaving them dependent on the support of Papen and his followers, which added six per cent to their voting strength in the Reichstag, raising them to some 51 per cent. The other half of the nation voted for deputies many of whom had been put in gaol or concentration camps by the day of the election as a result of the arrests made following on the Reichstag fire at the end of February.

Chapter 7 Retribution, 1933–1934

1 *Mein Kampf* (edition 1969), p. 106.
2 Rauschning, op. cit., p. 59 *et. seq.*
3 *Hitler's Table Talk*, p. 62.

4 *The Speeches of Adolf Hitler*, I, 484–5, 507–8, 865–6.
5 Rauschning, op. cit., p. 154.

Chapter 8 Dictator, 1934–1939

1 See Speer, op. cit., pp. 103, 113, 60.
2 Eva Braun's fellow schoolgirl, now married to a schoolmaster in England, made this statement for Roger Manvell.
3 Rauschning, op. cit., p. 74.
4 Henderson, *Failure of a Mission*, pp. 43, 266.
5 See Manvell and Fraenkel, *Goering*, p. 211
6 See Anthony Eden, *Memoirs: Facing the Dictators*, p. 141.
7 See *Ambassador Dodd's Diary, 1933–38* (Gollancz, London, 1934), p. 173.
8 For this and subsequent quotations in the following pages, see Rauschning, op. cit., pp. 87, 88, 91, 171, 251.

Chapter 9 The Violent Peace, 1936–1939

1 See Bullock, op. cit., p. 322.
2 Schmidt, *Hitler's Interpreter*, p. 41.
3 Idem, pp. 50–51.
4 François-Poncet, *The Fateful Years*, p. 209.
5 Dahlerus, *The Last Attempt*, pp. 119–20.

Chapter 10 Hitler as Strategist: the Period of Success, 1939–1942

1 Ciano, *Ciano's Diaries, 1939–43*, p. 162.
2 Idem, p. 220.
3 See Bullock, op. cit., p. 592.
4 Hitler had not really bargained for the emergence of Tito and his partisans. Their relentless guerrilla warfare necessitated the presence of rather more German troops than Hitler could afford to employ in already 'conquered' territory. The delay caused by the Yugoslavian campaign delayed the attack on Russia by many weeks, using up the summer period, and substantially contributing to the fact that the ill-equipped German armies became bogged down in the Russian winter.
5 Dietrich, *The Hitler I Knew*, pp. 210–12.
6 Speer, *Inside the Third Reich*, p. 262.
7 Goebbels, *The Goebbels Diaries*, pp. 87, 92, 141.
8 Franz Halder, *Hitler as Warlord* (London, 1950).

Chapter 11 Hitler's Europe: Master Race, Slave Labour and Genocide, 1941–1945

1 See International Military Tribunal: *The Trial of the Major War Criminals.* Vol. VI, p. 219.
2 See Bullock, op. cit., p. 694.
3 See Manvell and Fraenkel, *Goering*, p. 244. 'Final solution' is only one of many euphemisms used to camouflage the genocide being perpetrated in the East. There were (for example) terms such as *Umsiedlung* (resettlement) and *Sonderbehandlung* (special treatment) that formed part of the official terminology used in the reports of the *Einsatzgruppen* (action squads) who conducted mass murder in Poland and Russia.
4 For Hoess, see Manvell and Fraenkel, *The Incomparable Crime*, pp. 61–63; Hoess's evidence given before the International Military Tribunal is fully quoted here.
5 For this and the following speech by Hitler, see *The Incomparable Crime*, pp. 31–3.
6 For Hitler's views expressed in *Table Talk* on racial purity and 'Aryan' supremacy, see especially pp. 258, 327, 440; on colonialism, pp. 25, 27, 42, 68–9; and on the place and position of women, pp. 91–2, 245–6, 251–3, 358–60.
7 It should be emphasized that during the first year and more of the regime, the great majority of those who offered resistance to Hitler were from the working class. Many found their way into the concentration camps. Many were members of the Social Democratic and the Communist parties. Many died through execution, beheading being the usual method of dispatch.

Chapter 12 Downfall, 1943–1945

1 F. W. Deakin, *The Brutal Friendship*, p. 206.
2 Ciano, op. cit., pp. 462, 536.
3 See Manvell and Fraenkel, *Goering*, p. 285 *et seq.*
4 Goebbels's *Diaries*, p. 200. See also Manvell and Fraenkel, *Goebbels*, p. 233.
5 See Bullock, op. cit., p. 711.
6 See Speer, op. cit., pp. 359 *et seq.*, 407 *et seq.*, 439, 471 *et seq.*, 483.
7 To appreciate how miraculous Hitler's escape that day really was (and he truly believed it showed the hand of 'Providence'), one should keep in mind the various fortuitous circumstances. It was a very hot day, and all three windows were wide open, thus reducing the effect of the blast. Colonel Schmundt (one of those killed) found the briefcase holding the bomb impeding his feet, and moved it to the

further side of the table's plinth away from Hitler, who was thus further protected from the blast; moreover, Hitler at the moment of the explosion was virtually leaning the whole of his trunk across the top of the table, reaching to a far point on the map. General Warlimont, who was among those present in the map-room, told Heinrich Fraenkel that had the explosion come only seconds earlier or later Hitler would at the very least have been severely wounded, as were several of the others, not to mention those killed.

8 See Nerin E. Gun, *Eva Braun* (1968), p. 207.
9 *Hitler's War Directives* (paperback edition, 1966), p. 288.
10 Idem, p. 290.
11 Speer, op.cit., p. 424.

Chapter 13 Aspiration in Death.

1 *Hitler's War Directives*, p. 294.
2 Guderian, *Panzer Leader*, pp. 341, 343.
3 See Speer, op. cit., p. 218.
4 Gerhard Boldt, *Hitler's Last Days*, p. 39 *et seq.*
5 *Hitler's War Directives*, pp. 300–301.
6 Manvell and Fraenkel, *Goebbels*, p. 277.
7 Boldt, op. cit., p. 122.
8 See Gun, op. cit., p. 236.
9 Traudl Junge, who was little over twenty years old in 1945, told Heinrich Fraenkel about a significant conversation she had with Hitler. 'Is there no chance, my Führer,' she asked, 'of our great movement being revived?' Hitler shook his head and explained that leadership such as his could happen only once every few hundred years. He added that the German people had proved unworthy of his leadership, and no longer deserved to survive. When Frau Junge recalled this thirty years later she added that, having been a very loyal party member up to this time, she became horribly disillusioned and, as it were, she was 'de-Nazified' on the spot.

Chapter 14 Aftermath

1 *The Testament of Adolf Hitler* (paperback edition), p. 79.
2 Trevor-Roper, *The Last Days of Hitler*, p. 253.
3 *Hitler's Table Talk*, p. xxxix.
4 Felix Kersten, *The Kersten Memoirs*, p. 168.
5 Schramm, *Hitler*, pp. 132–3.

Appendix

Another book which, in our view, seeks unwarrantably to exonerate a top leader from implication in the Jewish massacre is Leonard Mosley's study of Goering, *The Reich Marshal* (Weidenfeld and Nicolson, 1974), in which, among other grave omissions, this specific order was not even mentioned.

Select Bibliography

Bezymenski, Lev. *The Death of Adolf Hitler.* New York: Harcourt Brace 1968; Pyramid 1969.

Boldt, Gerhard. *Hitler's Last Days.* London: Sphere Books, 1973.

Bormann, Martin. *The Bormann Letters.* London: Weidenfeld and Nicolson, 1954.

Bullock, Alan. *Hitler: a Study in Tyranny.* London: Odhams Books, 1954; revised 1964.

Ciano, Galeazzo. *Ciano's Diaries 1939–43.* London: Heinemann, 1947.

Cross, Colin. *Adolf Hitler.* London: Hodder and Stoughton, 1973.

Dahlerus, Birger. *The Last Attempt.* London, 1947.

Deakin, F. W. *The Brutal Friendship.* London: Weidenfeld and Nicolson, 1962.

Dietrich, Otto. *The Hitler I Knew.* London: Methuen, 1955.

Domarus, Max. *Hitler: Speeches and Proclamations.* Neustadt, 1962–63.

François-Poncet, André. *The Fateful Years.* London: Gollancz, 1949.

Goebbels, Joseph. *Kampf um Berlin.* Berlin: Eher, 1934.

——. *My Part in Germany's Fight.* London: Paternoster Library, 1935.

——. *The Goebbels Diaries.* London: Hamish Hamilton, 1948.

——. *The Early Goebbels Diaries 1925–26.* London: Weidenfeld and Nicolson, 1962.

Guderian, Heinz. *Panzer Leader.* London, 1952.

Gun, Nerine. *Eva Braun.* London: Leslie Frewin, 1968.

Hanser, Richard. *Prelude to Terror; the Rise of Hitler 1919–23.* London: Rupert Hart-Davis, 1971.

Halder, Franz. *Hitler as War Lord.* London: Putnam, 1950.

Hanfstaengl, Ernst. *Hitler, the Missing Years.* London: Eyre and Spottiswoode, 1957.

Heiden, Konrad, *Der Fuehrer: Hitler's Rise to Power.* London: Gollancz, 1944.

Henderson, Nevile. *Failure of a Mission.* London: Hodder and Stoughton, 1940.

Hitler, Adolf. *Mein Kampf*. Translated by James Murphy. London: Hurst and Blackett, 1939. New Translation, with an Introduction by D. C. Watt. London: Radius/Hutchinson, 1969, 1972.
——. *The Speeches of Adolf Hitler, 1922–39*. Edited by Norman H. Baynes. London: Oxford University Press, 1942.
——. *Hitler Directs His War*. Edited by Felix Gilbert. New York: Oxford University Press, 1950.
——. *Hitler's Table Talk 1941–44*. Introduced by H. R. Trevor-Roper. London: Weidenfeld and Nicolson, 1953. New edition, 1973.
——. *The Testament of Adolf Hitler*. Introduction by H. R. Trevor-Roper. London: Cassell and Co., 1961. Icon Book (paperback) 1962.
——.*Hitler's Secret Book*. Introduced by Telford Taylor. New York: Grove Press, 1961.
——. *Hitler's War Directives*. Edited by H. R. Trevor-Roper. London: Sidgwick and Jackson, 1964. Pan (paperback) 1966.
Hoffmann, Heinrich. *Hitler Was My Friend*. London: Burke, 1955.
International Military Tribunal. *The Trial of the Major War Criminals*. London: His Majesty's Stationery Office, 1947–49.
Irving, David. *Hitler's War*. London: Hodder and Stoughton, 1977.
Jetzinger, Franz. *Hitler's Youth*. London: Hutchinson, 1958.
Kubizek, August. *Young Hitler*. London: Allan Wingate, 1954.
Langer, Walter. *The Mind of Adolf Hitler*. London: Secker and Warburg, 1972.
Lüdecke, Kurt G. W. *I Knew Hitler*. London: Jarrolds, 1938.
Manvell, Roger and Fraenkel, Heinrich. *Doctor Goebbels*. London: Heinemann, 1959; New York: Simon and Schuster, 1960.
——. *Herman Goering*. London: Heinemann, 1962; New York: Simon and Schuster, 1962.
——. *The July Plot*. London: Bodley Head, 1964; re-titled, *The Men Who Tried to Kill Hitler*, New York: Coward-McCann, 1964.
——. *Heinrich Himmler*. London: Heinemann, 1965; New York: Putnam, 1965.
——. *The Incomparable Crime*, London: Heinemann, 1967; New York: Putnam, 1967.
——. *Rudolf Hess*. London: MacGibbon and Kee, 1971.
——. *The Canaris Conspiracy*. London: Heinemann, 1969; New York: McKay, 1969; Pinnacle, 1972.

——. *The Hundred Days to Hitler*. London: Dent, 1973.
Maser, Werner. *Adolf Hitler, Legende, Mythos, Wirklichkeit*. Munich: Bechtle, 1971.
Papen, Franz Von. *Memoirs*. London: Deutsch, 1952.
Payne, Robert. *The Life and Death of Adolf Hitler*. London: Cape, 1973.
Pridham, Geoffrey. *Hitler's Rise to Power: the Nazi Movement in Bavaria 1923–33*. London: Hart-Davis, MacGibbon, 1973.
Rauschning, Hermann. *Hitler Speaks*. London: Thornton Butterworth, 1939.
Reitlinger, Gerald. *The Final Solution*. London: Valentine Mitchell, 1953.
——. *The SS, Alibi of a Nation*. London: Heinemann, 1956.
Schacht, Hjalmar. *My First Seventy-Six Years*. London: Wingate, 1955.
Schmidt, Paul. *Hitler's Interpreter*. London: Heinemann, 1951.
Schramm, Percy Ernst. *Hitler, The Man and Military Leader*. London: Allen Lane, The Penguin Press, 1972.
Shirer, William L. *Berlin Diary*. New York: Knopf, 1941.
——. *The Rise and Fall of the Third Reich*. New York: Simon and Schuster, 1959.
Smith, Bradley F. *Adolf Hitler: His Family, Childhood, and Youth*. Hoover Institute, Stanford University, California, 1967.
Speer, Albert. *Inside the Third Reich*. London: Weidenfeld and Nicolson, 1970.
Taylor, A. J. P. *The Origins of the Second World War*. London: Hamish Hamilton, 1961.
Toland, John. *Adolf Hitler*. New York: Doubleday, 1976.
Wheeler-Bennett, J. W. *Munich, Prologue to Tragedy*. London: Macmillan, 1948.
——. *Nemesis of Power*. London: Macmillan, 1953.
Wykes, Alan. *Hitler*. Ballantine War Leader Book. New York: 1970.
Zoller, A. *Hitler Privat*. Düsseldorf: Droste Verlag, 1949.

[illegible] London [illegible]
[illegible]
[illegible] London [illegible]
[illegible] *The Life and Death of* [illegible]
[illegible]
[illegible] London [illegible]
[illegible]
[illegible]
[illegible] 1976.
[illegible]
[illegible] London [illegible]
[illegible]
[illegible] New York [illegible]
[illegible]
[illegible]
[illegible]
[illegible]
[illegible]
[illegible]

Index